GRANITE AND GRIT

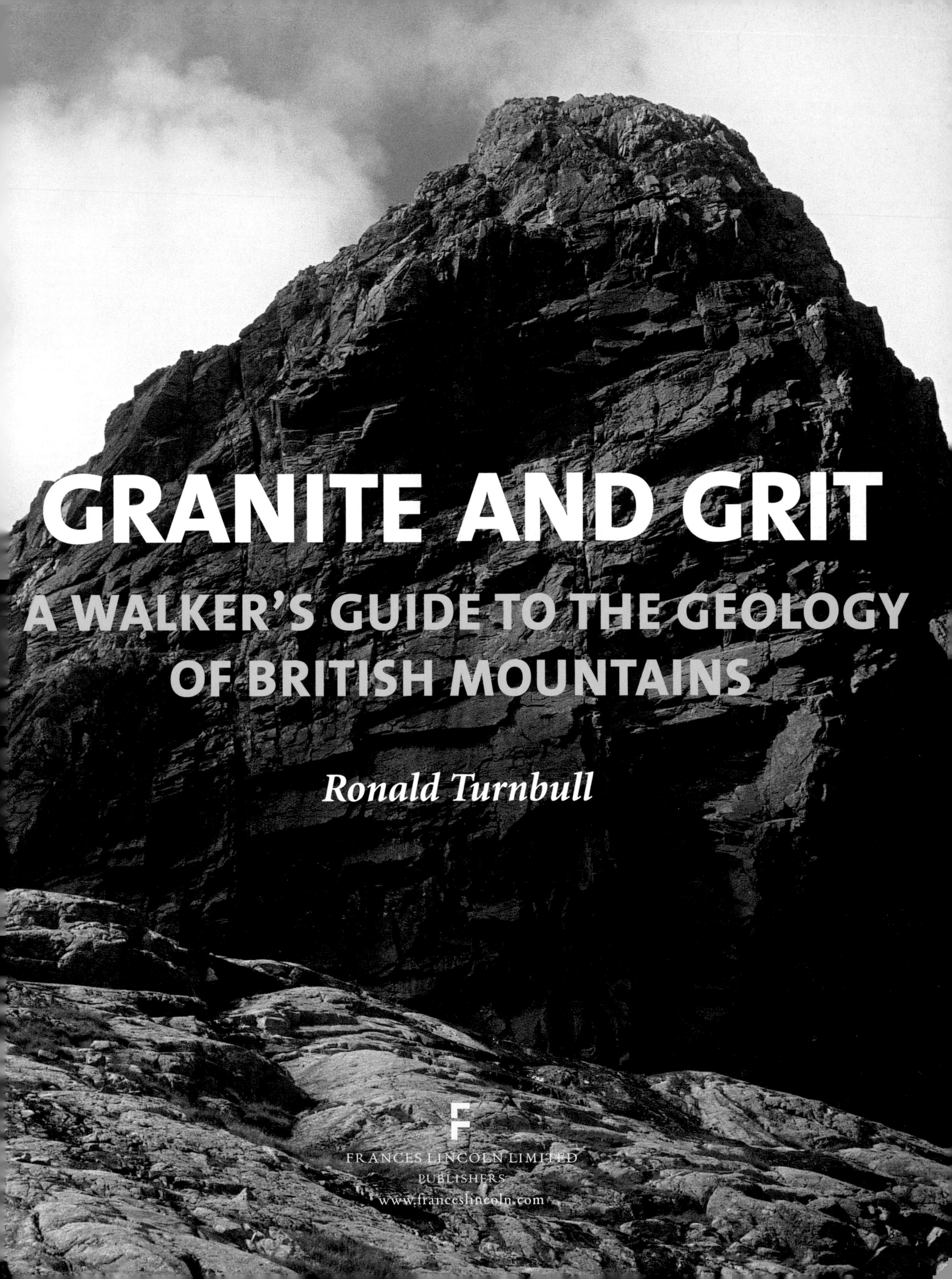

GRANITE AND GRIT

A WALKER'S GUIDE TO THE GEOLOGY OF BRITISH MOUNTAINS

Ronald Turnbull

F

FRANCES LINCOLN LIMITED

PUBLISHERS

www.franceslincoln.com

Frances Lincoln Limited
4 Torriano Mews
Torriano Avenue
London NW5 2RZ
www.franceslincoln.com

Granite and Grit:
A Walker's Guide to the Geology of British Mountains
Copyright © Frances Lincoln Limited 2009
Text and photographs copyright © Ronald Turnbull 2009
First Frances Lincoln edition 2009
First published in paperback 2011

A catalogue record for this book is available from the
British Library.

ISBN 978-0-7112-3180-1

Printed and bound in China

1 2 3 4 5 6 7 8 9

CONTENTS

INTRODUCTION   7

1. THE CRUNCH OF CONTINENTS   13
Various earth-shattering events of the last two billion years:
Scotland crashes into England; the UK drifts north through
tropics; the nudge from Africa; the opening of the Atlantic

2. THE WORK OF ICE   27
Glaciers carved the shapes as we see them today

3. GNEISS TIMES   37
The Lewisian Gneiss, in the Outer Hebrides and Wester
Ross; landscape of knock and lochan; a moment in the
Malverns

4. THE MONSTERS OF TORRIDON   47
Sandstone lands of Wester Ross; buried landscapes;
the origin of our oxygen

5. QUARTZ AND QUARTZITE   53
Beinn Eighe and the Grey Corries; the Moine Thrust

6. SQUASHED STONES: SLATE TO SCHIST   61
Metamorphism, rocks cooked and crushed; shale to slate to
schist; the Mountains of Moine and the Dalradian schist

**7. GREYWACKE AND THE RUGGEDNESS
OF RHINOG**   71
How ocean-bottom sludge became the rock of the Rhinogs

8. SHALES AND UNDERWATER MUD   77
More ocean sludge in the Howgills, Isle of Man, mid-Wales
and the Southern Uplands; the life and times of the
graptolite; Charles Lapworth in Dobbs Linn

9. ALL-TERRAIN LAKELAND   87
Volcanoes and slate, grey shale and granite; four different
sorts of country but only one Lakeland

**10. RED-HOT FLYING AVALANCHE:
IGNIMBRITES IN SNOWDONIA**   97
Various cataclysms above Llyn Idwal

11. WALKING THE FAULT   105
Faults, and a walk along one in particular, the Rossett Gill
Fault of Lakeland

12. ANDESITE AND RHYOLITE   113
More volcanoes, at Ben Nevis and Glen Coe; collapsing
cauldrons

13. GRANITE LANDS   121
Cairngorms, Dartmoor, Arran, Mourne, Galloway –
very different but all of them a bit grim; the cause of tors

**14. STONE ARRIVING SIDEWAYS:
DOLERITE INTRUSIONS**   137
The Whin Sill in the north Pennines, Arthur's Seat in
Edinburgh and God vs Mr James Hutton

15. THE SANDS OF TIME   147
The Old Red Sandstone of the Brecon Beacons; the New
Red Sandstone fails to make mountains

16. MOUNTAIN LIMESTONE, MILLSTONE GRIT   155
Yorkshire and the Peak District; lime to grit to shale:
the Yoredale Series

17. THE BLACK MAGIC OF GABBRO   165
The Tertiary Volcanic Province; the Black Cuillin of Skye

**18. BASALT LANDS AND THE OPENING
OF THE ATLANTIC**   173
The Death of Gaia; Lakeland Lavas, black rocks of
Snowdonia, and the Quiraing on Skye; a round-up of the
red-hot rocks

**19. A TWO HUNDRED MILLION YEAR
WALK OVER DUFTON PIKE**   183
Breaking the Law of Superposition behind Dufton Pike,
with a visit to the Great Whin Sill

CONCLUSION   193
My country, your country, further reading and more things
to see

READING ABOUT THE ROCKS   198
GLOSSARY   200
INDEX   202
INDEX OF PLACES   206
ACKNOWLEDGEMENTS   208

Introduction

INTRODUCTION

This is not a geology book. Well okay, this is a geology book. But I'm not a geologist: I'm a hillwalker who likes to know what's going on under my feet.

My early hill days were spent in Lakeland, where the Borrowdale Volcanic was, as far as I was concerned, all the rock there was. And very nice too, with its evocative shades of greeny grey through grey to greyish purple, its rough texture and many cracks, its occasional crinkly quartz. Happily I scrambled among the rugged rocks at the top of Helm Crag; and a year or two later, I was getting an even firmer grasp of Lakeland rock on the roped climb up Bracket & Slab on Langdale's tremendous Gimmer Crag.

Several years passed, and brought school visits to Snowdonia. Tryfan and Amphitheatre Buttress only confirmed that the proper sort of rock was rough, grippy, and purplish grey in colour. There was also gritstone. But Stanage is only 20m high, and scarcely counts; gritstone's rounded holds, hand-jamming cracks, and uncouth colour could be considered as an aberration.

ABOVE: Quartzite ridge of Beinn Eighe, Torridon.
BELOW: Raven Crag, above Langdale. The rough grey rocks of the Borrowdale Volcanic Series, and similar volcanic rocks of Snowdonia and Glen Coe, are so good that we almost don't need any other sort to climb upon.

ABOVE LEFT: Quartzite boulderfield on the Grey Corries, Lochaber. Quartzite is tough, but also brittle. It breaks into sharp-edged blocks that scar the boots and make for remarkably harsh walking.
ABOVE RIGHT: Galloway granite, on Craignaw. As overlying strata are eroded off, granite expands and breaks away in layers parallel to the ground. This can give a pavement-like surface that's a welcome change from the surrounding tussocks and bog.

It took a family purchase of a holiday cottage in Alligin village in Wester Ross – at a price that would get you a top-end mountain bike today – to open my eyes, and my fingers, to three sorts of stuff that were quite different, never came out of any volcano, but were still great to climb about on. There was the Torridonian sandstone: huge walls of purplish red, crossed by steep grass terraces from which black slime oozed to cover the holdless, smooth and gritty rockfaces in between. And yet, where the steepness of it eliminated those soggy terraces, where the sandstone rose near-vertical and clean, it was warm in the sunshine, gritty to the grip, and well covered in rounded handholds. And oh, the grandeur of it; as I sat alone on the third stance of Cioch Nose Direct, with my rope snaking upwards over an overhang, and an eagle soaring its timeless spiral between the toes of my boots.

Above the grim purple-coloured slabs of the Torridon side-slopes was the ridge of Liathach, a stone walkway interrupted by implausible towers of pillow-shaped squashy lumps. Then, at the end of the ridge, a single stride takes you off the brown and onto pale grey quartzite: quartzite, whose square-cut boulderfields make the worst walking ever, whose ridgelines are tottery affairs of balanced blocks. But the sharp-cornered quartzite screes of Beinn Eighe allow a descent from ridgeline to valley in 20 minutes or less. And the quartzite crags of Coire Mhic Fhearchair are in a sense the opposite of the underlying sandstone. Instead of gritty roughness, here is the almost-glassy smooth – but instead of roundedness, an abundance of small sharp-edged handholds. Quartzite's the rock that *is* all it's cracked up to be – and on Thin Man's

Ridge, confronted with a cornice of small impassable overhangs, one of those cracks took us right through the rockface to a high-perched cave on the back side of the ridge.

Then again, on the moorlands below the big hills was an eerily beautiful landscape of low humps and a hundred sparkling lochans. It's the gneiss of the Western Isles, 2.5 billion years old, making it half as old as the Earth (and the Universe itself, right back to the Big Bang, is only six times as old as the Lewisian Gneiss). The Lewisian Gneiss is grey at first glance, but look closer and there are dozens of colours woven into its subtle stripes, just like the Harris tweed that comes from those same islands. And like Harris tweed, the gneiss is rough and warm and cuddly under the hand.

Mountain ranges elsewhere are of one, or at most two, sorts of stone: the limestone of the Pyrenees, the granite of Yosemite or the Tatras, the andesite of the Andes. There are, by my count, 17 different sorts of stone that form the hills of England, Scotland, Wales and Northern Ireland. We have the granite of Dartmoor and the gabbro of the Cuillin (plus one small corner of Lakeland); the black basalt of Mull and the creamy limestone of Ingleborough. Some are great to climb on, some form high grassy ridges for the walker, some simply make extraordinary shapes.

Are the Earth Sciences irrelevant, are they unexciting? Just an hour ago, my computer table trembled for several seconds and a low rumbling noise came in through the window. My wife checked to see if our central heating had exploded; my son texted his friends in a nearby village, who had also been shaken and rumbled. A quarry, a chemical works? Both seemed, on December 26th, unlikely – though there is the ageing Magnox reactor at Chapel Cross power station. But no; we have in fact just been struck by the Dumfries earthquake of Boxing Day 2006. A neighbour interviewed by Radio Scotland describes herself as 'really frightened', while wondering whether Santa was trying to break in through her roof-slates 24 hours overdue.

As I write, the British Geological Survey (BGS) website has yet to register our wee tremor. But it does have a map of UK earthquake hotspots, which include Comrie in Perthshire, and Anglesey. Comrie is on the Highland Boundary Fault but on the whole earthquakes don't follow the boundaries of the former tectonic plates described in Chapter 1, and the BGS thinks they reflect rather the way we're still gently rising, a millimetre or so a year, since the last Ice Age melted off the top of us.

When you walk up a hill, the vegetation alters gradually from bog myrtle to heather, then stays heathery for half an hour, then changes gradually to grass, and some time after that to moss. The rocks sometimes change in the same way – from limestone, say, to gritstone, as you wander along a Yorkshire dale. But more commonly they change quite suddenly and surprisingly. Walking up Slieve Donard from Newcastle, I noticed that the character of the stream had changed altogether; instead of little romantic waterfalls, it was running down grey slabs in wide watersplashes. I backtracked down the path, to see in the riverbed the actual line where dark shale butted up against smooth pale granite. I could even stand with my feet in a few centimetres of water and 250 million years apart . . .

Red rocks lean up against grey, with only a crack between. Is one of them a red-hot intrusion; or have they been brought together by faulting; or does the narrow crack represent some millions of years of missing time? Most geology textbooks stay within walking distance of the car

park. Up on the summits, we can look at the land, walk up closer to see the individual stones, and try to make sense of it all on our own. We can be, indeed, as the heroes of early geology.

One day in 1778, James Hutton (1726–97) took a boat trip out along the coastline south of Edinburgh to look at rocks. What he saw was red rocks leaning against grey in an 'unconformity' – indeed, Hutton's own Unconformity, photographed opposite. At Siccar Point (grid reference NT813710, north of Berwick on Tweed) Old Red Sandstone, layered slightly off the horizontal, lies against dark greywacke layered roughly upright. What Hutton realised was that this could be explained using only everyday items such as sea-waves and rain, given enough time. But the time required was a lot.

First, the greywacke should be laid down, a grain at a time, on the seabed, and compressed under its own weight into rock (1 in my diagram). Some time later, that seabed should shift, tilting and rising into the open air (2). Plausibly, this would be a single event of folding and crumpling, as I've shown in my drawing. Thirdly, erosion by rain and wind (and perhaps some ice and the invading sea) exposes the cut-off ends of the greywacke beds, after which more tilting puts the slope onto that exposed cut-off (4).

ABOVE LEFT: Glen River, on Slieve Donard, flows over granite.
ABOVE RIGHT: Downstream, Glen River flows over dark shale.
LEFT: The line of contact in the riverbed, where granite (left) meets shale.

OPPOSITE RIGHT: Seven ages to create the unconformity at Siccar Point: see text.
OPPOSITE LEFT: Siccar Point, Berwickshire. Below, Southern Upland greywacke stands almost upright; on top of that, slightly sloping Old Red Sandstone; on top of that, the author. Photo: Clare Melinsky.

Next, the whole business sinks back under the sea, and reddish sand trickles down, grain by grain to form the beds of sandstone (5). Once again, the whole caboodle tilts and rises into the air (6). Seventh and finally, the sea eats into it all to expose the join to the eye of Mr Hutton.

But even those seven stages aren't all of it. For the greywacke is formed of sand, and the sand is the eroded remains of some even earlier rock. Given that the rocks he found all seemed to be formed out of previous rocks, Hutton proclaimed 'no vestige of a beginning, no prospect of an end,' and supposed the Earth to be infinitely old. This was an over-simplification; but over-simplification is sound science, provided we stand ready to embrace the complications as they come along. Mr Hutton will be back in Chapters 13 and 14.

Those early geologists descended into coal mines, and peered into the cuttings of the newly built canal system. But up on the mountaintops, the rocks are on open display, rising in crags, lying in screes and boulderfields, and with only a light covering of lichen or moss. The hillwalking birder gets to see an eagle once or twice a year, and an amateur naturalist gets to spot a pine-marten approximately as often as never at all. Even a stonecrop takes some seeking out; but a stone is never further away than under your feet.

So this book concentrates on the hills of 600m (2000ft) and more, where the rocks are obvious. People who hang about at altitude have the advantage when it comes to looking at stones; and even more, when scrambling or climbing on the crags themselves. You don't need a hand lens to distinguish the Birker Fell Andesite from the Buttermere Mudstone; not if you're a walker on a wet day coming down Fleetwith Edge. This ridgeline is pretty steep and the path has more bare rock than loose scree. The andesite of the upper ridge is a compact, dark-grey volcanic lava that provides blocky handholds and is comfortingly rough underfoot (it's part of the Borrowdale Volcanics, Chapter 9).

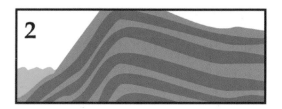

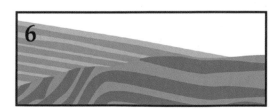

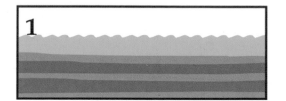

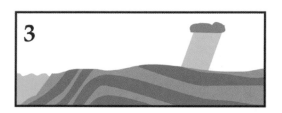

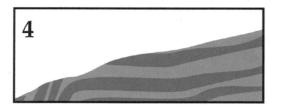

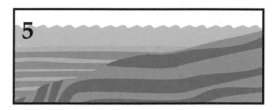

hacking away the ends of spur lines, filling valley floors with hummocks of rubble. Watch the basalt spilling out at a brisk walking speed across the surface of Mull. Stand on the edge of the Highlands, and feel the earth move as Scotland crashes into England.

The story of the rocks starts with James Hutton standing on the Old Red Sandstone at Siccar Point. But in another sense it starts at the bottom – where the oldest rocks are – and works upwards towards the really recent past of only 50 or 100 million years ago.

Reading the rocks from the bottom up turns out to mean, very roughly, starting at what is mapwise the top – the far north of Scotland – and working erratically southwards. (Indeed, the jagged route through the UK of these chapters could be the path of a boulder of grey gneiss transported south by successive ice ages.) The opening chapters are set where the really old rocks lie, in the Scottish Highlands. Lovers of Lakeland will find their rocks – so delightful to climb on but the UK's most awkward to understand – only in Chapter 9. They could leap straight to that chapter. On the other hand, Wester Ross, where not one but three of the opening chapters are set, doesn't just have striking rocks helpfully marked apart in red, white and grey. Those colour-coded stones also happen to form some of our most magnificent mountains.

The book opens, though, with a brief history of the last billion years. Where have our continental fragments come from, and what have they bumped into on the way? Chapter 1 is to refer back to, like the plot outline of a complicated and violent Italian opera. (Just why have these two characters suddenly arrived from opposite sides of the stage, crashed into each other, and started making mountains?) At the other end of the timescale, all our hill scenery (apart from Dartmoor) owes its shape of today to the Ice Age. That ice-shaping may be the most recent scene in the story so far, but I've put it in Chapter 2.

From the gneiss to the Ice Age, the rocks, boulders and screes of the UK are more varied and enticing than those of any other country. This book is your User's Guide.

You can relax and enjoy the superb view along the Buttermere–Crummock valley. Contemplate, if you like, the classic U-shape of this glaciated trough with its two ribbon lakes; observe how corries have formed only on the north-east-facing left-hand valley wall. But then at the 500m contour you step down onto the Buttermere mudstone, which is part of the Skiddaw Slates. The mudstone is also a compact, dark-grey rock: but although it looks the same, it feels completely different. Instead of being blocky it is round-edged and slaty; it is also unpleasantly slippery.

A few steps below, the ridge levels off. Having just appreciated with your feet the difference between Lakeland's two main sorts of stone, you can now relax a little and look at the corresponding different sorts of hill. Haystacks, on your left, is made of the Borrowdale Volcanics; ahead, Littledale Edge and Grasmoor are of the Skiddaw Slates.

The more you know, the more you see. The ice that once ground its way down to Buttermere village was invisible for ten thousand years and more; but once you're aware of it you spot it everywhere, sandpapering down the rocks,

1. The crunch of continents

1. THE CRUNCH OF CONTINENTS

You can't look long at the rock exposed in Britain's mountains before you start to realise that something very big has been going on. See Snowdon from the Miners' Track and it's not, as you'd expect, the top point of one of the great folds in the rock strata – what's called an 'anticline'. It is actually the opposite, the low point of a fold, or 'syncline'. (Think of anticline = arch, syncline = sink.) More detailed examination of Snowdon will even show fossil seashells on the summit.

Again, all along the quartzite lands of the north-west Highlands, lines of bent strata swoop upwards across the hillside. They get cut off by the skyline that's the present-day summit level when they've only just started on their upward arc. It's apparent that things have been moving up and down; and that there's an awful lot of hill missing.

And what about those folds and wrinkles? Mountains aren't carpets, to ruckle up when the cat jumps off the sofa. Or rather, they are: but it has to be a very big cat. Examine the schist boulder propping up the door at the Batavaime Hut in Glen Lochay, Perthshire. Were those squiggly lines originally the flat, stripy strata of some sort of sedimentary rock? They certainly look like it. In which case, this stone has been squashed but not crushed, deep underground, by something very large and moving very, very slowly.

In one of the Narnia books by C.S. Lewis, the four young people go geologising in a deep and strangely divided trench in the mountains. It's only the following morning that they see the hillside as a whole and realise they've been exploring the letter E, in an important carved message saying 'Under Me'. It was just too big for them to see.

OPPOSITE: Clogwyn Mawr, on the north-west ridge of Snowdon. Deep-ocean sediments raised and folded by the Caledonian collision. Photo: John Gillham.
BELOW: Hut doorstop, Dalradian schist: Glen Lochay, Perthshire.

The study of the Earth has been rich in such moments: insights waiting for the first person to open his eyes wide enough to see them. Hutton looked at Siccar Point, and saw the immense age of the Earth. Agassiz looked at Scotland, and saw the Ice Age. Alvarez looked at a few centimetres of strange clay, and saw the meteor that wiped out the dinosaurs.

And in 1915, Alfred Wegener took a pair of scissors to his atlas, and worked out the theory of continental drift. Ever since the time of Hutton, it had been an embarrassment to geologists that, while erosion all too obviously was turning mountain tops into sea bottoms, there was no way at all of turning sea bottoms back into mountains. But what was even more embarrassing was that the answer was not supplied by a geologist, but by Wegener – who was a weather forecaster.

MOUNTAIN BUILDING AND MARMALADE

Let's boil up some marmalade in a very large pot on a gas ring. (After all, it's going to turn out a lot nicer than what you buy in the shop.) Once it comes to the boil, hot marmalade bubbles up in the middle of the pan, spreads outwards, and sinks down the sides again. All the peel, plus one or two pips which sneaked into your mix, stay floating on top; but they get pushed outwards, so that you get clear marmalade in the middle, and the peel piled in a ring-shaped raft around the edge. The marmalade is now mixing itself, so you can stop being so frantic with the stirring spoon, and start testing it by dripping it on the cold saucer you've got ready in the larder.

The Earth, on the other hand, is a marmalade pot without any edges. So the hot marmalade rises, and the cooler marmalade sinks, at arbitrary and unpredictable places. And the scum on top, which is the continents and us, just floats around in large lumps which occasionally bump into each other. Sometimes the upward currents start up at a new point, and if that happens to be underneath a continent, then that continent splits apart and a new 'marmalade ocean' opens in the middle. The African Rift Valley is one place where that's just starting to happen, and in a mere 50 million years, the Red Sea's going to be the Red Ocean, as big as the Atlantic.

I think our marmalade should be done by now. Just pass me the saucer, and let me push my finger into the sticky blob. Yes, it's set perfectly; see the way it wrinkles around the tip of my finger? Now look again, through a very, very powerful magnifier. Is my finger now Italy? And aren't the Alps, exactly, the wrinkles as Italy pushes into the semi-solidified Europe?

Once you've seen it, it's quite obvious that the Alps are where Italy is ploughing inexorably northwards, and that the Himalaya are a slow, slow, ongoing collision of India with the rest of Asia. But the evidence is much more detailed and specific. Particularly iron-rich rocks preserve traces of the Earth's magnetic field from when they solidified. This fossil magnetism tells us which direction, and how far away, the magnetic pole was then from that particular bit of continent. Plotting the video in reverse we find not just shorelines but rockforms matching up, and even more convincingly, the fossils of land animals and freshwater fish.

By the 1960s, geologists were forced to realise that the weatherman had got it right for once. And the writer of the oldest geology book on my shelf, published in 1975,

BELOW TOP: Italy pushes its way north-west and Europe gets crumpled up. Result: the Alps. **BELOW BOTTOM:** Piz Badile from the west.

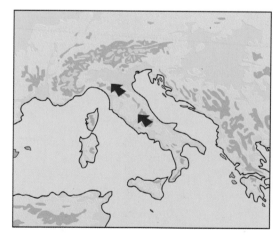

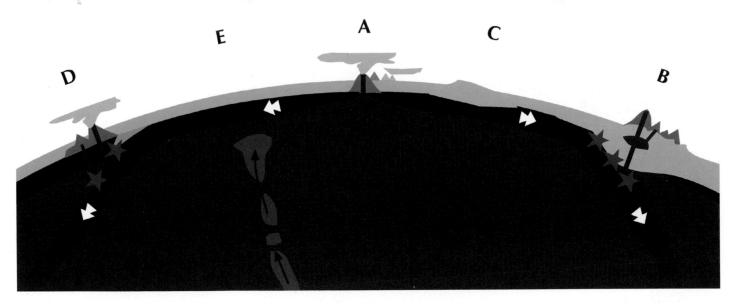

is already complaining that every geology book, including his own, has to carry a subduction diagram. Here's the first one for this book . . .

There are two sorts of crust. Ocean crust rises out of the Earth's mantle at the mid-ocean ridges, spreads sideways, and sinks back into the mantle below. Continental crust corresponds with the peel and the pips of the boiling marmalade. It's made of lighter stuff, and it stays up on top.

New mountains are made in three ways. At [A] in the diagram, separating plates allow new magma up to form a mid-ocean ridge. The resulting mountains are mostly underwater, but currently rise into the air in Iceland. At [B], a continent edge is being ruckled up by an ocean plate subducing (or possibly subducting) in underneath. Friction heat is also creating volcanoes. This could be the Andes.

The continent [C] is about to collide with [B], and that is going to cause some really serious and vigorous mountain building. Such collisions are happening at the moment in the Himalaya and the Alps: Everest is currently rising at several metres a century, though as it rises it also falls down. At [D], ocean crust is sliding in underneath more ocean crust, rather than continent: the friction heat between them creates a volcanic island arc, such as modern-day Japan.

By happy chance, the scrap of planet that's currently the UK has experienced one full-on continental crunch and the edges of another. All three sorts of mountain building have happened here, as well as the odd-ball volcanoes caused by the sort of hot-spot that's about to happen at [E] in the picture. We are also blessed with a small chunk of original continental crust in the Outer Hebrides, and even two bits of ocean bed shouldered onto dry land at Ballantrae in Ayrshire, and at Lizard Point.

A VERY BRIEF HISTORY OF BRITAIN

At one time or another Britain was at the bottom of a warm coral sea; a red desert covered South Wales; tropical tree-ferns grew all over Yorkshire. There came an episode of

volcanoes. Then everything got covered in ice. All this can get confusing, even before you start examining the evidence of it underfoot.

So let's start with the simple outline. Four, or maybe four-and-a-half, important events have affected the UK.

1. Somewhere in the southern hemisphere, a bit of continent containing Scotland (plus parts of America) crashes into England-and-Wales (plus other parts of America). This creates a Scottish-border mountain range of Himalayan size: its roots will eventually give us the rocks of the Highlands, Snowdonia and Lakeland.
2. The combined new country drifts north, through the hot, dry southern tropics, across the hot, damp Equator, and through the hot, dry northern tropics.
3. Africa crashes into the corner of Spain, building another huge mountain range just to the south of us. The UK crumples, raising among other places the Pennines, and also receives sand and gravel washed down out of the new mountains.
4. It's time to lose the Americas. The Atlantic Ocean opens, initially just off the UK's west coast. Interesting Iceland-like rocks form from Mourne to Mull.
5. The final, half-important, event is the Ice Age. Geology textbooks in another hundred million years won't even mention the Ice Age. But for us at this particular moment, it's created the current shape of every British hill.

The rest of this chapter repeats all this less briefly. The whole story, over four billion years and in its 11 separate sections, is fairly involved. So this section isn't meant as a straight read-through, but more as a reference section for the rest of the book. Later, when I say 'Moine Thrust' you can look back and go: yes, that's right, we'd just crashed into England; and when I mention 'coal' you can check we were indeed crossing the Equator just then.

ABOVE: Precambrian schist in the central Highlands: Bidean a' Choire Sheasgaich.

PRECAMBRIAN
4500–545 Ma (million years ago)

The invention of writing is what makes the difference between the mysteries of archaeology and the over-abundant data of history. The start of the fossil record, half a billion years ago, is the same. Geology is divided into the Precambrian – 4 billion years of it before the first hard-bodied sea creatures – and the remaining half-billion years of the Cambrian, Ordovician, and the other eight periods. If those following ten periods are geological 'history', the Precambrian is geological 'archaeology'.

It was 4.6 billion years ago that the Earth's surface started to solidify. We have in the Outer Hebrides a fragment of continental crust from almost back at the beginning, though its rocks, the Lewisian Gneiss of Chapter 3, have been severely mangled ('metamorphosed') along the way. From later in the Precambrian come the grey schist rocks of the central Highlands (also metamorphically mangled, see Chapter 6) and the well-preserved sediments of the Torridonian sandstone, described in Chapter 4.

CAMBRIAN
545–495 Ma

Radioactive dating now means we can put actual dates on at least those rocks formed from melted magma (the igneous rocks). But for 200 years, rocks were sorted according to their fossils; and it's still cheaper to find a fossil than to run some rock-dust through a mass spectrograph. So rocks are arranged according to their fossils. Considered as time, the great geological divisions are 'periods'. Considered as layers of fossil-bearing rocks, they are 'systems'.

The systems are defined by their fossils, and the dates attached to them are still somewhat insecure. In the USA, the top of the Cambrian is dated at 490 Ma.

The start of the Cambrian Period (the bottom of the Cambrian System) is marked by the worldwide arrival of sea creatures with hard limestone shells, and the start of the fossil record. The most useful creatures for rock-sorting are brachiopods, a sort of seashell, and trilobites, a sort of sea-woodlouse. From here onwards, things are much easier to sort out.

The important Cambrian rocks of the UK are the quartzite of the north-west Highlands (Chapter 5), and the grey sediments of the Rhinogs in Snowdonia (Chapter 7).

Cambrian quartzite forms several distinctive mountains in Scotland's far north-west including Arkle (**RIGHT TOP**) where it is folded almost double by later mountain building of the Caledonian collision, and Foinaven (**RIGHT BOTTOM**)

ORDOVICIAN
495–443 Ma

The novelty fossil of the Ordovician is the graptolite. It's a colonial plankton floating around the oceans and deposited in the deep ooze of the ocean subduction trenches. It's so unspectacular that it was originally mistaken for scribbly marks on the rocks, hence its name, from the Latin *graptos* meaning writing.

As the 500,000th millennium BC dawns, Britain is somewhere in the southern hemisphere, and in two bits. An ocean called Iappetus separates 'Scotland' from 'England and Wales'. There were subduction zones, and the ocean trenches that go with them, at both edges. The two trenches gathered grey silt and sludge, which would eventually form grey slates and sandstones, and smooth-sided, only slightly craggy mountains: the Skiddaw Slates, the Southern Uplands of Scotland, and the Isle of Man. But above the mud-filled oceans stood volcanic island arcs: and these would eventually become a more rugged sort of mountain ground, Snowdonia and the Lake District.

But for the time being, the grey sludge is still under the ocean, and so indeed is most of the volcanic lava. Serious mountain-building is still required to raise these rocks, and also to crush, compress, and firm them up nicely.

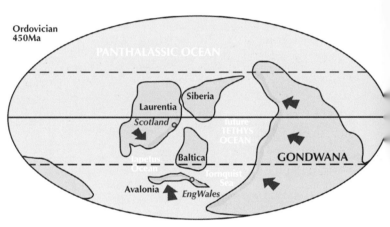

SILURIAN
443–417 Ma

In fossil terms, the end of the Ordovician is marked by a major extinction, with 60 per cent of known species plunging into oblivion. But in the UK, the rocks of the Ordovician merge pretty imperceptibly into the Silurian. The mountain rocks of the Silurian period are represented by more grey ocean sediments in the Southern Uplands, and shallow-water sediments around the mountains of Lakeland and Snowdonia.

But things were about to get more exciting. From 440 Ma, Scotland and England-Wales were crashing together. This 'Caledonian Orogeny' reached its height at the end of the Silurian. The newly risen mountain ranges along the Anglo-Scottish border (as well as in adjacent north America and Scandinavia) were as high as the present-day Himalaya, but about twice as wide. In the north, that range was formed of raised and compressed schists of the previous Scotland. In the south, the island arc off the shore of England was crushed and elevated – the mangled volcanics fated to form Lakeland and Snowdonia. Squashed between, deep-ocean sludges had nowhere to go, as their ocean disappeared, but up. These are now the rocks of the Southern Uplands.

OPPOSITE: The world 450 million years ago. Brown areas are continental crust, but possibly covered by shallow seas. Ordovician-era rocks from a volcanic arc off the north coast of Avalonia would eventually form Lakeland (**LEFT**, Esk Pike and Great End) and Snowdonia (**BOTTOM**, Snowdon from Glyder Fawr). But they would have to wait 50 million years to rise again into mountains during the Caledonian Collision – and they owe their shapes of today to the Ice Age.

BELOW: Rocks of Silurian age happen to form only rather unspectacular hills in Britain: Southern Uplands (Queensberry, **BOTTOM**) and southern Lake District (seen from Lingmoor Fell, **BELOW**). However, the Caledonian collision, at the end of the Silurian, would raise and compress pre-existing rocks (Ordovician and earlier) into what would eventually become the Scottish Highlands, central and northern Lakeland, and Snowdonia.

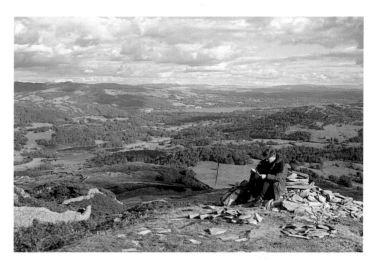

DEVONIAN
417–354 Ma

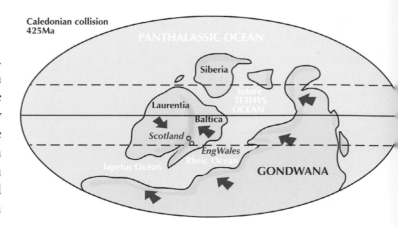

Caledonian collision
425Ma

PANTHALASSIC OCEAN
Siberia
Laurentia
Baltica
future TETHYS OCEAN
Scotland
EngWales
Iapetus Ocean
Rheic Ocean
GONDWANA

Originally, this period was called the Old Red Sandstone. And over north-east Scotland, in the Scottish Lowlands, in south Wales and (of course) in Devon, the rocks of this age are indeed red sandstones. As the map shows, the newly united UK was several thousand kilometres south of the Equator, in the dry latitudes which today hold the Namibian desert. And in that dry desert climate, the Caledonian Mountains were eroding vigorously, generating lots of red desert sand. Flash floods carried red sand and pebbles down in great rivers, whose deltas spread into wide, shallow seas.

The Old Red is a soft rock, so even where it did later get raised into hills and mountains, it has eroded away again. The Old Red Sandstone (ORS) reaches 600m (2000ft) in these later days only in the Brecon Beacons. (OK, plus a couple of points in Caithness, and a hill called Uamh Beag just south of the Highland Line.)

And the ORS isn't just typical in Britain. As the map shows, similar conditions produced similar red rocks across much of what is now north America and north Europe (and were then the Old Red Sandstone continent). Even so, calling the whole period the 'Old Red Sandstone' is misleading. Half the world didn't get any of the red sandy stones. Even here in Britain, there are other rocks as well. Under the southern Highlands and Lakeland, the mountain-building Caledonian collision was grinding to a halt, but still generating underground heat. Upwelling magma congealed, and eventually emerged as granite in Ennerdale and Eskdale; same-age granite makes many mountains of the Scottish Highlands, including Ben Cruachan and the Cairngorm range; also the Cheviot, and one hill, Mynydd Mawr, in Snowdonia. At the same time, surface volcanoes formed the lavas of Ben Nevis and Glen Coe.

To refer to 'Old Red Sandstone granite and lava' is unhelpful in the end. So the period now takes its name from Devon, where ORS makes the friendly hills of Exmoor.

Just as the ORS continent was drifting north, out of the desert zone, something awful happened to the world's wildlife. Whatever it was killed off 60 per cent of the species we know about, conveniently ushering in a new set of fossils and the next geological period.

The typical Devonian rock is red, because produced in dry desert conditions, and is a sandstone or conglomerate formed from outwash of the huge new Caledonian mountain chain.
BOTTOM LEFT: Countless sea-bed layers of Old Red Sandstone in a riverbank at Jedburgh, Scottish Borders.
BOTTOM RIGHT: Not all Devonian rocks are red sandstones. Some, like those in Glen Coe, are volcanic.

CARBONIFEROUS
354–290 Ma

At the time when the Devonian was still known as the Old Red Sandstone, the following period was called after three typical rocks. First and underneath, the Mountain Limestone; in the middle, the Coal Measures; and on top of the Coal Measures, the Millstone Grit. There's no such place as 'Carbonivia', and the present name for the period is just 'coal measures' translated into Latin.

It was world geography that gave us these three rocks. A southern hemisphere ice age was just ending, putting water back into the sea; at the same time, new oceans were being born and their new mid-ocean ridges were also pushing the ocean waters upwards. The sea washed back and forwards across Britain.

At the time, Britain was just crossing the Equator. To start with, under a shallow tropical sea, coral reefs formed, and as the sea deepened the coral creatures energetically built upwards towards the light. And so we got the fossil-rich Mountain Limestone of Yorkshire, the Peak District, and the Mendips.

BELOW: As well as the Mountain Limestone and the coal fields, the Carboniferous has given Britain the Millstone Grit of the Peak District. Climber on 'Flying Buttress', Stanage Edge.

The sea sank, to leave a swampy lagoon with forests of giant fern. Collapsed into the silt and crushed by later rocks above, these swamp sediments became the Coal Measures. Later, the sea rose or the land sank (or both), and a huge river delta covered northern England. Its coarse sands formed the Millstone Grit.

At the end of the Carboniferous all this tropical relaxation on the beach was to be horribly interrupted. Africa was approaching from the south, and starting to crunch into the southern corner of Spain.

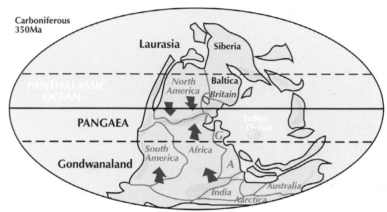

Carboniferous 350Ma

PERMIAN
290–248 Ma

The new mountain range to the south is called the Hyrcanian or Variscan. Its remnants today form the Appalachians in America, and the Atlas in north Africa (Africa and America being still attached during the Permian). The range continues as the Pyrenees, and stretches west to the Urals.

The geologist Sir Roderick Impey Murchison (1792–1871) had already named the Devonian and the Silurian periods. If he was to appear even slightly cosmopolitan, any new period would have to be named outside the UK. So he headed for the Urals, and named this period after a place called Perm. The Tsar of All the Russias was gratified, and presented Roderick Impey with a diamond-studded snuff box, which you can see in the Natural History Museum in London.

With Africa now attached to the Old Red Sandstone continent, the entire land mass of Earth forms a single supercontinent, called Pangaea. Closer to home, the Africa crunch (or Hyrcanian Orogeny) folded and crumpled Cornwall, Somerset and the south-west corner of Wales, and pushed the UK definitely above sea level. The friction heat of the descending continental edge created magma blobs which rose to become the granite of Cornwall and Devon.

In the Devonian, the UK lay in the 'Kalahari' dry desert zone south of the Equator: the then-new Caledonian mountain range was generating sand and pebbles for the Old Red Sandstone desert. In the Permian, all this was exactly the other way up. Britain was in the 'Sahara' zone, 25 degrees north of the Equator. The new Hyrcanian range to the south was eroding away northwards. The result was, accordingly, the New Red Sandstone. It's not at all easy to tell it from the Old Red Sandstone; it lies most noticeably in a ring all around the Lake District.

ABOVE LEFT: Desert sandstone from the Permian. Since the Ice Age, the small stream has carved a gorge 30m deep.

From the start of the Permian, to the end of the Cretaceous 200 million years later, not a rock was formed that today stands above 600m (2000ft) in the UK apart from two hills: Yes Tor (**LEFT**) and High Willhays, the two high points of Dartmoor, are made of Permian granite.

TRIASSIC
248–205 Ma

The Permian ends with the biggest mass extinction of them all, with 95 per cent of known species extinguished. The trilobites vanish, as do those useful graptolites. Many of the giant reptiles and amphibians die out, making space for the newly developed dinosaurs. The ammonite also makes its appearance. The ammonite is so style-conscious that it changes its spiral shell every few hundred thousand years; this makes it very useful for dating whatever rocks it died in. Geologists, accordingly, are very fond of ammonites.

So at the end of the Permian the fossils alter completely. But, in the UK at least, the rocks remain the same; a slightly newer version of the New Red Sandstone. Thus these two periods often get lumped together as the Permo-triassic.

The end of the Triassic is marked by another mass extinction; 80 per cent of species went, including many of the ammonites. But the dinosaurs made it through.

JURASSIC
205–142 Ma

Two geological periods have now eroded down the Hyrcanian Mountains to not much (geologically speaking, the Pyrenees are mere stumps). The UK as well has been worn down to desert plains, which are periodically invaded by the sea. So the typical Jurassic rock is an alternating limestone/sandstone, depending on whether the sea is clear or carries river-sand and mud from some nearby coast.

A band of limestone/sandstone Jurassic rocks forms the North Yorks Moors, runs southwards into the Cotswolds, and emerges splendidly in the sea cliffs of Dorset. But as it nowhere rises above 600m (2000ft), this book will ignore it on the whole.

The UK's highest Jurassic rocks are at 400m: in the North Yorks Moors (**BELOW**), Carlton Bank. But its sediments do give 74 slightly different shapes of ammonite. **RIGHT:** A 20cm one at Quantoxhead, Somerset.

CRETACEOUS
142–65 Ma

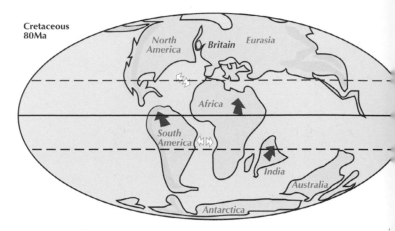

The super-continent Pangaea was now breaking up. The formation of various new mid-ocean ridges raised sea levels (perhaps by 300m) during this period; the fact that the globe was warm and ice-free also helped. So worldwide we find shallow seas rather than continental land. In those warm seas flourished a form of microscopic limey slime, and its corpses falling on the floors of the shallow seas formed chalk. After 80 million years the world cooled down, and for that or some other reasons the chalky slime died out.

So the Cretaceous is marked by chalk, which is actually what the name 'Cretaceous' means. At a rate of 2mm per century, 500m of the stuff was dumped over most of UK. But chalk is soft and erodes away easily. From the Yorkshire Wolds to the South Downs, the hills it forms are low and rolling; there are no cliffs or rockfaces. Chalk is porous, so there are no gorges or ravines, although the rolling hills did receive some shaping by streams during the Ice Age, when subsoil was frozen and so waterproof. Actual chalkfaces are only seen at the seaside, where the waves can carve into the soft rock even faster than it can crumble and fall down again.

With characteristic perversity, the evil magus and mountaineer Aleister Crowley (died 1947) achieved some climbs on Beachy Head with the aid of an ice-axe. Otherwise, while all rocks are absolutely fascinating, chalk manages to be slightly less fascinating than any other. I wouldn't go so far as to call chalk boring. The reason it doesn't get a chapter in this book is merely because it nowhere rises to the 600m contour.

The end of the Cretaceous is marked by a 6cm layer of strange clay that's rich in the heavy element iridium. While the earth was molten, such heavy elements naturally sank to the middle. This iridium arrived, much later, from outside: it's the vaporised remains of the 10km meteor that hit a place called Chicxulub in the Yucatan peninsula, covered the earth in darkness for several years, and extinguished the dinosaurs and two thirds of all the land species on earth. By switching to a completely fresh set of fossils, it also conveniently inaugurates the next geological period.

BELOW: Old Harry Rocks, on the Dorset coast.

TERTIARY
65–1.8 Ma

The early geologists divided the rocks into just three eras: those created by God on the third day of Creation (identified by Bishop Ussher as Tuesday, October 25th, 4004 BC); the outwash from Noah's Flood; and more recent rocks. These were Primary, Secondary, and Tertiary. Alan Sedgwick's detailed and astonishingly accurate work in Dentdale, Yorkshire, was entirely steered by this classification; just one example of how a wrong theory is much, much more useful than no theory at all. The term 'Tertiary' survives as a sort of nomenclatural fossil into the present day.

With the dinosaurs out of the way, not to mention the ammonites, the Tertiary world will be dominated by flowering plants, grasses, and us, the mammals.

The UK during the Tertiary drifts gently northwards, through a hot, wet, sub-tropical climate, to its current position in the cool damp Atlantic edge.

But for that Atlantic edge to exist, we need a new ocean! The big event of the Tertiary was the opening up of the Atlantic. To start with, the mid-ocean ridge was just off the

After the Permian, Triassic, Jurassic, and Cretaceous have managed to raise just a single UK 2000-footer, we were beginning to think it was all over . . . But ocean-floor spreading in the very last of the geological periods, the Tertiary, has given us the Mountains of Mourne, Arran and Skye (**ABOVE**, Sgurr Thuilm looking to the Cuillin Ridge). Meanwhile, at the other end of Europe, Africa was squeezing the Mediterranean Ocean out of existence, and raising its seabed to form fine limestone holiday destinations (**BELOW**, the White Mountain coast of Crete).

west coast of the UK. So, while the Scottish Highlands are blessed with three different sorts of mountain from the remote Precambrian, we are also blessed, in Skye, Arran, and the Mountains of Mourne, with mid-ocean ridge eruptions of a mere 50 million years ago. And what a blessing it is: Mull and Mourne are fine enough, but many mountaineers would consider Skye as worth the rest of the UK combined.

The Tertiary was also to bestow good mountains on the other edge of Europe. For during the Tertiary, and continuing currently, the Mediterranean Ocean gradually closed up, and various subcontinents such as Italy were crunching into the southern edge of Europe. This is the Alpine Orogeny. Africa is bigger than India, and by the time it's finished arriving, in another 100 million years or so, the Alps will make the current Himalaya look like hummocks . . .

In the meantime, the rising of the Alps is causing a few folds and ruckles here in the other corner of the European continent. In creating the Matterhorn and Eiger, the arriving Africa has also gently raised the Lake District, thus allowing the Ice Age to carve it into its current attractive shapes.

QUATERNARY
1.8 Ma–present

When you meet people, the thing you see is the make-up and the clothes. The same is true of mountains. The current outward shapes of the UK's hills are caused by the Ice Age that's going on at the moment. It's ice that's carving out corries, shaping valleys, and exposing all the crags that we'll be examining and scrambling over in the next 18 chapters.

We're currently in a brief gap in the Ice Age – a gap that if we're lucky could continue for a few more tens of thousands of years. Not only does this let us inhabit these islands, it lets us look at our rocks with the ice off. The following chapter describes the currently absent ice and the styling effect it's had on the mountains – clothing them, as it were, in crags and corries. In the rest of the book, as we gradually become intimate with the landscape, we shall persuade it to take its clothes off for us.

BELOW: Ordovician lava flows in Llanberis Pass, raised as mountains in the Caledonian collision, re-raised in the Tertiary Period, and shaped by the recent glaciers. The Quaternary-period human being is currently rearranging Earth's climate and sea levels, and possibly starting in on its sixth big mass extinction.

2. The work of ice

2. THE WORK OF ICE

Back when we were young, a friend and I found ourselves at Bel Alp, above the Rhone Valley. After several days of training climbs, we wanted to tackle some of the large but reasonably easy mountains of the Bernese Oberland further north. These could be reached by a whole day of hitch-hiking around the range. Instead we decided to walk it; especially as this would mean traversing the full length of the Great Aletsch Glacier, Europe's longest at 23km (14 miles).

Well, not quite the full length. We already knew enough that we didn't consider ascending the very tip of the glacier. 'Snout' is the appropriate word for the unwholesome place where the milky-grey torrent, loaded with ice particles and stones, emerges from its dirty hole to rush down the rock slabs below. Those slabs are ice-smoothed, as this is where the glacier has until recently been – 100 years ago, the Great Aletsch was 26km (16 miles) long. The smoothed-off rocks are covered in the loose gravel and boulders dropped by the melting ice. The river rushes down the slabs in constantly shifting braided channels. In the river bed the boulders clash together, and a cold breath rises off the water.

Fortunately we didn't need to visit any of this, as Bel Alp is already above the glacier. From there we descended above the glacier's west bank. This slope has been undercut by the glacier; so it's actively eroding, which is to say steep, and covered in scree, gravel and loose rocks. But the Swiss have always been industrious on behalf of tourism, and a well-crafted path zigzags down to the glacier.

BELOW: Boval Glacier, in the Engadine Alps, Switzerland. Transverse crevasses occur as the glacier crosses a hump (level with the walker's elbows); the medial moraine right of centre formed where the glacier combines with its tributary Morteratsch Glacier on the ice plateau above. The further bank, left side of the picture, shows the recent shrinkage of the glacier. Alpine glaciers have been retreating since 1850, but very much more rapidly in the last ten years.

Here one does not simply step off a grassy meadow with wildflowers onto a sea of gleaming ice. The eroding slope we've descended has dropped its rocks onto the glacier edge; and all the way up the glacier other eroding slopes have been doing the same. From the path foot we don't even see the glacier, but just a heap of loose rubble. This is the moraine. It's moraines that make most Alpine scenery between the meadow tops and the snowline so conspicuously ugly. As the glacier moves down the valley, the rubble constantly shifts about; it is loose and uncomfortable to walk over. A gap opens underfoot, and we look down into a rubble-choked crevasse, and we realise we're actually on the ice.

But in 50 metres we reach the edge of the moraine, where we sit down on the final loose boulder to strap on our crampons. This lower part, where the ice is not snow-covered, is called the dry glacier. No name could be less appropriate. Water is everywhere. Streams run across our path, in beds that aren't just eroded out of ice but are also built up out of watersplashes into fresh ice. The effect is like underground streams in limestone caves, but forming and dissolving in days rather than centuries, and much more brightly lit.

The streams swirl away into ice-sculpted holes, continuing below with a merry chattering: this is the *moulin de glacier*, the glacier watermill. Elsewhere, water lies in sculpted circular pools, blue or green depending on the depth: these are the *marmites de glacier*, the glacier cauldrons. Large boulders shade the ice beneath them, and stand on stalks as everywhere else melts away. Occasionally one of these will collapse under the sun, and with this and the clatter of the moulins, the icefield in the warm mid-morning is a noisy place.

And then there are the crevasses. The Aletsch Glacier is a couple of kilometres wide, and runs fairly evenly, so that crevasses are not a serious obstacle to movement – except when we have to stop and peer into them and say: 'Gosh, look at this one.' Down in the crevasse the ice fades from white through blue-green to black darkness. Where two meet, the blade of ice between is melted through like sugarwork on a fancy Swiss creamcake.

The glacier slopes up as smooth and uniform as a concrete roadway, if that roadway was bulldozed with a 2-kilometre blade. Two black stony stripes run along it like lane markings. Far ahead we can just see the bright cones that are the back sides of Eiger, Monch and Jungfrau. Up there, three smaller glaciers join to make the Aletsch. Where two tributaries meet, their two edge moraines combine and are carried down-valley as one of these rubble-stripes, the medial moraines.

BELOW: Upper Morteratsch glacier, with the beginnings of a corrie forming above the small icefall. Note the bergschrund at the top of a small hanging glacier on the right (directly below the blue sky) where another corrie is forming. Two mountaineers, on the sunlit plateau below the icefall, supply scale if you can see them.

The glacier bends left. This means that the right-hand side of it, being under tension, will open into transverse crevasses. Accordingly we keep left, and it's only after passing it that we look back to see the small lake trapped at the angle, between glacier and the mountain – the Marjelensee. In the landscape of bright ice and black rubble, its blue-green water studded with small icebergs is something of a shock. (Since we visited, this lake has drained itself away through holes in the ice.)

After a couple of hours, the sun gets hotter but we're getting up the glacier and the ice underfoot is colder; the

running waters now cease. Another couple of hours, and we come to where snow lies over the ice. Now for the first time the glacier is the colour it should be – purest white. The snow is soft under the sun and we take off our crampons. At the same time, we put on the rope. Snow lies over the crevasses, bridging them: this will be convenient tomorrow in the pre-dawn chill, but is dangerous now, as the snow-bridges are soggy and soft. An alert eye can spot a crevasse as a slight dip running across the snowfield. But in the heat and weariness, eyes are not always alert.

After being on the Aletsch Glacier for about nine hours, the final problem is getting off it. Far overhead, the Konkordia Hut squats on a ledge that's almost too small for it. To avoid falling rocks and avalanches, it's been sited on a steep convex buttress high above the glacier. Between those unmoving rocks and the moving ice there will be a particularly large and awkward crevasse known as the *bergschrund*. But before we get that far, paint-spotted rocks guide us across the moraine, over the rubble-choked *bergschrund*, to where a few wildflowers grow among the stones and boulders.

Before the glacier shrank, the bottom part of the hut's buttress used to be inside it. So the rockface has been smoothed by ice to featureless bulges. There are sloping ledges, and paint spots to show the way, and here and there a chain is stapled to the rock to haul the weary body upwards. (Since our visit it's been equipped with a metal stairway like a fire escape, with 400 steps and a handrail; for the Swiss are industrious, and it wouldn't do to lose a paying bednight because someone got turned back by black ice on the rocks, or maybe slipped off and fell to the glacier.)

What has all this to do with Scotland? Today most of us are aware that Scotland was recently ice-covered, and that every bit of good mountain ground is good precisely because it has been shaped by glaciers. It takes an effort to project ourselves back into the innocent attitude when this idea

BELOW LEFT: Erratic boulder on Beinn a' Bhuird, Cairngorms. Left there by playful giants; washed upright by Noah's Flood; carried by a now-absent glacier; none of the theories is immediately believable.

BELOW RIGHT: Glacier-scratching has usually been eroded off again by subsequent wind and weather. Here it shows on rocks recently exposed by a busy footpath in the Lake District. This rock bar at the foot of Goats Water (SD2670 9733) also shows, a few metres away, a convincing block tuff (Chapter 9).

BELOW: The Hotel des Neuchâtelois, summer home of Louis Agassiz from 1840 to 1845.

was just silly. But the bergschrund of the imagination is even harder to cross in the uphill direction . . .

Ice is smooth and slippery, so it can't possibly make scratch-marks on the rocks, let alone gouge out the Lairig Ghru. Then there are those erratic (or 'wandering') rocks, perched mysteriously on ridge tops that in some cases are made of a quite different sort of rock. How did they get there if not swept up by Noah's Flood – which, mark you, is in the Bible. God's book doesn't say anything at all about glaciers.

On the other hand, Mr Agassiz, who does have quite a lot to say about glaciers, happens to have been born only a hundred miles north of the Great Aletsch Glacier. When he observed ice-scratches and moraines on the plains of Neuchâtel, along with the ice-moulded outcrops called *roches moutonées*, he did know what he was looking at.

In 1838, top geologist Adam Sedgwick of Dent went to Dublin expecting a lecture on fossil fishes, on which Louis Agassiz was the world expert. Instead he had to sit through 'a long and stupid hypothetical dissertation on geology, drawn from the depths of his ignorance . . . I hope we shall before long be able to get this moonshine out of his head.' Britain's other leading elderly geologist, Roderick Impey Murchison, agreed: 'Grant to Agassiz that his deepest valleys of Switzerland, such as the enormous Lake of Geneva, were once filled with snow and ice, and I see no stopping place.'

In 1840 Agassiz converted a large moraine boulder into a comfortable hut, the 'Hotel des Neuchâtelois', on the Unteraar Glacier (immediately

east of the Aletsch Glacier). He spent five summers on the ice and made an early ascent of the Jungfrau.

Meanwhile, the Oxford professor William Buckland, who actually at 56 was even older than Sedgwick and Murchison, was wondering if some features of Scotland could be more easily explained in terms of glacier ice than of Noah's Flood. He invited Agassiz over to have a look. The two toured the Highlands, everywhere finding evidence of ice and being particularly thrilled by the parallel roads of Glen Roy, which they correctly interpreted as the shores of an ice-dammed lake at various depths. The tour ended at Edinburgh's Blackford Hill, just below the City Observatory. Here Agassiz found clear scratch-marks at the cliff base, and exclaimed to the assembled geologists plus the editor of *The Scotsman*: 'This is the work of ice!'

The Glacier Theory may have some merit, agreed the Edinburgh Geological Society in 1841 – 'but is not applicable to Scotland, at least in general.' It is traditional to see Murchison and the Edinburgh Geological Society as intellectual fossils, preserving ancient attitudes in rock-solid minds. In fact, the middle-aged and younger geologists discussed the theory fiercely in the oyster houses and coffee shops, then went off into the mountains to have a look. It was not academic argument, but the moraines near the head of Llyn Idwal in Snowdonia, that convinced the young Charles Darwin in 1842. By this time he had seen real glaciers in Patagonia.

We, today, accept the Agassiz glaciers because we've been taught them in school. We, like Murchison and Sedgwick, believe what we've been taught; but we're better than them because what we've been taught is actually true. Isn't it?

A *roche moutonée* is a 'sheepified rock', glacier-smoothed on the up-valley side, glacier-plucked on the down-valley side. It somewhat resembles a sleeping sheep, but actually takes its name from an antique French wig stiffened with mutton-fat. But I've yet to come across one so convincing that I had to say, yes, a glacier came here and did that. Then again, the Dartmoor tors eroded out from underground without anybody having to bring them: so why not the erratic boulders?

The glacier-smoothed rocks, as in the picture of Loch Avon earlier in the chapter, are rather more convincing; especially when the crags higher up are visibly not so scoured. But it's the scratch-marks on the rocks that really make me believe. The glacier, as we saw in the Bernese Oberland, is full of rubble: it's not the ice itself, but the stones and rocks frozen into it, which drag across the valley floor and sandpaper away the sides. Ten thousand years, and rain, and lichen have erased many of the marks: the best place to see them is on rock freshly exposed by a path. It was an ice-scratched rock below Goats Water that made me acknowledge: 'Yes, I can now see the long-vanished glacier.' And happily, the scratches do seem to be running up-and-down the valley rather than across it.

But once we do believe in the glacier, we see its left-behind signs all over the place. Corries, aretes and U-valleys are the defining features of mountain landscape. Moraines, tamed and covered in heather, swarm across the valley floors. Long ribbon lakes run out into the lowlands.

Rubble under the ice gets rolled into balls and cylinders, in the same way as when you rub two very dirty hands together. If the ice melts in place, the rubble remains as the

ABOVE: Steep sided, U-shaped glacier valley: Langdale, looking down to Windermere.
LEFT: Ribbon lake: Wastwater from Great Gable.

swarms of drumlins seen in Mickleden at the head of Langdale (see picture page 112) or Wasdale (left).

Glaciers don't like to bend about, and will bite away the end of a side-ridge rather than wind their way around it. And so we see ridgelines that start steeply before abruptly easing off. The Rhyd-Ddu route on Snowdon is one of countless examples: such 'truncated spurs' make an uncomfortably steep finish to many a mountain day out. Glaciers don't want to stop going downhill. So when they get to the bottom, they gouge out the valley floor to make a hole which gets filled by a ribbon lake.

Snow on prevailing south-westerly winds builds up on north-east slopes to form a small corrie glacier. The ice doesn't just sit there, but actively gouges out the hillside by a process still not completely explained. The resulting corrie has a steep head-wall and, in all the best specimens, a tarn in the bottom. Corrie glaciers attacking a ridge from both sides produce a fine, sharp-crested aretc.

Sometimes a gentle ridge is crossed by a steep-sided rocky notch. It could be a river gorge, except that rivers run down valleys, not across ridges. Indeed, it is a river gorge. For the river has run along the side of the now-absent

Rainfall just won't do it: real mountain scenery is carved out by ice.
TOP: A ridge with corrie glaciers chewing at its base on both sides becomes a sharp-crested arete. Sgurr Thuilm, Skye Cuillin.
ABOVE: Coire Ardair on Creag Meagaidh, Scottish Highlands.

ABOVE AND RIGHT: Chalamain Gap: a river gorge that goes nowhere at either end and lacks any river; this meltwater channel makes an awkward ten minutes on the way down from Braeriach, Cairngorms.
BELOW RIGHT: Erratic boulder on Craiglee, Galloway Hills.

glacier and escaped across the ridge. The resulting meltwater channel will often be entirely senseless in terms of today's drainage. Downstream, the meltwater river may run back into the glacier to flow inside the ice, thus vanishing suddenly off the underlying ground. If it does visibly continue, its channel will today be carrying a much smaller stream than it seems to deserve.

At the end of the last Ice Age, summit plateaux emerged from under the ice into tundra-type conditions. During the brief warmth of day, water seeped into the cracks: at night, it froze and expanded. Ice that had formerly protected the summit stones was now the force that broke them apart. Over a few hundred years, such freeze-and-thaw turned rocky summit plateaux into boulderfields. Similar freeze-and-thaw chips at cliffs to create scree. Both these processes continue today, at a much slower pace.

'When a new doctrine is presented,' says Agassiz, 'it must go through three stages. First, people say that it isn't true, then that it is against religion, and, in the third stage, that it has long been known.' After Hutton's realisation, at Siccar Point, of the incredible age of the Earth, the glaciers of Agassiz were the second great mental shock to hit geology. There would be several more such surprises to come: the drift of the continents, the all-destroying meteor impact that ended the Cretaceous period. It's always interesting to cultivate an innocent mind and ask: why was this idea so surprising, and why did they finally decide to go along with it?

Or maybe those poised boulders really were left by giants tired of playing geological golf?

JUST AFTER THE ICE

TOP: At the end of the last Ice Age and after, freeze-and-thaw turned rocky summit plateaux into boulderfields. Bowfell, Lake District.

MIDDLE LEFT: Similar freeze-and-thaw chips at cliffs to create scree. Great Hell Gate, on the Wasdale face of Great Gable.

BOTTOM LEFT: On the summit plateau of Beinn Bhrotain, Cairngorms. Nobody has kicked over these stones since frost action first split them apart; over 10,000 years their corners have been eroded away by rainwater.

ABOVE: Frost striping in scree, Coniston Old Man. This is an exotic effect of the tundra climate. Larger stones carry coldness deeper into the ground, to create frost heave which lifts them at the expense of their neighbours. The result is a sort of very slow convection current within the scree or stonefield. Easily disturbed by footfalls, the effect is only seen where you're unlikely to be.

3. Gneiss times

3. GNEISS TIMES
The Lewisian Gneiss, in the Outer Hebrides and Wester Ross

BELOW TOP: Banded gneiss, Barra.
BELOW BOTTOM: Lewisian Gneiss on Lewis itself: slopes of Mealaisbhal.

The scale is different in the Outer Hebrides. The land is more than half water, with many pools, lochs and inlets. The sea is half land, with islands of all sizes and rocky reefs decorated with cormorants. That sea is huge. Westward it stretches over the curve of the horizon for another 3000km (2000 miles) until you reach Nova Scotia or Greenland. Eastward, small islands rise near at hand and larger ones in the distance, until a row of isolated brown spikes along the skyline is the UK mainland, Europe and the Rest of the World.

The ocean may be enormous, but the mountains are rather small. The biggest is 799m (just over 2500ft) and they go down to almost nothing at all. The bit that's missing from the mountains is the dull heather at the bottom. Harris mountains start being mountainous straight above the shoreline, and stay rocky right to the top. That top may not be very high in feet or metres, but you still get to see an awful

TOP: Garnets 1cm wide in the gneiss of Roineabhal, South Harris.
ABOVE: Scandinavian-type scenery: Leverborough (An t-Ob) from Roineabhal, South Harris.
FOLLOWING PAGE: Knock-and-lochan country of South Harris, seen from Bliabhal.

lot of ocean. A mainland Munro takes all day. A Western Isle mountain takes (apart from the two days boat and bus to the bottom of it) just a couple of hours.

The Sound of Harris ferry makes a simple straight line on the map. This is a cartographic convention. Depending on the state of the tide and the currents, it winds among rocks and islands like the convolutions of one of the more advanced Scottish country dances – *The Duke of Perth*, say, or *The Reel of the 47th*. Just sit at the side and let the experts get on with it. Even so, as we steamed at a thrusting 20 knots straight towards a brown reef just 50m away, I did glance up at the bridge to make sure the experts really knew what they were doing. Through the wide window I could see the captain seeing the brown rocks, and a moment later the great red-painted tin bucket swerved do-si-do, set to partners with an old iron marker post, and started heading back in the general direction of Berneray.

As we were playing reel-of-three with the islets of Eriskay and Berneray, the sun suddenly came out. This turned our progress into a white paintbrush swept across a turquoise sea, and set me dashing down from the port railing, across the car deck, and up to the starboard railing to try and orient the sun, the sea and the ship in relation to the sparkling islets and the grey conical hills of Harris. At the same time I was rearranging the afternoon ahead so as to include as many as possible of those grey cones . . .

What's special about the Western Isles is the light. The air is clean, really clean, in a way the mainland only gets at sunrise on a Monday morning. When the western sun does shine, it shines not just downwards but also back up out of the sea, and again upwards out of the sea on the other side of the mountains. The effect is of pre-industrial, almost medieval air, like illuminated manuscripts rather than real scenery. It's embarrassing when you bring back the pictures; those accustomed to the industrial landscapes of Ben Lomond or the Lake District will assume you just fiddled the colour saturation in the Photoshop computer program.

What the special and somewhat implausible lighting effect shines on is a special and somewhat implausible land. This book will wander through the blobby shapes of the Yorkshire limestone, the bleak white gravel of the quartzite, the monster sandcastles of Torridon. But it's appropriate to start here on Harris, on a hill called Roineabhal, on a rock called the Lewisian Gneiss that's two thirds as old as the Earth itself.

Even on the map, the place is weird. Eastwards, grey rock is sprinkled with silver water in a sort of emulsion, so that you can't tell whether this sort of scenery should be 'knock and lochan' or 'lochan and knock'. Knock, or in Gaelic *cnoc*, is an upright rounded hummock scraped by the glacier that rampaged westwards out of the Highlands over all but the highest summits of the Western Isles. A lochan is a small lake.

And in terms of weirdness, the map does not mislead. The picture of Leverborough from halfway up Roineabhal is the one you show your friends and ask: 'Where in Europe are we?' The low boxy houses are scattered like seaweed across isthmuses and peninsulas reaching into a long, complicated sea inlet. In the middle of the village, the inlet shifts up a few feet and becomes a wide, complicated freshwater loch. Abrupt fells rise from a flat sandy plain, and out to sea is all islands. Your friends will say Scandinavia for sure.

And in a way they'll be right. The mountains are named in Norse, though this is slightly obscured by an overlay of Gaelic spelling. The rigid inflatable may have replaced the

longboat, but whale bones still lie in the front gardens of Leverborough. In Gaelic, the whale is the 'Pig of the Sea' and though it no longer feeds the islands, the unpolluted seas still yield lobster and crab.

The other main industry of Leverborough is geologising Roineabhal. Though the geologists up there didn't seem particularly pleased about it. 'Anywhere else,' they complained, 'we check out an outcrop, then walk along to the next outcrop, and what's in between we simply make up. But here, it's out in the open, every single bit of it.'

And they showed me in the grey rocks the blood-red garnets, as big as my thumbnail, whose presence reveals the past like dents and scratch-marks on a battered old pickup truck. From the rocks of Roineabhal you may be looking out across the Atlantic, but the Atlantic itself has only existed for one twentieth of the time these rocks have been around. They may be cool now under the gentle Hebridean rain, but to form these wine-dark garnets, they have passed through the heat and pressure of almost the very bottom of the Earth's crust, 20 or more kilometres underground.

The times when there was writing are known as history: the much longer, but undocumented, earlier ages of humanity are lumped together as prehistory. The writing in the rocks is fossils; and everything before the fossils was lumped into a single period, the Precambrian. With radioactive dating it was realised that this Precambrian was five times as long as all the other geological periods added together. The uncertainty in the timescale while the Lewisian Gneiss was being heated and hammered into shape: that uncertainty is roughly the same as the entire span of standard geology from the Cambrian to the present day.

ABOVE LEFT: Stripy gneiss knoll above Wester Alligin, Torridon. Liathach (Torridonian sandstone) is behind. Near the right edge of the picture, an erratic sandstone boulder.
ABOVE RIGHT: Scourie Dyke in gneiss: An Dun, near Gairloch.
BELOW: Strone Ulladale, Harris: the UK's largest overhang, climbed using pitons and etrier ladders in the 1960s. In 1987 the Scoop, the 'natural' line straight up the centre, was climbed without artificial aid.

ABOVE: Diabaig Pillar (its climb is graded E2 5b). These gneiss crags above Loch Diabaig have become some of the most popular rocks in Wester Ross. Beyond, typical knolly gneiss moorland.

Gneiss resembles Scotch broth, in that it's been heated and boiled about for so long that it's irrelevant what the original ingredients were. Typical gneiss is stripy grey. The paler bands are feldspar, grey from a smoke of other minerals dissolved into it at pressures of several tonnes to the square centimetre. The darker bands are mica, which has assembled itself into stripes to take up less room. All is well welded, with no tendency to split along the stripe-lines.

But typical gneiss is hard to find. Some has almost melted, on its way to starting all over again as pink granite. Black blobs and swirls are Scourie Dykes. These are ancient magma squeezed out by volcanoes whose remains are now somewhere on the other side of the world – some books put them in what's now Brazil. These dykes arrived 2400 million years ago, before the very, very old gneiss but after the very, very, very old gneiss; so they help the geologists start sorting out how it all happened. Around Scourie itself, the dykes have not been mangled by any later earth movements. Further south, the dykes are broken and fragmentary. Further north, they come chopped to bits like tomatoes in a can.

The gneiss rock is hard and tough – much tougher than old boots, which after a week of wandering over these rough hillsides will need to be replaced by some new ones. The knocks of the knock and lochan are lovely to walk on, gently rounded and grippy-rough: that is, until you find on the other side of the knock your way blocked by the next lochan. Between the knocks, the waterproof rocks ensure black bog and orange tussock-grass. But where the rock rises above the knock and lochan, it is compact and complicated; rough, sound, and covered in small holds. Mostly we like what we're used to, and few live on the Lewisian. However, some broad-minded climbers consider the Lewisian Gneiss the best climbing rock of them all.

MALVERN GLORY

BELOW: Precambrian England was an ocean away from Precambrian Scotland; but aeons of continental bashing about have produced similar ancient rocks there. All along a strip of western England, much later earth movements have brought those ancient rocks to the surface. The Malverns are small but genuinely mountainous, and are made still more mountainous by the way their sides have been quarried into for their tough stone.

England's exposure of ancient gneiss is at Worcestershire Beacon (**OPPOSITE TOP**). A faultline associated with the distant arrival of Africa has raised this tough old rock high above the softer and much younger sandstones which form the level plains below. Here, too, are blocky-looking lavas from volcanoes of so long ago that their geography is pure guesswork (**OPPOSITE CENTRE**, at Clutter's Cave). Broken up and complicated by faults and folding, the band of ancient rocks extends northwards to

Shropshire, where a surprising small outcrop of Ordovician quartzite, at Stiperstones, is pictured in Chapter 5. Where gneiss is crushed and heated to the verge of melting down and starting all over again, the rock called pegmatite is formed. This has the same quartz-felspar-mica composition as granite, but with individual crystals, formed over thousands of years, which may be centimetres or even metres across. The pegmatite at Gullet Quarry has quartz crystals some 20cm long (**BOTTOM RIGHT**).

THE ROCKS OF WESTER ROSS

ABOVE: Banded gneiss, Diabaig beach.
RIGHT: Geological mapping (1957) of places and pictures in Chapters 3–5.

KEY: oldest rocks at bottom

Precambrian

45	Torridonian sandstone
34	Mica schist
31	Moine schist (undifferentiated)
2	Intrusions into gneiss (Scourie dykes)
3	Lewisian gneiss

Cambrian and later

13	Late intrusions (dolerite)
64	Triassic sediments
63	Jurassic sediments
48	Durness limestone (Cambrian)
47	Fuciod Beds (Cambrian)
46	Quartzite (Cambrian)

In the north of the map, Lewisian Gneiss rises to its highest point, the Munro of A' Mhaighdean. An exhumed hill ridge of Lewisian Gneiss runs from the striped knoll (see pictured page 42) across the narrows of Loch Torridon, where it has been breached with difficulty by the Torridon glacier. On the south shore, the gneiss hill reappears below Beinn Shieldaig.

Above the Torridonian sandstone (brown on map), two small outliers of quartzite are the caps on the two Munro summits of Liathach, with Beinn Eighe's more extensive quartzite capping lying to the east. Disparities between the two sides of Loch Maree reveal the fault exploited by the glacier that formed the loch itself. Land north of the loch has dropped by about 1km relative to the south, so that at the foot of Beinn Eighe's Mountain Trail, Lewisian Gneiss looks across at quartzite.

North of Kinlochewe, the Moine Thrust has shoved gneiss over the top of Torridonian sandstone; while to the south-west, it has placed a sandstone cap onto Meall a' Ghiubhais. The piled layers of sandstone and quartzite on Sgorr Ruadh are mapped at bottom right, and pictured from Maol Chean-dearg on page 58.

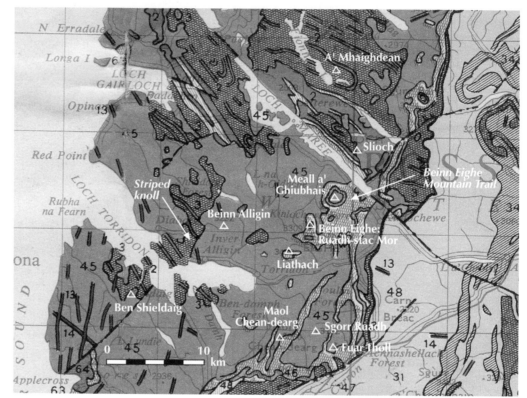

BELOW LEFT: A quartzite mountain, an Ruadh Stac.
BELOW RIGHT: A sandstone mountain, Liathach.

4. The monsters of Torridon

4. THE MONSTERS OF TORRIDON
Sandstone lands of Wester Ross

In the tourist leaflet, Torridon is described as the 'Place of Transference'; and it'll transfer any walker from a well-balanced lowlander into a rain-drenched, midge-bitten, demented howling mountain man (or woman, as the case may be).

It's easy to get depressed when another day dawns grey between the slate-black clouds and the slate-black sea a few metres below. Your spirits will be as low as your altitude as you plod along a coast path that's not a path at all but a series of black peat-wallows between nasty gneiss boulders. As damp noontide eases into wet afternoon you get lost among the knock and lochan on what was meant as a gentle low-level walk. Meanwhile your breathables have suffocated, and inside your boots the Gore-tex lining has turned up its toes and surrendered. At day's end your bright purple gaiters are rigid with black bog-slime, the people in front have filled up the Youth Hostel's drying-rack, and the pub is three miles away around the head of the loch.

Is it enough to be merely wet, miserable and cold? In order to be wet, miserable, cold and scared as well you just have to head up onto the Torridon ridges.

From the compass, rain trickles down your arm to pool in the elbow of your waterproofs. The swirling of the mist suggests great cliffs lurking all around. Fat white streams burst out from under snowfields. In poor light the sandstone turns to sadstone: it goes a nasty dark purple, with a coating of slime that laughs at your Vibram soles. Starting from sea level, it's a long, long climb to the ridge, even

ABOVE: Torridonian sandstone on Liathach.
BELOW: Am Fasarinen Pinnacles, Liathach.

if you don't get lost among the crags. And when you get there, what?

Wind roars like a river among the rocks, and there's the edge of a frightful drop for that wind to blow you over. There's a scrambly bit that's gritty and loose and has fresh sleet lying all over it. Getting blown off the edge is the quick way down; and given the slippery rocks, saturated turf and chilled limbs, the slow way down can be very slow indeed. Just don't think about the warm fire, malt whisky and dry socks 1000 metres below. That way madness lies.

And yet the Torridonian madness can take an exactly opposite form. The magical transference takes place in the time needed for a pale patch overhead to become sun, the cloud to break open and show bits of moor and a distant waterfall. The dismal scene is whisked away into the sky. What replaces it is purest melodrama.

Most Precambrian rocks are metamorphic, mauled about by a billion years of colliding continents. The surprising thing about the Torridonian sandstone is its survival as sandstone, still with its beds almost as level as they were laid. The terracing (here emphasised by snowfall on Beinn Alligin) represents strata of softer mudstone, laid in still waters when the lively river systems were elsewhere. The grassy terraces break up the climbing, and also dribble black slime down it, so that the faces of Alligin and Beinn Bhan shown here do not tempt summer climbers. However, where the sandstone crags are continuous and therefore slime-free, superb climbs such as the Cioch Nose of Sgurr a' Chaorachain resemble Derbyshire gritstone scaled up to mountain size.

ABOVE: Coire na Poite of Beinn Bhan, Applecross; scrambling on An Teallach; Beinn Alligin from the north.
BELOW: Cross-bedding in Torridonian sandstone. The sand and gravel were carried down out of a now non-existent mountain range by vigorous streams and flash floods.

Now you can actually see the holes you're going to fall into. They are lined with dark crag, and have the sea at the bottom. The sandstone rises in lumps, layer on layer, to ridges that

TOP LEFT: The contact of Torridonian sandstone (below) with Cambrian quartzite, seen on the summit ridge of Liathach (NG939582). A sprinkling of red Torridonian gravel a few centimetres up into the quartzite suggests that this may be an unconformity, with missing time between the two rock layers. Nothing in this photo, though, suggests that the time gap is actually some 700 million years – equivalent to all ten geological periods from the quartzite to the present day.

TOP RIGHT: The Torridon conglomerates contain dark pebbles of volcanic rocks not part of the Lewisian, or of anything else currently existing in the UK.

ABOVE: Photomontage of Slioch across Loch Maree. The low gneiss hill immediately above the loch, centre, has re-emerged after a billion years buried under red sandstone. On the right, the faultline of Gleann Bannisdale has brought quartzite down level with Slioch's sandstone. The Moine Thrust (see Chapter 5) has brought more Lewisian Gneiss in from the right over the top of the quartzite.

stand jagged against the sky. Of mainland Britain's ridge-scrambling, about one third is on these four monster mountains. The Beinns Alligin, Dearg and Eighe each have a stretch that attains Grade 1. Liathach has nearly a kilometre of scrambling over the famous Fasarinen Pinnacles.

Between the tricky bits are miles of rocky ridge. Natural sunlight colours the sandstone a cheerful red. The rock gives rough rounded holds to hand and foot, and stands in wobbly-looking towers with flat tops and ledges, like a trifle that's been poured out a bit too warm. Other parts are quartzite, a completely opposite rock. Quartzite is yellow-ish-grey. It is smooth, even slippery, to the foot, but breaks into nice sharp edges for the hand. Sometimes it breaks too much and comes right off the mountain.

Some bits of the ridges are single-track, like the Highland roads. If someone comes the other way, one of you must retreat to a passing place. Below the crest the sandstone slopes are high, steep, slimy and not to be contemplated. Brownish scree, bright green moss and white snow patches complete the picture, with silver water gleaming far, far below.

Across Loch Torridon the hills of Applecross would, in any other range, be counted as proper mountains. Here they take on a supporting role as interesting shapes against the sunset. Beyond them, a crumpled bit of horizon is the Isle of Skye. Crazy towers and pinnacles stand in line, one behind the other, and beyond them all, the sun sinks golden into a western sea.

Next day the cloud's down and it's back to the coast path in the rain.

THE THREE TIERS OF TORRIDON

The thing about Torridon is its stark simplicity. There's the Lewisian Gneiss, which is grey, and forms the basement layer. The gneiss is rough, lumpy, and quite amazingly old. On top of that there's the purplish-red Torridonian sandstone, which is also old, but not quite so amazingly old as the gneiss. Even so, while the New Red Sandstone is old, and the Old Red Sandstone is really old, the Torridonian Sandstone is much, much older than that. What is really amazing about the Torridonian is that it has survived 1000 million years of crashing continents unmetamorphosed, unmangled, here and there just slightly tilted sideways.

Then, 500m further up again, there's the white Cambrian quartzite, which is just young enough to have some fossils in it and to stand at the very start of what we could call normal geology.

The contact at the top, where the sandstone meets the quartzite, is a fairly ordinary unconformity: the same sort of thing that we saw at Siccar Point in the Introduction. That is to say, the Torridonian sandstone was worn down by wind and weather, and then finally, as the land sank, by the incoming sea. The quartzite was then placed on top as a sedimentary, underwater layer.

The contact at the bottom, where the Torridonian stands on the gneiss, is altogether more intriguing. The tough Lewisian Gneiss has been eroded, but certainly isn't laid flat; and the red sandstone was laid down on land. Its rough gritty texture, the big pebbles in it, show that it has travelled only a short way since it crumbled out of some big red decomposing mountains somewhere. Plot the contact very carefully, allowing for the fact that everything has tilted seaward since the sandstone landed (this plotting has been done in detail at Scourie further north). You discover that the top of the buried gneiss forms a landscape of canyons 500m deep, floored with loose boulders, down which the red mountain debris rushes in flash floods, into which red sand blows on pitiless winds.

Later, in Chapter 15, we will be looking at the Old Red and the New Red Sandstones: laid down as our bit of land passed through desert zones to south and then to north of the Equator. But in Torridonian times, everywhere was desert. There was no grass or trees to slow down the wind; pebbles 2cm across are rounded in the style of sand-grains, showing that they were blown across the rocky surface. When rain fell, there was no soil to hold it, for soil is made by plants. Above Loch Sligachan on Skye, the Mad Burn drains a corrie of bare rock and stones. Two hours after the rain starts, that burn is in raging spate, and if you just crossed it there's no way you're getting back to Glen Brittle. In Torridonian times, every burn was a mad burn.

The world was probably hotter then: the atmosphere was full of CO_2, the greenhouse gas. The day was shorter, and the moon, being closer, was twice the size in the sky. It raised high tides four times as high as those of today, in an ocean that tasted not of salt but of soda water.

Far out in the west, on land that has subsequently moved away to become Greenland and North America, the big, red, decomposing mountains stood against the sunset. Here in the foothills, mountain storms brought a roar of waters down the great bare-rock wadis; waters which stood for a few days or months in wide sterile lakes on plains of sand and gravel. Over millions of years, the land sank under the weight of sediments, allowing ever more sediments to build up on top – the Torridonian red sandstones are up to 5000m deep.

And yet this bleak reddish-black world did contain life. Life – but not as we know it. Prokaryotes are simple single cells, each one little more than some DNA with a membrane around it. If life's first great leap was in coming into existence in the first place, the second was when various of these simple cells colonised one another to form eukaryotes. Eukaryotes are large complex cells with nucleus (the DNA bit), chloroplast (the photosynthesising organ), and mitochondrion (the food processing plant).

Prokaryotes have been referred to as cyanobacteria, or as blue-green algae. But in fact prokaryotic and eukaryotic bacteria are more different from each other than we are from yeast. Indeed, they are more different than us and bacteria.

Across the bottom of shallow seas and lakes, the prokaryotic bacteria formed what's been called a lawn or carpet, but was more like a layer of slime, stiffened with a little calcium carbonate (chalk). As the sea drops silt, the slime climbs up through it to form reef-like mounds called stromatolites.

ABOVE: The best outcrops of banded ironstone are on ancient continental crust in South Africa and Western Australia. This UK outcrop is on An Groban, Wester Ross (NG838749). Rainwater has weathered some of the originally black iron oxide to ordinary rust.

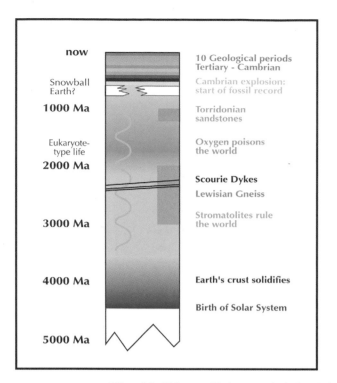

now

Snowball
Earth?

1000 Ma

Eukaryote-
type life

2000 Ma

3000 Ma

4000 Ma

5000 Ma

10 Geological periods
Tertiary - Cambrian

Cambrian explosion:
start of fossil record

Torridonian
sandstones

Oxygen poisons
the world

Scourie Dykes

Lewisian Gneiss

Stromatolites rule
the world

Earth's crust solidifies

Birth of Solar System

ABOVE AND BELOW: Life, and the Universe, with the ten geological periods crammed into a multicoloured band at the very top. Ma = millions of years ago. Snowball Earth = an intriguing theory that the world and its oceans froze over completely for 200 million years just before the explosion of fossil life at the start of the Cambrian. Evidence includes deep rocks apparently made of glacier rubble on Islay and on Schiehallion, at a time when Scotland was in the tropics.
ABOVE RIGHT: In a dry desert atmosphere, flash floods wash kilometre depths of sand and gravel out of a decomposing mountain chain: Death Valley, California. Or Wester Ross, 1000 million years ago.

The green slime didn't have sex so it didn't evolve. It stayed much the same, ruling the Earth in a soda-water ocean for 3000 million years. This is ten times longer than the dinosaurs, and roughly 1500 times as long as human beings have existed so far. In a 'living fossil' moment that makes the coelacanth seem like a Johnny-gone-lately, in 1956 stromatolites were found still alive and smelling like cowpats in the brackish waters of Shark Bay in Western Australia.

Geology popularisers tend to get very excited about stuff like the silty slime layers, which is, to anyone who hasn't been looking at rocks for three undergraduate years, two

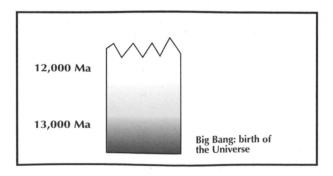

12,000 Ma

13,000 Ma

**Big Bang: birth of
the Universe**

post-graduate years, and a bit more after that while waiting for the next research grant, invisible. The interleaved layers of slime and lime which make up a stromatolite are indeed present in the Torridonian sandstone, but an inexperienced eye just doesn't see the stuff. However, the Precambrian slime carpet has left its sign in the rocks in another way. A way that, if it's invisible, is invisible by being so huge and conspicuous.

Stromatolites made their living by photosynthesis: using energy from sunlight to break up carbon dioxide, then using the carbon to build their bodies. The polluting by-product is oxygen.

As anyone who's attempted to maintain rusty motor cars will know, the chemical element which enthusiastically scavenges oxygen is iron. Iron dissolved in seawater seized hold of the oxygen and formed the black, powdery oxide of iron called magnetite. This dropped to the ocean bottom, where it formed stripy-layered banded ironstone. After 1.5 billion years of this, the stromatolites had converted all the ocean iron to ironstone, and were making oxygen faster than fresh iron was being washed into the sea. Oxygen started to pollute the atmosphere. Now it could attack iron compounds lying about on land, turning them the cheerful orange of the iron oxide we call rust.

Life's first work was the conversion of Earth's atmosphere, charging it with dangerous and unstable oxygen. The challenge of coping with, and then exploiting, an air poisoned with oxygen was what led to the complex eukaryotic cell, the first multicelled organism, and eventually to us. We think of green as being the colour of living things. But nearly a billion years before the first ferns emerged on land, the life colour was oxygen plus iron: the rusty-red of the Torridonian sandstone.

5. Quartz and quartzite

5. QUARTZ AND QUARTZITE
Quartz thoughts

There are quartz and quartzite, silicon and silica, not to mention silicate and silicone. Quartz is silica but silica isn't necessarily quartz.

ABOVE: Quartz crystals on display at the Natural History Museum, London.
BELOW RIGHT: Quartz vein in Borrowdale Volcanic rocks: Haystacks, Lake District. As the presence of this quartz suggests, a very large lump of granite is 5km below.

Silicon is one of the chemical elements; and of the 120 elements, it's the commonest, along with oxygen and aluminium, in the Earth's crust. (When the Earth was molten, the heavier elements, such as nickel and iron, sank to the middle. They still remain there, causing the earth's magnetic field. The lightest elements, like hydrogen, ended up as gasses in the atmosphere, where they diffused away into space. This leaves the crust mostly made of silicon, aluminium, oxygen, carbon and nitrogen.)

Pure silicon, chemically abbreviated Si, is shiny stuff with peculiar electrical properties that turn out to be very useful in the insides of computers. But chemically speaking it's rather reactive, and in the ground is always combined with other elements. The simplest and commonest such combination is silicon dioxide, SiO_2, known as silica. As silicon is the commonest element in the crust, its compound silica is the commonest compound.

More complicated compounds, with silicon, oxygen, and something else, are *silicates*. The feldspar which is the second mineral in granite; the mica which gives the granite its black specks; the olivine that darkens basalt and other 'mafic' rocks; the garnets in the Lewisian Gneiss – all of these are silicates of one sort or another. Indeed, apart from silica itself, just one of the common rock-forming minerals is *not* a silicate: calcite, which is calcium carbonate, examined in the limestone chapter. (And *silicone*, used in fire retardants, sealants, and breast implants, is a long-chain molecule – a polymer – based on a chain of alternating silicon and oxygen atoms. Apparently if you burn silicone you end up with powdered sand.)

Those silicate minerals will be important in chapters to come. For now, we need to look at the simplest and commonest silicon compound, silica or SiO_2. Let silica cool slowly and solidify and it forms regular crystals, hexagonal in section and pointed at both ends. This crystalline form of silica is called quartz. Quartz is white, shiny, and slightly translucent. It is hard, and tough, and resists erosion and weathering.

It's a basic ingredient of many sorts of rock; but in particular, forms the groundmass of granite (granite's other two minerals being feldspar and biotite mica). When other rock minerals are eroded away, the quartz survives to form ordinary beach sand – and then, in the normal course of geology, sandstone. It's a small addition of iron that turns beach sand yellow. Quartz crystals with other impurities can come out in a range of colourways. Among the semi-precious stones, several are actually impure quartz: cairngorm, rose quartz, amethyst.

Quartz has the lowest melting point of any common mineral. So when magma bubbles up under a chunk of country, the quartz in the magma itself or in the overlying rocks comes boiling out. It can also travel upwards dissolved in superheated steam. It seeps through faultlines and cracks, cools, and recrystallises. So veins of pure white quartz show that there have been hot rocks below; as often as not, a big lump of granite.

BELOW: The Ordinary Route on Idwal Slabs, Snowdonia. The climb follows a faultline all the way up the slabs. Quartz was originally intruded between two bedding planes, of which the upper one has eroded off. It supplies small but useful extra holds on the slab alongside the faultline crack.

RIGHT: Flint is silica in another shape. Originally the silicaceous skeletons of sponges and other sea creatures, it's been dissolved in seawater and precipitated out again in lumps into the chalk of Dorset.

On the other hand if you cool silica quickly, so that it can't crystallise, it forms a supercooled liquid. If the silica is pure, and is cooled quickly enough, that supercooled liquid is ordinary window glass. Some volcanic lavas are mostly made of silica, and the rock called obsidian is a kind of dark glass that's 70 per cent silica plus impurities of iron and aluminium. Lumps of pure window glass can also be formed by lightning strikes on beaches.

There's a third way to make solid silica. Silica – whether quartz or window glass – is slightly soluble in water; more so if the water is hot, pressurised, and acid, but slightly even in the sea. If dissolved silica precipitates out, it forms a hard, whitish, structureless lump. In fact, it forms flint; or again, with minor impurities, jasper, agate, onyx and so on.

FROM QUARTZ, QUARTZITE

ABOVE: Quartz vein in quartzite rock: Grey Corries, Lochaber.
BELOW: Quartzite country at the back of Beinn Eighe, Torridon. Darker sandstone forms the lower part of the right-hand, and highest, summit, Ruadh-stac Mor. Another patch of darker sandstone appears as a moorland outcrop directly below Sgurr Ban, second summit from the left.

Edward de Bono, the inventor of lateral thinking, was asked for a recipe for one of those celebrity recipe books. His dish was composed entirely of one ingredient: a clever (but perhaps only slightly delicious) combination of various differently prepared styles of egg. Specifically, a boiled-egg omelette, glazed with egg yolk, and stuffed with scrambled egg.

Quartzite is the same sort of thing, done with silica. It's made up of crystals of quartz, cemented together with silica; much as de Bono's untempting supper was lumps of boiled egg bound together with egg. Compress ordinary sandstone, and the sand grains start to melt at the edges and fuse together; quartzite is metamorphosed sandstone. And thus I came to my first enlightenment over the rocks of Torridon. Liathach and Beinn Eighe are Torridonian sandstone, with a pale-coloured cap of quartzite. The quartzite on top is simply the sandstone underneath, with something horrible having happened to it.

Teenage brains are resilient, luckily. Because that first enlightenment was quite, quite wrong. The Cambrian quartzite is not squashed sandstone at all. It actually formed under the ocean; and it has the fossil worm-holes to prove it. It's made of ordinary quartz sand, cemented together with silica out of the seawater. At the Natural History

A QUARTZITE COLLECTION

ABOVE: On Ruadh-stac Mor, the main summit of Beinn Eighe, looking south to Choinneach Mor. Choinneach Mor (meaning 'big mossy') is topped with the less infertile shales of the Fucoid Beds, which contrast with the sterility of the crags and the foreground mountain. The compact quartzite below it, Eastern Ramparts, has many good but hard climbs.

BELOW LEFT (TOP AND BOTTOM): A sedimentary rock (quartzite from Beinn Eighe) and a metamorphic one (quartzite from the Grey Corries). But which is which?

BELOW RIGHT (TOP): Tunnels made by marine worms are easily spotted, not quite so easily recognised as the fossils they are. The bedding cuts across the worm-holes, which are about 1cm across. Spidean Coire nan Clach, Beinn Eighe.

BELOW RIGHT (BOTTOM): A boulder of the yellowish Fucoid Beds in quartzite stonefield, Beinn Eighe.

BELOW CENTRE: Where today's rock surface corresponds with the actual tunnel tops, there shows a wider and slightly splayed marking, though to call the result 'trumpet rock' perhaps overdramatises it. Beinn Eighe Mountain Trail.

ABOVE: Grade 2 scrambling on the Giant's Staircase of Coire Claurigh, Grey Corries.
BELOW: Photomontage of Sgorr Ruadh from Maol Chean-dearg. Sandstone in the foreground is ice-smoothed and shows glacier scratches if you walk down there (not visible in the photo). Sandstone continues across the valley to the col left of Sgorr Ruadh. Up the skyline to Sgorr Ruadh summit the walker crosses quartzite, sandstone, quartzite and sandstone again. Continue to Fuar Tholl (back right) and you cross another band of quartzite before the sandstone summit, where the Mainreachean Buttress with its fine climbs (top just visible) drops to the left.

Museum in London, you'll even find quartzite classed as a sort of sandstone.

The first, fundamental, start to understanding our stones is: sedimentary, metamorphic, igneous. This is useful, and illuminating. But quartzite complicates it. Quartzite can be sedimentary (fallen to the sea bed and squashed); or it can be metamorphic (changed by heat out of something else). The Cambrian quartzite of Wester Ross is sedimentary. The Dalradian quartzite of the Grey Corries is just the same stuff, but it's metamorphic.

Sorry about that.

QUARTZITE QUALITIES

The cap of pale quartzite lying across the top of Beinn Eighe in Torridon, or Carn a' Mhaim in Glen Nevis, is often mistaken for snow: so say the guidebooks. In fact it's pale grey, and quite easily distinguishable from the white stuff out of the sky. It's also quite easily distinguishable from other sorts of stone.

Quartzite may not look like snow, but it's paler than any other sort of rock. It's also, as rocks go, one of the hardest. Where other rocks crumble, or wear down into rounded lumps, quartzite may crack but stays square. Its whiteness and its angularity make it probably, of the common rocks, the easiest one to recognise.

Being made of quartz, it has the shine of quartz and also the toughness. It does not crumble away into soil, and quartzite moorland is bare rock and bare gravel, all in ghostly pale colours. So that, two paragraphs down the guidebook from the phrase about 'mistaken for snow', invariably come the words 'lunar landscape'.

By rights, the Giant's Staircase scramble, on the end of the Grey Corries range, shouldn't exist at all. The map marks simply a steepish slope, with no hint of crag. And the slabs that line the hollow behind the Grey Corries are so gently angled that you simply put hands in pockets and walk up. Or you would, if they were made of granite or Borrowdale Volcanics or anything but quartzite. Up on the Grey Corries ridge, the quartzite forms flat pavement, like a city street surprisingly raised 900m into the mountains. But tilt it at 45 degrees, and its smoothness makes a scrambling challenge, while its small but sharp handholds make sure the challenge isn't going to get too serious.

But first you have to find it. So ramble in through the Lairig Leacach, a place that feels slightly like a faded old photo, because of the pale grey colour of the quartzite rocks above. Explore the lost hollow behind the Grey Corries. At its end, running into the gap between Stob Ban and Stob Coire Claurigh, the grey and slightly shiny slabs rise in two tall steps. Rock at 45 degrees can feel surpris-

ingly exposed, especially when it rises for 20m before the next grassy ledge. Or you can choose shorter slabs, with slightly less scare-factor, and an easier sort of scramble. You top out on a bare rock terrace, only to find you haven't topped at all, as the third step rises behind. It's steeper than the first two, more exposed, but easier because of its chunky footholds.

And then, for the afternoon, there's more quartzite: as much of it as you can take, along the classic Grey Corries ridge. It's flat on top, it's blocky in the boulderfields, the sharp edges will slash your boots. Yes, it's quartzite, all right?

CAMBRIAN QUARTZITE: SEEING IT AS SEDIMENTS
It isn't always impossible to tell whether the quartzite you're walking is a sediment or the result of metamorphism. The sedimentary quartzite of Torridon is from the Cambrian; and the Cambrian is in a sense the 'beginning' of geology precisely because it has the possibility of fossils. The fine-grained, hard-edged quartzite holds impressions well, so that the great clawed beasts of the Cambrian totally overshadow the Jurassic ammonite 'industry' of Dorset.

Or they would if there were any great clawed beasts of the Cambrian. What the Cambrian did have was worms, living in the seabed. Worms don't have bones but they do have wormholes. These you can see, but don't necessarily see

as fossils, more as a useful texture, a sort of non-slip surface like lavatory tiles, here providing grip across the shiny slabs of Beinn Eighe.

Only the upper, younger layers of the Cambrian quartzite are the 'pipe rock' that has the fossil wormholes. But in those rocks they are everywhere, the most easily spotted fossil of them all.

THE MOINE THRUST
Over the last three chapters, I've laid out the simple colour-coded scheme of the North-West Highlands. A basement layer of grey Lewisian Gneiss; 600m of red Torridonian sandstone; and a pale capping of quartzite across the top. The scheme is simple enough that we can follow it even when it isn't actually working . . . For the gneiss/sandstone/quartzite forms a narrow band up Scotland's north-west coast, but only half of that band follows the straightforward scheme. On the inland side, things get very seriously scrambled.

What are we to make, say, of the ridge of Sgorr Ruadh on the southern side of Loch Torridon? Ascending, we pass from sandstone onto quartzite; all well so far. But half an hour up the ridge, the rock is again red, rounded and sandy; fifteen more minutes, and it is again sharp-edged and white and quartzite. The summit is sandstone, now steeply tilted eastwards. Continuing inland, down the ridge but up the

ABOVE: The Stiperstones of Shropshire, England's only quartzite, and the UK's youngest, belonging to the Ordovician period. Though you can't tell from the picture, this is a sedimentary quartzite. Its beds have been tilted steeply by movements of a nearby faultline.

sandstone strata, we meet quartzite for the third time at the base of Fuar Tholl. Above that again, sandstone rises in its finest form, the magnificent Mainreachan Buttress, to this second summit.

On top of that, we might expect (if not now totally confused about everything) some more quartzite. And it can indeed be found, at the far back of the hill on the slopes down into Strath Carron. But, in case we thought we understood what was going on, we find down there some of the basement gneiss as well – and on the far side of Strath Carron is a different rock altogether, the folded, metamorphosed, mica schist of the central Highlands.

The schist is the subject of the following chapter. For now, we note its abrupt beginning, cutting across the complications further west. And the way that something very heavy, carrying that schist on its back, has crushed and shoved the sandstone and quartzite.

That very heavy thing was England. Some 200 million years after the quartzite of Wester Ross was formed, a continent called Avalonia, with England on its edge, arrived from the south in the Caledonian collision. The rocks of the central Highlands were crushed and folded into schist, and pushed forward for dozens of miles over the top of the gneiss, the Torridonian sandstone, and the quartzite. The resulting faultline, running from the corner of Skye to Loch Eriboll on Scotland's north coast, is called the Moine Thrust.

Near the coast, Liathach and the western end of Beinn Eighe have been untroubled by these earth movements. The sandstone strata of Beinn Alligin lie level, undisturbed by the arrival of the southern country. But at the front of the arriving central Highlands, the sandstone and the quartzite are not just crumpled up, but broken and lifted on top of themselves, several times over. In a similar way, layers of ice pile up in front of a large icebreaker.

Travel northwards for two hours by car, and on Ben More Assynt you'll find ancient Lewisian Gneiss sliced between two layers of quartzite. At the head of Loch Glendhu, a neglected but very walkable path between the two bothies of Lochdhu and Glencoul gives an excellent view of the rock sandwich. The geological trail at Knockan Crag, near Elphin, gives a simple view of the strata: oversimple, complains my geology book, which revels in the complex overthrusting and the paradoxical strata, and seems almost disappointed when the time comes to pass eastwards into the plain grey schists of the central Highlands that are in the following chapter.

6. Squashed stones: slate to schist

6. SQUASHED STONES: SLATE TO SCHIST

The trouble with starting the history of the rocks at the start is that the most complicated sorts of stone get mentioned first, and the simpler stuff is right at the end. Gneiss (Chapter 3) is a mangled and messed-up form of schist; schist is a mangled and messed-up form of shale and slate. The intense pressure and heat of a continental collision cooks a straightforward sort of stone into something that's harder; harder underfoot and also harder on the brain.

ABOVE: The heat and pressure that put the cleavage into the slate will often obscure the original bedding structure; here, however, the original bedding can still be seen. Note how the stone has no longer any tendency to break along that bedding. Path stone from Black Combe, part of the Skiddaw Slates of Chapter 9.
BELOW: Cathedral Cave, Little Langdale, Cumbria. The purplish-coloured slates quarried here were formed from a fine-grained volcanic ash.

The progression is from ordinary mudstones and shales, through slate, to schist, and then, at pressures deep in the earth's crust, eventually to gneiss. The oldest rocks tend to be the most ravaged: the ones that are less crumpled also tend to be younger. The gneiss, which is the end-point of this metamorphic progression, occupied Chapter 3 above. Next-less-squashed, the schist, is the later part of the current chapter. But to make sense of that schist, it's necessary to start with the original shales and mudstones (belonging to Chapter 8, below) and then pass onwards through the slates.

STAGE 1: SLATE

Take some shale, laid down in the sea as clay mud drifts gently from the shoreline just visible on the far horizon. Shale is sedimentary, and splits apart along the bedding planes that are the layers as they originally fell to the ocean floor.

The shale just lies there on the ocean floor, gradually getting deeper and deeper. After 50 million years of this, the shale might suppose that just getting gradually deeper was

ABOVE: The rocks of Glyder Fach, Snowdonia, were originally laid as volcanic ash-fall tuffs. Fifty million years later, earth movements of the Caledonian mountain-building event squashed them. The resulting cleavage fracture-pattern gives Castell y Gwynt its spiky outline.

what it was all about. However, there's a continent coming, and continents mean change. The shale is made of clay minerals: flat platy crystals of mica, long thin ones of quartz and alumina. As the stone is compressed, these minerals get realigned at right angles to the direction of stress. It's now easy for the rock to split along the planes between the minerals: those planes that are across the direction of the original compression. Indeed, if you see a skilled slate splitter at work, the block of rock seems to fall into sheets as easily as opening the pages of a book.

This new sort of stripiness, and new way of falling apart, is called the 'cleavage'. It cuts across the original bedding and usually hides it. If the original rock was not a shale but a smooth and uniform mudstone, the resulting slates will be good enough to go on your roof.

But the very best starting-point for slates is a smooth and uniform sediment formed of volcanic ash ('tuff'). Among and around the volcanic mountains of Snowdonia and the Lake District, the earth movements that raised the mountains have also turned tuffs into slates. Quarries at Honister and Llanberis supplied waterproof rooves for the cities of the Industrial Revolution. They also ensured that the mountain villages would be not only walled but also topped off

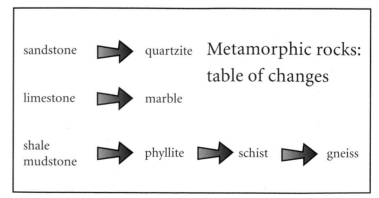

sandstone ➜ quartzite

limestone ➜ marble

shale mudstone ➜ phyllite ➜ schist ➜ gneiss

Metamorphic rocks: table of changes

with local stone. The small farms with their barns are obliged to harmonise with the landscape: they're made of exactly the same materials.

STAGE 2: SCHIST

The earth buckles and rises; the slates are buried more deeply, and more fiercely crushed. As the temperature rises, molecules are mobilised and old crystals start to grow, new crystals start to form: still at right angles to the compression.

First comes chlorite, which is greenish, and gives a greenish or silvery sheen to the resulting rocks as they break apart along the cleavage planes. That rock is called phyllite.

As the temperature still increases, more minerals start to mobilise. The most important one, from a walking-on-it point of view, is mica. Mica was already there in the clay mudstone we started with; it realigned itself as the shales were compressed into slate and phyllite. But what makes schist, schist – and is referred to as schistosity – is when, as the rocks hot up some more, the mica starts to redeploy into big, visible crystals along the cleavage.

Well up inside the clouds on Gleouraich above Glen Shiel, we were looking at the ground because there was nothing else to look at, and my companion stopped suddenly: 'What's this? It's a bendy rock.' Jammed sheets of what looked like thick discoloured plastic were sticking out of the stone. Trodden on, they yielded below the boot. We were on the mica schist, and here was the mica.

Silica, three molecules of oxygen and one of silicon, is the basis of most continental rocks. It can join together in chains, giving the pyroxene family of minerals. It can join in double-chains, giving the amphiboles which, with pyroxene, go to form dark volcanic rocks like basalt. Alternatively, silica can combine into sheets, and then it makes mica.

ABOVE LEFT: The halfway stage between slate and schist is a rock called phyllite. Its silver sheen makes it quite easy to recognise, as at Edinample Falls, by Loch Earn in the southern Highlands (**ABOVE**).
BELOW: A mica crystal about 25mm wide, formed in orange microgranite of Cross Fell in the Pennines.

SCHIST OF THE CENTRAL HIGHLANDS

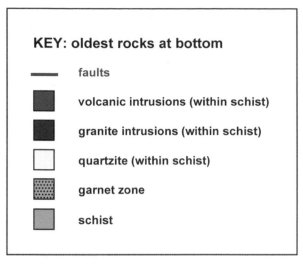

KEY: oldest rocks at bottom

— faults

volcanic intrusions (within schist)

granite intrusions (within schist)

quartzite (within schist)

garnet zone

schist

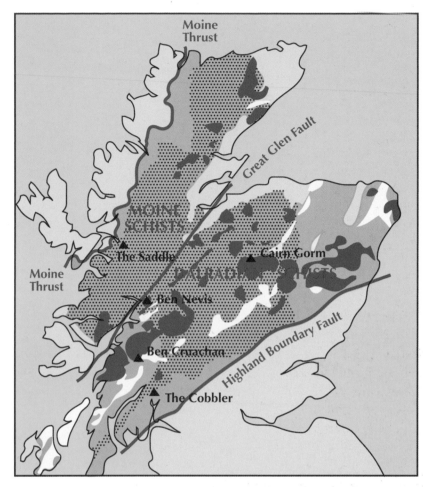

BELOW: The shininess of schist shows on the Saddle, Glen Shiel. The climbing here is across the cleavage, so that there are plentiful incut holds, making this Forcan Ridge one of Scotland's superb scrambles.

Strictly, mica isn't a mineral but a family of minerals. The biotite sort of mica is the black specks in granite. But white, shiny mica, called muscovite, grows along the cleavage planes to distinguish the mica schist that covers central Scotland.

The mica delivers a shine to the schist that's particularly noticeable if you look sunwards across the rocky knolls on a hazy August afternoon. It also means that schist can be slippery, especially when wet.

As the temperature and pressure go on increasing, garnet starts to crystallise within the schist. It forms deep red lumps the size of peas, beans, or sometimes of even bigger garden vegetables. The striking colour makes them an exciting find;

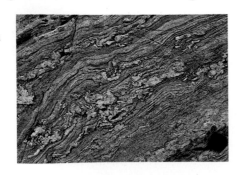

ABOVE: Mountains of the Moine: Sgurr a' Chaorachain south of Strath Carron.
RIGHT: Seen closeup, the ordinary grey rock of Scotland shows quite a bit of colour, as well as the swirly texture imparted by the collision with England 400 million years ago.

it helps, too, that they count as jewels, or at least as semi-precious stones. As with fossils, look for clean, unweathered rocks. But you'll only find garnets towards the centre of the compression zone. For geologists, the real excitement of the garnets is that they mark where a precise level of heat and pressure has been attained – where the schist has, as it were, *really* hit the fan at 450°C, at depths varying from 4 to 20 km (2 to 12 miles).

STAGE 3: GNEISS

Even more pressure and heat will transform the schist onwards into the gneiss, subject of the earlier Chapter 3. What makes the gneiss nice, is the further minerals that form, binding the cleavage back together again. Mica crystals rearrange themselves in distinct bands within the rock; so gneiss is stripy and the mica slipperiness is obliterated. The stripy cleavage remains as a pretty pattern, but no longer makes a plane of breakage.

This as far as it goes. Any more heat and pressure will melt the gneiss completely, and after that it must reform as a new rock; no longer metamorphic at all, but igneous. Granite is the likeliest result.

MOINIAN MOUNTAINS

Between the Skye Road and the Skye railway lies an area
known to geologists as the 'Moine schists'; to Munro-
baggers as 'Sections 11 & 12'; and to others, scarcely known
at all. This large parcel of ground offers perplexities to the
geologists: before being baked and crumpled by being
shoved westwards over the top of the Torridon mountains,
and then by the arrival of England from the south, these
were sediments subsiding into a deep ocean – but what
ocean? Are these rocks very, very old, or are they in fact a
great deal older than that?

It offers perplexities also to the Munro-bagger. There is
the locked gate that stops you driving up Glen Strathfarrar;
there are the stalking paths that vanish into Lochs Monar
and Mullardoch. There are the two exceedingly inconvenient
ridge-end peaks just south of Loch Mullardoch.

There's the problem of a name for it all. You can't call it
after a deer forest: it lies over 14 different deer forests. You
can't call it after a glen: it is three glens, Strathfarrar, Cannich
and Affric. You can't call it after the centre you climb it
from as there is no such centre, only various edges. (The
Achnashellach Hills? Not really. It'd be as sensible to set out

from Dalwhinnie to climb Ben Nevis as to climb An Socach
from Achnashellach.)

There's the problem of partition. How do you break up,
into day-length or even week-length portions, an area of
six principal ridges, 36 Munros and 17 Corbetts? Not all of
us have the time or even the shoulder-muscles to march
in at Cluanie with a fortnight's food and a return ticket from
Strathcarron. And so it's all too easy to leave yourself,
when you come to your advanced Munro-bagging
years, with a long walk in just for the rather unexciting
Maoile Lunndaidh.

They have no pretty valleys, these mountains of the
Moinian schist, this nameless Monar-Mullardoch. Bleak
reservoirs, not glittering sea lochs, penetrate the hills. Here
are no car parks for the folding chairs and the picnic table,
because there are no roads. And for the climber and mountaineer, here are no high terrifying crags. It's country, above
all else, for walking: for walking long and hard.

You can walk through it. North to south, weaving among
the ridges, it's 50 miles of stalkers' path, riverbank and bog

67

from Achnasheen to Cluanie by way of Iron Lodge.

Or you can go over the top. What walkers want is ridges. The impact with England – the Caledonian Orogeny, 400 million years ago – has left the area crumpled along east-west lines, and here are 60 miles of ridge. The ridges are sided with grass, and with the Moinian schist, or, as hillwalkers call the stuff, 'ordinary grey rock'. The grass is steep, and 600m high. The ridge top is mossy, with a little path, and some-times enough grey schist to scramble over, though not usual-ly enough to get scared about. The ridge top is sharp: sharp enough that you see down both sides of it at once. The way ahead swoops down, and as it rises the strata of the ordinary grey rock are buttressing the northern side in a strong rising diagonal. The green moss and the grey schist rock blend together, and the strong diagonal is like the weave-line in those stout tweed breeches worn by walkers 50 years ago.

There's another thing they do for you, the green and the schisty grey. They do their steep ascent, and from a distance it looks fierce. When you get to it, there's a little stream fold-ed among the rocks, and gentle grassy bits, and the grey slabs are flattish and just waiting to be walked up. But – it's a big but – the slope may be likeable: it isn't low.

These hills are vigorous hills. They are not for the not particularly fit, or for those who want just a little walk. They'll give you a ridge that swoops 200m down and up again all day long, and is still swooping a day and a half later; and maybe a May snow shower to speed you along the way. Say you've had enough and drop off the ridge, and they'll give you peat hag and bog, and half a day of gloomy glen to Achnasheen or Achnashellach. Say you want more, then, and stay up on the ridge. Now they offer a bright lochan with banks of grass to shake out a tent onto; or a little grass-bottomed hag, just out of the wind, and a sunset spiked from underneath with 50 Munros.

These are not little hills and not pretty hills. 'The ugly,' said Gauguin, 'can sometimes be beautiful. The pretty, never.' These hills are high lumps above a shapeless reservoir. They can indeed be beautiful. But to appreciate the beauty you need not good eyesight but good legs, and a small green tent.

DALRADIA: THE LAND OF GREEN PICNIC PLACES

South of the Great Glen, Scotland's schist changes its name – it's now the Dalradian – but not its nature. It's still crinkly grey, slightly slippery when wet; it still makes mountains that are knobbly rather than stark.

Gneiss and quartzite are tough rocks and hardly break down at all; granite breaks down into coarse gravel and sand. But schist is a complicated, messy rock, originally made of mud; and it breaks down into stones and silt, to make that complicated messy stuff called soil. The Moine mountains are topped with grey moss, but in the Dalradian of the southern Highlands, the green grass runs right over the tops. The hills of Perthshire in particular have few precipice moments, but in among the crinkly grey outcrops is an abundance of green and sheltered picnic places. Sometimes the original ocean sediments included a bit of seashell, so that the schist soil donates some lime to the present-day mountainside. And so on Ben Lawers and at the head of Glen Isla, the green picnic places are decorated with tiny wildflowers.

The other difference in Dalradia is in the scale. The hills are closer to the England impact zone, so even more crumpled. The ridges do not stride from one side of Scotland to the other, but form into convenient hill days and horseshoes. And the grey itself is not unvarying. Suddenly it can shift into quartzite; a glare of white rock, tumbled screes, and any picnic will be not on grass but on a flat bare stone, hopefully without too many sharp bits.

A later chapter is devoted to the volcanic outbursts at Glen Coe and Ben Nevis. The same underground melting also gives granite at Ben Cruachan and Glen Etive, and interrupts the monotony of the eastern Grampians with the magnificence of the Cairngorms. Along the ridge of the Mamores, you'll be stepping from granite to schist to quartzite – between the two tops of Na Gruagaichean you pass over all three sorts of rock.

HISTORY OF THE SCHIST

Sediments are fairly straightforward: granites and volcanics are exciting. The messy metamorphics of central Scotland

BELOW: Garnets up to 2mm wide, in mica schist.

were the last of all to be mapped. As rocks go, they're hard underfoot and under the climber's hand. They are hard also in the head. They've been severely bent about and crushed, three times: the Caledonian Orogeny, when England met Scotland, was just the end of it all. It's not just the garnets, but a sequence of distinctive minerals that have formed at different levels of heat and compression. And these minerals are different in the east (where there was not so much heat but even more compression) and in the west (where things were hotter, but not so deeply buried). They are different also across a single hillside or along a single glen, as metamorphism is different in the elbow or in the forearm of a fold.

So garnets are not everywhere among the red spots on the map. In fact, they are pretty difficult to find. That's a good thing. The longer you spend failing to find any small red specks, the more time you spend inspecting schist in all its differences. Along the cleavage, you get the shine of the mica. The other way, you see the intricacy of the folds, and the folds within the folds.

The rock changes, also, according to what it started from. Where the original mudstone was of a sandy sort, the schist becomes psammite; a subtly textured, paler rock without the glitter. In the Nevis Gorge, impure limestone among the ingredients has resulted in streaky folds of blue and orange among the grey. At the edges of the Highlands, outside the garnet zones, the glitter-mineral is chlorite rather than mica, and the rock is the less-altered phyllite, silvery among the path stones like a fish.

The ordinary grey schists, when you look at them, turn out quite extraordinarily rich in their variety, and also sometimes quite colourful. The question of how best to hill-walk them remains a tricky one. Its billion-year history does seem to suggest, though – walk slowly with a big rucksack across the Moine; and gently with a picnic over the Dalradian schists south of the Great Glen.

A SCHIST SELECTION

ABOVE: The slipperiness of schist: Anyone aspiring to lead Clan Campbell must stand at the true summit of the Cobbler (Ben Arthur) above Arrochar, Scotland's toughest summit outside Skye. The front of the summit is a separate block, and the least difficult route passes from the boulders at left, through the tunnel behind this block, to the exposed ledge on the right. At its end, this ledge becomes a rising ramp: the angle is easy but there are no specific footholds. It's the descent of this ramp, especially in the wet, that makes this one of Scotland's accident blackspots. The foot-smoothed mica schist is all too easily slipped off.

ABOVE RIGHT, TOP TO BOTTOM: Blue/orange schist above Nevis Gorge, Fort William; shiny schist on Stuc a' Chroin, southern Highlands; psammite (below) and greyer, shinier, mica schist above, Creag Meagaidh Reserve in Badenoch; folded schist above Nevis Gorge; river pebbles in Ariundle Oakwood Reserve, west of Fort William.

7. Greywacke and the ruggedness of Rhinog

7. GREYWACKE AND THE RUGGEDNESS OF RHINOG

ABOVE: Two greywacke beds, each about 2 metres thick, Southern Uplands.
RIGHT: A broken piece of greywacke reveals its sandy nature.

Greywacke is the harshest of rocks, rounded, rough and gloomy grey. Its looks just reflect its origin, as it forms from underwater mud at the bottoms of deep ocean trenches.

Greywacke counts as a sort of sandstone, composed of an assorted mixture of coarse and fine grains. However, deep oceans have no oxygen. So greywacke shows no cheerful rusty-red or orange colour, but a dark deep-ocean grey. Its individual grains are sharp-edged, as there's no desert wind or brisk freshwater current to rub the grains together, just the slow stirring of the mud currents. To get the very toughest sort of concrete, builders mix sharp sand together with

an aggregate of both fine and coarse particles. Nature has done the same in making greywacke. Greywacke doesn't separate into handy slabs, nor does it welcome the carver's chisel. The stonewaller of the Southern Uplands, who has to deal with the stuff daily, develops a sore elbow and a short temper as well.

Here's how sandstone ought to happen. A large river delta slides into the sea. The pebbles and gravel drop out at once, but the sand is carried on out to sea before sinking to the bottom; the silt and mud are carried even further. And so, a few kilometres offshore, sand falls, and keeps on falling for some thousands of years until an earthquake diverts the river, or the seabed rises. Thus, eventually, one bed of ordinary sandy sandstone; and, further offshore, a bed of silty mud.

Greywacke isn't like that at all; so it presented a bit of a mystery. Its beds are a promiscuous mix of sand, gravel, grit and silt. They are also, in places, unduly thick: a single bed may be many metres deep, with no internal bedding structure at all. Desert sand is yellow or orange, as the New Red Sandstone. Sand recently carried out to sea can be more brownish, as the Old Red Sandstone and the Torridonian. But greywacke is grey.

Rocks are formed by processes visible around us today. But the process that forms the greywacke is different and was, until 1929, completely unseen. And the greywacke, though technically just another sort of sandstone, makes a different sort of mountain altogether. That different sort of mountain is the Rhinogs.

A DIFFERENT SORT OF SANDSTONE: A DIFFERENT SORT OF HILL

The Beast of Bodmin Moor looks pretty scary from afar, but when you get up close it's nothing but a pussy cat. The Rhinogs of southern Snowdonia are the opposite. They don't look much on the map: a mere 15 kilometres by 5 (9 miles by 3), barely 750m high, and nowhere particularly steep. But the nearer you get, the worse they become. Look

at them through thick mist at a range of a few metres and their true class and quality appears.

What sort of beast is this Rhinog, with its wrinkled gritstone hide,

ABOVE: Pebbly greywacke, Muldonoch, Galloway Hills.
BELOW: Rhinog landscape, caused by individual, massive layers of submarine mudslide. With the apex of the Harlech Dome out of picture on the right, these beds dip gently to the left (west). Rhinog Fawr and Llyn Cwmhosen across Bwlch Dwrs Ardudwy. Photo: John Gillham.

its sulky disposition, its reluctance to get out of your way? It's a beast with more teeth than brains. You're walking over a perfectly innocent low rocky mount when it suddenly snaps out and takes a bite from your leg . . .

Enter its den by way of the 'Roman' Steps from Llyn Cwm Bychan. Here a built path of slabs laid edge-to-edge gives comfort to the feet, but already the low cliffs of the enclosing ravine are beginning to unsettle the mind.

Try not to think of Cambrian bandits with heather in their beards, mouths stained with bilberry juice. Convince yourself, if you can, that they're not about to leap down on you with death threats expressed in poetical Welsh. Their goatskin garments are grey among the grey rocks, and they fade in and out of the grey mist until your nerve breaks, your feet falter and you stumble off the Steps . . .

. . . into a waste of heather and round, rough-sided stones. In no time at all your ankle's in a hole. Your rucksack drags you down, your leg bone snaps, and by tomorrow morning the ravens have your eyes out and are pecking at your skull.

But it doesn't take bandits to drive you into the boulders. All you need is a desire to reach Rhinog Fawr. Desire inflamed, perhaps, by the words of 1930s author Patrick Monkhouse: this hill 'is grunt and sweat all the way . . . it will extract more perspiration per yard than any other in Wales, with the possible exception of the other side of the same mountain.'

The path is only a place where the heather's been rubbed away to show the holes. It leads around, down, by

TOP: As mud stops sliding, the heavier particles settle first. A well-exposed greywacke bed should show graded bedding, getting finer as it goes up. Sometimes it's easier to see this indoors in a nice clean museum, such as the Natural History Museum, London. Rock sample 20cm thick.

ABOVE: Small turbidity currents, 15–20cm thick. To have been fossilised intact, these flows must have been sludgy rather than watery ones. Greywacke at the back of Blencathra, Lake District.

crag and angle and finally up to a black pool. No paddling here; the banks and bottom alike are broken boulders. This is where you lose the path, and it's a bad place to be without one. Here I have known a man become cragbound on horizontal ground.

This particular man was a mountain-runner from a country where mountain means nicely graded paths with red and white paintmarks. The event, a five-day race the length of Wales, had already, after an afternoon on Tryfan, left him with a new word of broken English – 'shkrambling' – and the broken skin of the shins to go with it.

Now far from home and mapless, wearing expensive but unsuitable flat-soled running shoes, wrapped in mist and unable to speak the language, he came to a stop. His only companions were two scruffy and bad-tempered Scots hill-runners. One of whom (the author) spoke bad German with a villainous Swiss accent; worse, when comprehensible at all, the fellow kept making bad British jokes; such as pretending to be enjoying this sort of stuff. Alois the mountain-runner knew better. He knew that what awaited him on the upper slopes of Rhinog was his death.

'What nonsense,' I assured him in German as cracked and uncouth as the rocks we stood on. 'Nothing awaits above but more boulders, and a jolly little crag; and it may be a bit windy, but the ground's just about flat and – whoops – look out for that loose bit.'

To head down off Rhinog Fawr there's this useful path. The useful path takes you by the foot, leads you gently forward, and then leaves you looking down some cliffs into Bwlch Drws Ardudwy. (You should have gone down that nasty stony gully on the right.)

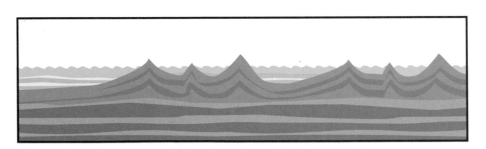

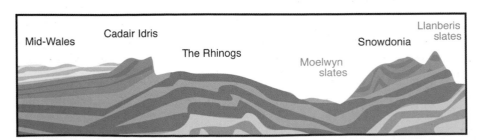

**Formation of the Harlech Dome
view South - North:
simplified and stylised**

KEY: oldest rocks at bottom

Silurian sediments: sandstone, shale, etc

Ordovician volcanic island arc: lavas and ash, some becoming slates after compression

Cambrian greywacke and mudstone: mudstones becoming slates after compression

Precambrian schist and gneiss (metamorphosed lavas and sediments)

Is this bwlch a nice warm friendly spot? 'I was tempted to visit this noted pass,' wrote the 18th-century Welsh traveller Thomas Pennant, 'and found the horror of it far exceeding the most gloomy idea that could have been conceived of it.'

These Rhinogs are part of the Snowdonia National Park. Does this mean that we can expect ice-cream shops, reconstructed footpaths and interesting leaflets? It does not. The bad-tempered Rhinogs are being left in their corner to sulk. There will be no car parks: get there at dawn for your two metres of muddy verge, or walk in from beyond some dismal bog. There will be no waymarks: in the Rhinogs you haven't really lived until you're lost. There will be no ice-cream.

You could go Rhinogging on a warm August day. You could linger among the bilberries. You could dip in the pools. You could take a direct line for the summit and enjoy the rough warm rock, the easy-angled scrambling. You could look down onto the lively green bogs and out to the sleeping sea.

But that wouldn't do at all. To do it properly, go there in the wind and in the rain. Go there in winter or early spring. Go there in unsuitable shoes. Get lost in the mist, get a rock rolled against your shin, get benighted among the boulders or the surrounding spruce.

That's the real Rhinog experience.

WELSH HEIGHTS AND THE OCEAN FLOOR

Rhinogs are Cambrian: not just for being a great lurk for a Welsh bandit, but being the place the Cambrian Period was actually named after. This makes them roughly the same age as the quartzite of Chapter 5. But in their harsh grey nature, they lump themselves in with the slightly less ancient grey underwater rocks of the Ordovician and Silurian: the Skiddaw Slates and the Southern Uplands of Scotland.

At the same time, the Rhinogs are harsher than other grey underwater muds. The relatively slender slabs used to make the Roman Steps are the exception. The Rhinog landscape is laid down in single beds, each one several metres deep, compact and featureless. These grey sands were laid down in an ocean edge, alongside a continent with a coastal mountain range. The subduction diagram on page 16 (B) gives the layout. Vigorous erosion from those coastal hills supplied the sand and grit. Each of the thick beds is the result of a single underwater event, and took only a few seconds to be laid.

A 'turbidity current' is a short-lived and extremely silty sea current. Or looking at it another way, it's an underwater

ABOVE: Grey mudstones and sandstones don't always slide around at 100kph. Conventional bedding gives this sandstone/mudstone junction on Pen Llithrig y Wrach, Snowdonia. The mudstone (above), but not the sandstone, has responded to continental crushing by cleaving into slate.

mudslide of an extremely wet and sloppy sort. Silt and grit run out of the river systems, and settle at the point where the river current fades into the sea. Gradually there builds up a shelf of river-delta mud and silt, each grain wafted into place by the last tendril of freshwater current far out from land. And then, jiggled by a distant earthquake, or simply by the final gram of mud, the whole thing sets off, along a front of dozens or hundreds of kilometres, down a slope as gentle as 1 in 20.

It's a black water-cloud of suspended mud, swirling and turbulent. As it goes it feeds itself by scouring even more grit and mud, eventually travelling at the speed of a railway train for hundreds of kilometres. And as it comes to rest, in a cloud of black silt, the heavier grit and sand sink first, settling in the bottom layers of the eventual rock bed.

It's hard to visualise all this unless you've actually seen it, which of course nobody ever has. A turbidity current first drew attention to itself in 1929, after an earthquake on the Grand Banks off the coast of Newfoundland. Over the next six hours, underwater telephone cables snapped in sequence, one by one, over a distance of 600 kilometres (350 miles).

A suspension of silt and grit is heavy from its internal rock, but flows as free as water. Later in the book (Chapter 10), there'll be the same thing in bright red, as hot volcanic ash flies downhill in an airborne avalanche. Powder snow gives the same quick and lethal downhill surge, this time coloured white. The turbidity current, violent but unseen across the ocean bed, is the grey-black version. The Rhinogs give the monochrome gloom, the lumped-up violence, of underwater mud in its most unfriendly mode.

8. Shales and underwater mud

8. SHALES AND UNDERWATER MUD

We go up the hills for the exercise; we go up them for the view. Then there's the good company, providing we've persuaded it to come along. There's sometimes a scary bit of scrambling, though not usually in the Southern Uplands. There's the great walking along the grassy summits; there are the wild goats and the occasional eagle.

What more could I ask, on a wet afternoon in the Moffat area? Well, I was going for the graptolites. And a half-hour into the walk, I found three of them. It took the best part of two hours to appreciate them fully and take the photos.

Dobbs Linn lies a half-hour's walk to the east of the much better known Grey Mare's Tail waterfall. No path leads into Dobbs Linn, just a narrow slit in the hill, walled with scree and bare shale. And around the second corner, water tails elegantly down a sequence of high slabs: a fall that's smaller than the Grey Mare but about six times as secret. Even so, the principal secrets here are inside the stones.

LIFE AND TIMES OF THE GRAPTOLITE

In 1864, Mr Charles Lapworth from Berkshire admired Sir Walter Scott and wished to inhabit Walter Scott country, so he took up a teaching post in Galashiels. Once there, his interest was aroused by the greywackes and shales of the country up-river from Moffat. This arousal of Mr Lapworth is, in a small way, rather mysterious. The Southern Uplands are not the most stimulating of hills. The greywackes of Moffat are thick and featureless; the tough black shales were known not to contain fossils.

Lapworth's refusal to be bored was rewarded. The black shales did contain fossils after all: the inconspicuous graptolites. The name means 'writing': when first spotted, graptolites were considered to be meaningless scribbly marks in the rocks. They were, in fact, clumps of free-floating ocean plankton. Even so, they failed to be quite as exciting as they should have been. Geologists elsewhere were finding fresh fossils every few metres as they went up through the rock layers.

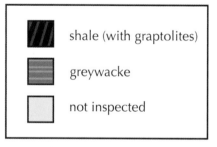

ABOVE: Black shale at Dobbs Linn. This is compressed deep-ocean mud, sandwiched between greywackes that are deep-ocean sand and gravel. This unglamorous mud holds the key to the Ordovician period.
DIAGRAM: First impressions of Moffat geology. Just shale and greywacke again and again.

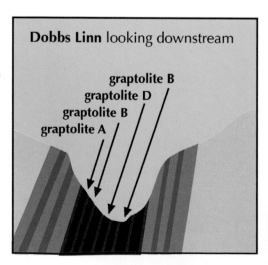

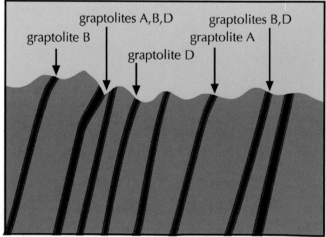

78

Dobbs Linn, in
Moffatdale, where
Charles Lapworth
uncovered the secret life
of Ordovician plankton.

What Lapworth found was a thin band of shale, with various graptolites; then a thick band of greywacke with, as expected, no fossils at all; then the same thing repeated, five or six times, with the same graptolites every time. Evolution seemed to have simply not happened, all the way up through thousands of metres of grey Southern Upland rocks.

Charles Lapworth decided he didn't find the Southern Uplands even slightly boring. He just needed to look harder. And then a bit harder than that. In the end he spent 11 years looking at shale in Dobbs Linn and the nearby hills. The moral is, that if you look at something boring for 11 years extremely carefully, you might find out something fundamental and fascinating. On the other hand, you might not. But Lapworth did.

ABOVE: Graptolite fossil (2cm long) from Dobbs Linn.
OPPOSITE: Loch Skeen, a glacier-formed tarn, is on the slopes of White Coomb, above Dobbs Linn.
DIAGRAM: After 11 years' examination, Moffat geology becomes more complex and much more interesting.

The greywacke on either side of Dobbs Linn is not two lots of greywacke but the same greywacke turned upside-down and repeated. The shale under the left-hand side of Dobbs Linn is the right-hand shale repeated, again with the order reversed. Across the wider countryside, all the six bands of shale are the same shale, sometimes the right way up and sometimes reversed. And far from the fossils being boringly the same over several kilometres, in the single (but repeated) shale band they change every few centimetres. Instead of a boring repetition of shales and grey sludge, Lapworth worked out a complex sequence of folds and faults. As a side-effect, he discovered 100 species of graptolite and the entire Ordovician Period.

Dobbs Linn is still the standard place for sorting graptolite sequences: one book describes a metaphorical 'golden spike' driven into the side of the ravine to mark the mutual boundary of the Ordovician and Silurian periods. Did Lapworth stumble, straight away, on the world's most convincing exposure of the Ordovician oceans? I suspect rather that no geologist anywhere else, in the century and a half since Lapworth, has put in the necessary 11 years . . .

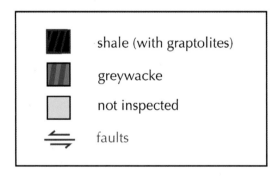

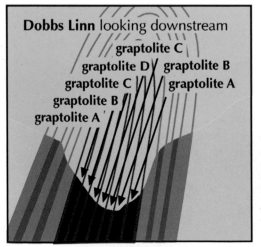

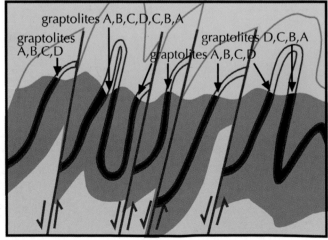

WALKING AT THE BOTTOM OF THE OCEAN

Once I'd poked among the screes to find a graptolite of my own, I carried on up some tussocks to Watch Knowe, followed the fence across the peaty levels beside Loch Skeen, and joined a nice straightforward path up Lochcraig Head. In terms of Southern Upland scenery, Loch Skeen is the exceptional bit. As I've said before, real mountain scenery is shaped by glaciers not rainwater – with tarns, aretes, truncated spurs and deep steep-sided valleys. The greywacke of the Southern Uplands forms such scenery only around Moffatdale; over Hart Fell, White Coomb and the Ettrick range. Loch Skeen, a glacier-formed tarn, is on the slopes of White Coomb. (The one other patch of mountain scenery, the Galloway Hills, is formed from granite.)

But above the glacier landscape of Loch Skeen, up on Lochcraig Head, is what the Southern Uplands are really all about: fences, and grassy summits, and great views stretching from the Pentlands to the extreme northern end of the Pennines. On the short grass caused by sheep and the 600m (2000ft) altitude, guided by the fences, I could stroll carefree, whistling a happy tune accompanied by the tweeting of the skylarks overhead. Small paths led me around and over White Coomb, and a fallen wall took me back to Loch Skeen's outfall.

Fossil-hunting slows you down, and the sun was already set by the time I gained the top of the Grey Mare's Tail. Around the head of this, the really famous waterfall, the wild goats were foraging for tourist sandwiches. The chasm is magnificent, and the pitched path of the National Trust is actually quite exposed. Clanking quietly in my jacket pocket were three little scribbly fellows from 450 million years before the birth of hillwalking.

PENSIVE SEDIMENTS

Just one of the insights that came out of Charles Lapworth's 11 years with the graptolites was that the Southern Uplands were an area of violent mountain building. With the aid of plate tectonics, we now understand the Southern Uplands as the impact area where Scotland crashed into England in an Act of Union dated to around 400 million years ago. As the two continents moved closer together, the deep sediments from the ocean trench between them were squeezed up like toothpaste, eventually to form the long Southern Upland range along the join. And elsewhere in the UK, dark underwater sediments were emerging to form new landscapes. Upraised mud is now mountains – or at least, hills – in northern Lakeland (the Skiddaw Slates), on the Isle of Man, in the Howgills and over most of central Wales.

Those sediments consisted of mud, silt, and the mixed-together sandy debris of the ocean-shelf mudslides described in the chapter about the Rhinogs. At the ocean floor they formed dark-coloured sedimentary rocks: mud becomes mudstone, silt becomes siltstone, and the mudslide sediments become the tough greywacke sandstone. A mudstone or siltstone which breaks apart along its bedding planes is called a shale.

The schist of Chapter 6 has been metamorphosed and hardened; but these mountains of mudstone, shale and slate have not. The Skiddaw Slates have been baked by some underlying granite, and have also been recently uplifted, so that erosion can really get its teeth into them: no such luck for the mudstone mountains. The bedrock here is well covered with glacial debris, peat, and gentle, waving grasses.

These hills are gentle to look at: 'more pensive by sunlight, than other mountains are by moonlight,' said Dorothy Wordsworth as she passed through the Lowthers of Dumfriesshire in 1803.

Thoughtfulness is a fine quality in a hill, but what walkers want is action. Action is not to be found in long, grassy, and – let's put it frankly – contemplative tops, but here and there on the steeper slopes, where they are water-carved into linns, gills and cleuchs, which is to say, the various sorts of little stream valleys. Go up a cleuch or a linn and at the worst you'll get nice photographs. At best you'll get soaked, scratched, scared, dirty, and your camera ruined in a waterfall. The slopes around may be smooth grass sprinkled with sheep pellets. In the gill you'll get trees, ferns, wildflowers, rare mosses and liverworts, plus (if the gill represents an upright-tilted shale layer) a pocketful of fossils.

Craig y Pistyll, below Nant-y-moch reservoir, has stones and small waterfalls, bright gorse and the bones of unwary sheep – because even the wild mountain sheep weren't expecting precipices here in central Wales. You won't find any decent rock climbing here (or anywhere else in mid-Wales much); but you will find a rock-type atmosphere. The walls rise on either side, the stream turns a corner, and you're in a trap with a waterfall at the top and no obvious escape.

But there's no need to starve to death slowly while gnawing those ancient sheep bones. Simply eat your usual sandwiches below the waterfall, then look on the ravine wall behind you for a short grassy path out onto the open hillside. And after that it's grassy grassy all the way to Pumlumon Fawr and grassy grassy all the way home.

SHALES AND UNDERWATER MUD

SOUTHERN UPLAND SCENERY FEATURES

OPPOSITE, LEFT: A cleuch, the narrow windy sort of stream valley (Cample Cleuch, Lowther Hills).

OPPOSITE, RIGHT: A scar, or eroded out stream valley (Craigmichen Scar, where Lapworth found more of the graptolite fossils).

LEFT: A gill, or precipitous white-water stream valley (Hang Gill, on Hart Fell).

FOLLOWING PAGE: The 'contemplative' Lowther Hills, Dumfriesshire, north of Durisdeer.

MUDSTONE MOUNTAINS

In the ocean between England and Scotland, sediments formed into mudstone, sandstone and shale. When the two countries collided, these rocks rose and now form various less exciting hill ranges. In places, their soft rocks have been hardened into slates. They form grassy slopes, sometimes steep-sided, but with few crags.

Cautley Crag (**TOP**) is the interesting bit of the Howgill Fells. On the Isle of Man, slates emerge at the summit of South Barrule (**ABOVE LEFT**). In mid-Wales, rolling hills, like Plynlimon (**ABOVE RIGHT**), fill the gap between Cadair Idris and the red sandstone escarpment of the Brecon Beacons.

LEFT: Brae Fell, at the Back o' Skiddaw. Here, underground granite has cooked and hardened the ocean-bottom muds. Even so, this is possibly the least thrilling of the four Lakeland landscapes wandered over in the following chapter.

9. All-terrain Lakeland

9. ALL-TERRAIN LAKELAND

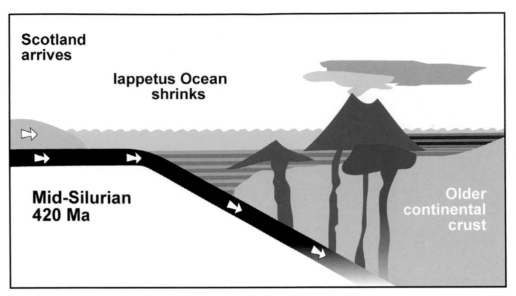

Scotland arrives

Iappetus Ocean shrinks

Mid-Silurian 420 Ma

Older continental crust

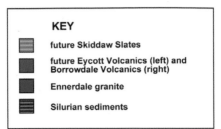

KEY

future Skiddaw Slates

future Eycott Volcanics (left) and Borrowdale Volcanics (right)

Ennerdale granite

Silurian sediments

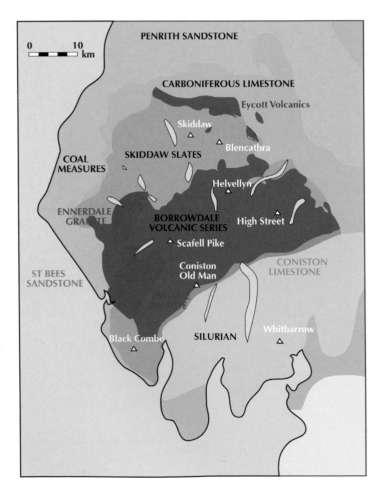

The Lakeland fells form the busiest and also the best mountain range in England – many would say, in the entire UK. And the best of Lakeland is the rugged lumpy landscape of Helvellyn and the Scafells. The mountains here are chunky ones: and every chunk is itself carved out and broken into further chunks. Not only does each great hill have its great crag buttressing its northern side: each small knoll has its own small outcrop as well. And so Castle Crag and Caw are not mere foothills. They are mini-mountains in their own right.

The grey-green or purplish-grey rocks are rough under the foot, or under the climber's fingers. The narrow valleys tangle together like string, to give more mountains to the square mile than anywhere else in Britain.

These knobbed and wrinkly hills are, it turns out, the crushed remains of a chain of volcanic islands. The purple-grey-green rock is called the Borrowdale Volcanic. The Borrowdale Volcanic Series (BVS) isn't just Borrowdale. It is also Helvellyn, and Haystacks, and Coniston Old Man, and Wansfell. It's what we think of as the 'real Lakeland': complex and knobbly, rough on the boot-leather but inspiring to the soul.

However, Lakeland is more even than that. Four different sorts of stone went to form the Lakeland fells. Volcanoes and slate; granite and grey shales: they combine to form a unique mountain kingdom, the UK's most-loved square miles.

SKIDDAW SLATES

Stand, say, on Great Gable, typical of those rugged central BVS fells, and look north: and you see an altogether different sort of hill. Grasmoor and Grisedale Pike and Blencathra are big and steep, but somehow smooth. They rise in straight lines to sharply pencilled summits.

It's odd to think, as you stand on the 931m summit of Skiddaw, that it started life as mud 6000m under the sea. Offshore, beyond the volcanoes that gave us the BVS, lay a deep ocean trench, such as we find today just east of Japan. The muds and sludges from the bottom of this trench were eventually compressed and raised to make the rocks of the northern hills.

Compressed ocean sludge makes (as in the previous two chapters) greywacke, shales and slates. At this northern brink of England, the mud was smooth, fine-textured mud, and the compression, when it came, was fierce. The result is that most of these northern edge rocks are more-or-less slaty; and they were named the Skiddaw Slates. But some of the Skiddaw Slates are shale; and some are elegantly

RIGHT: Skiddaw Slate exposed on Bowscale Fell.
BELOW: Skiddaw is a gently shaped hill, with long, smooth scree-slopes now covered in grass and heather.

slump-folded greywackes; so the official name today is the Skiddaw System. As the actual summits of Blencathra, Skiddaw itself, and the Grasmoor Group, are entirely slaty, I've stuck to the familiar older name.

The reason slate is slaty is the platelike crystals of mica, forming across the direction of stress. Freezing water gets into the cracks of the Skiddaw Slate, and breaks it into little round

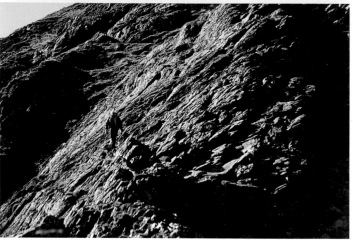

TOP: Cairns made of Skiddaw Slate, like this one on Skiddaw Little Man, tend to slide apart.

ABOVE: The slaty gleam on Sharp Edge, Blencathra, correctly suggests that it is smooth and a bit slippery – more so in the wet.

pebbles. Platelike crystals of mica are smooth and slippery: so the rocks are poor to grip, especially when wet. No serious rock climb is on Skiddaw Slate, although there are some good scrambles, and the cairns on Skiddaw flop down into wide loose heaps. The surrounding farmland is hedged rather than walled.

The Skiddaw Slates are, as rocks go, flexible and bendy (the geological term is 'competent'). When squashed by the arrival of the Scotland-continent from the north, they tended to squeeze and fold like slow-motion Plasticene. The result is a mountain that's much the same all through. Rainwater, frost and glaciers break it down into regular cones and pyramids.

So Skiddaw Slate mountains have high, smooth sides, running down into scree. The compensation is that Skiddaw Slate mountains get classic sharp ridges. Striding Edge may

be on good Borrowdale Volcanic, but almost all the rest of Lakeland's real ridges are on the Skiddaw Slate of the Grasmoor group and Blencathra. Sadly, only one of those ridges is on Skiddaw itself.

As you stop for lunch on Skiddaw's Longside Edge, you can see the difference between the lumpy shapes of the Borrowdale fells to the south and the smooth, Skiddaw-slate lines of the Grasmoor group opposite. Behind you, Skiddaw itself appears to be made entirely of the distinctive slaty screes; while the slippery Skiddaw rock is right there under your rucksack. If you're used to the rough rocks of Langdale and Wasdale, be a little careful on Skiddaw, especially when it's wet.

SILURIA IN THE LAKES

The south-east corner of Wales is tough country, as the Roman Governor of Britain, Publius Ostorius Scapula, found out. And the Silurians who lived in it were even tougher. So tough they named a geological era after them. It's the Silurian rocks that create the rugged and somewhat unconquerable Silurian sort of scenery. In Lakeland it's the southern bit, between Windermere and Coniston, separated from the high fells by the thin grey line of the Coniston Limestone. (Those high fells are of the preceding Ordovician period: named, incidentally, after an even tougher Welsh tribe.)

Silurian rocks are, on the whole, unexciting. In the Southern Uplands, they're a southern extension of the Ordovician ones. In Wales, they're the lower ground to south and east of the Harlech Dome. And here in Lakeland, they are sedimentary, and softer, below the brink of the exciting Borrowdale Volcanics.

LEFT: Crinkly Silurian sediments in Grizedale Forest, southern Lakeland.

The Good Lord didn't mean these Silurian lands for actually walking on, else he'd have paved them with the good Borrowdale Volcanic. This is country for seeing from overhead; from Coniston Old Man, or Wansfell, or

ABOVE: The gentler Silurian country of southern Lakeland. Windermere seen from Loughrigg.
BELOW: Coniston Limestone, on Timley Knott above Torver.

Loughrigg. Or even from little Latterbarrow, with its tall stone cairn like a drystone factory chimney, its views across a froth of oak tops which are grey under the evening rain like decomposing foam rubber.

But the earth movements of the Carboniferous period, while raising Lakeland's dome, also raised this Lakeland Siluria. The glaciers which carved Scafell also carved the smaller and softer Claife Heights. Coniston Water, Esthwaite and Windermere are, undoubtedly, lakes: and this southern country is also, in its softer way, Lakeland.

The sediments have been compressed into slates, and tilted up steeply against the high fells. This means that as you walk uphill away from Coniston Water, you are passing continuously downwards onto older, lower, rocks, until you finally reach the craggy slopes of the BVS. Along the boundary, in a line some 200 metres wide along the foot of the steep ground, lies the Coniston Limestone. Because it's actually rather low in lime, it's the same grey colour as the BVS whose erosion formed it in the first place. But in terms of texture, it is, as the picture shows, a pretty peculiar rock.

LAKELAND'S GRANITE

BELOW LEFT: Scale Force, Lakeland's highest waterfall, tumbles off the edge of the Ennerdale granite into the more easily eroded Skiddaw Slates below.

BELOW CENTRE: Skiddaw granite underlies the northern fells, and crops out in Sinen Gill on the side of Blencathra (grid ref NY300281).

BELOW RIGHT: Ennerdale granite, above Scale Force.

BOTTOM: Lakeland granite fails to form the great bare slabs and oblong-blocked crags that we'll see in Chapter 13. It fails to form tors. Instead it makes Lakeland-type landscape, but with a pink tinge. Dalegarth Falls, Eskdale.

LAKELAND GRANITE: PRETTY IN PINK

The pink rocks of Ennerdale (**ABOVE**) are properly 'granophyre'; they are fine-grained, and show the granite speckles only under a lens. But starting at the south side of Wasdale, the Eskdale granite (**BELOW**), while still surprisingly pink, shows also the visible black and white speckles that a granite should have.

Three different sorts of stone: rough lavas, smooth slates, and soft lowland sediments – yet somehow Lakeland casts a charm over them all, wrinkling them into friendly small shapes, decorating them with oakwoods and waterfalls. And it pulls the same trick on the Lakeland granite. Elsewhere, granite is grim; the granite chapter, later in the book, is a celebration of the austere. But there's nothing austere about lower Eskdale, with its ravines and villages and tiny tarns up among the outcrops. In Lakeland, even granite looses its gravity and becomes a jolly rock . . .

Granite weathers grey, so that you may at first not notice it among the other grey rocks, unless perhaps you're aware of a certain roundedness of the boulders in the boulderfield. In the path, though, the footworn pebbles are pink; and the streambed has a mix of pink and pale grey like a young girl going to her first posh party. The stream sides, too, where the water keeps them clean, are tinged with pink.

Lakeland's granite lands are good for streams. Where granite lies above softer Skiddaw Slates, waterfalls form, including Lakeland's highest, Scale Force. To reach the foot of that fall, above the footbridge, you'll clamber over rough round rocks, whose hospitable footholds are again tinged pink; and further up the hill, where wind and rain scour away the lichen, there are outcrops of almost strawberry ice-cream colour. Up on Iron Crag, you'll be shadowed by a drystone wall, its rounded lumps carefully nested together, in the same surprising shade.

Iron Crag at 640m is the high point of the pink, for Lakeland granite makes no spectacular high fells. But it does make spectacular low ones. Along the north side of Eskdale, the granite resembles none of the conventional granite lands (Arran, Galloway, or Cairngorm). Here are a hundred

midget mountains, each well-sized for somebody's back garden. If anything, it's the knock and lochan of the Lewisian Gneiss, but reinterpreted with grass instead of bog between the rockpiles.

Below them, old mine paths lead down through bracken to the oaks of Eskdale. There the little railway runs alongside the river whose waters have the green clarity that granite gives. But under their green mosses, those gorge walls peep pink.

LAKELAND VOLCANICS: THE BVS

But in the end, we come back to Borrowdale. These are the proper rocks, the authentic greeny-grey Lakeland. Perfect to climb on; superb at generating mountain shapes; they are not, it has to be said, the easiest of rocks to read.

Snowdonia was mostly made underwater, with big thick layers that you can get familiar with (the Pitts Head Tuff, the Lower Rhyolite, and the rest filling the following chapter). But Lakeland's volcanoes were up in the open air. Ashfalls spread wider, and in thinner beds. Sometimes the ash fell into the lakes left by collapsing magma chambers, to form bedded sediments with ripple marks. The Great Slab on Bowfell is simply the most noticeable of these. But half a kilometre away, the same ashfall makes tuffs of the more normal sort, or, closer to the volcano top, welded hot-avalanche tuffs. Or there's a landslide, and you find yourself climbing up tuffs with big broken lava-chunks in them. As if the several textures of tuff were not enough, many of the great crags are lava flows; others (Dow Crag is one example) are lava intrusions, squeezed out underground.

And then, any remaining simplicity is destroyed by the faulting. The map of central Lakeland shows a fault every few hundred metres. So even where there have been big distinctive rock-making events, the faulting has broken them to bits.

Take, for instance, the Wet Side Edge member; easy enough to see on the map, because of its distinctive mauve shading. It represents a fall of dark-coloured andesitic ash, some 300m deep, and formed a layer from Yewbarrow and Borrowdale right across to the Coniston fells. For a geologist of say 400 million years ago, the Wet Side Edge member would have been a nice marker, a dark band running around the 500m contour.

But now what's happened to it? The middle section, underneath Scafell Pike, is underground anyway, because of the great down-fold of the Scafell Syncline. And as it happens, that underground bit isn't even there but has melted away into the underlying granite lump. What's left of the

LAKELAND'S VOLCANIC

TOP LEFT: An upstanding stone, formed from a fall of volcanic ash ('tuff') on Broad Crag, east of Scafell Pike.

TOP RIGHT: Gable Crag, from Green Gable. Gable Crag is part of the same lava flow (the Scafell Dacite) that formed Scafell Crag. Around the other side of the mountain, the Napes buttresses are of ashfall tuff, a much friendlier-feeling rock.

ABOVE: Tuffs are wonderfully rough-textured. Scrambler on the south-west side of Coniston Old Man.

Wet Side Edge member, the faulting which raised the Lakeland dome has shattered into a dozen separate strips. Over the present position of Upper Eskdale, it has been eroded away altogether and swept into Windermere.

So trying to work out what everything started off as can be like detecting the individual ingredients of a fruit cake after it's been through the cake-mixer and after that, the oven. Sometimes you'll spot a particular distinctive ingredient – a currant or a scrap of peel. But mostly, just relax and enjoy the flavour of the rugged, multicoloured, richly blended mix.

ABOVE: Contrasting crags, seen from Hollow Stones. In shadow on the right, the grim Scafell Crag, formed from lava flows. Its rocks are steep and solid; they also face north, so are sunless and often damp; and the crag carries some of Lakeland's most serious climbs. On the left is Pikes Crag of Scafell Pike. While the lower apron of this is formed from the same Scafell Dacite, the steep upper part is a rough-textured and grippy tuff. It also catches the sun. The result is a selection of enjoyable and easy-graded climbs (V Diff and Severe) like Arete, Chimney and Crack.

BELOW LEFT: Scafell Crag detail, from the West Wall Traverse.

BELOW: Barn in Buttermere village. The pinkish blocks of granite (strictly, Ennerdale granophyre) are easy to find but hard to work. The gaps have been filled with BVS slate, possibly cast-offs from the Honister quarries at the other end of the valley. Some rounded BVS lumps from a riverbed have also found use. Surrounds for windows and doors are dressed blocks of altogether more amenable sandstone, presumably from St Bees.

TUFF STUFF

The rock of the high fells is mostly compacted volcanic ash, but with various textures.

TOP LEFT: Lapilli tuff, where the 'lapilli', a sort of airborne volcanic gravel, have fallen into the ash. Larger pumice lumps, also fallen in afterwards, have been slightly flattened by the weight of overlying ash. The pumice is softer than the ash, and some of the pumice lumps have eroded out leaving oval holes. Boulderfields at head of Goats Water.

TOP RIGHT: Block tuff; a landslide on the side of a volcano leaves a mixture of broken blocks in a heap of ash. Path at foot of Goats Water (SD267974).

ABOVE LEFT: Tuff sediments, where ash has fallen into water, which was probably a caldera lake. Fallen block in Little Narrowcove: the lowest beds are now at the right-hand side.

ABOVE RIGHT: A fine-grained tuff sediment has been compressed by earth movements into a tough, good-quality slate. Cove Quarry, Coniston Old Man.

BELOW LEFT: Ignimbrite, a welded together mixture of volcanic ash with pumice fragments that have been flattened into thin strips. It's the result of a *nuée ardente*, an airborne avalanche of gas and red-hot fine fragments. Stone built into path culvert between Goats Hause and Coniston Old Man summit.

BELOW CENTRE: Rhyolite tuffs (and for that matter, lavas) are paler, due to their higher quartz content; andesite ones are darker. By chance, frost shattering has brought together lumps of both sorts near the summit of Wetherlam.

BELOW RIGHT: Welded tuff. Pumice lumps and smaller lapilli have been flattened by overlying ash while still semi-molten; more so than in the example at top left, but less so than in the ignimbrite at below left.

10. Red-hot flying avalanche: Ignimbrites in Snowdonia

10. RED-HOT FLYING AVALANCHE: IGNIMBRITES IN SNOWDONIA

The stories from Snowdonia are violent and exciting ones. There's the Afanc, the monster who lives in Glaslyn and has a taste for fresh and nicely rounded female hillwalkers. There's the final battle between King Arthur and his treacherous nephew Mordred: a battle that took place, according to one rather implausible legend, on Bwlch y Saethau, the Pass of the Arrows, between Snowdon and Y Lliwedd.

But the birth of Snowdonia itself makes all this seem small-time. Snowdonia burst into the world in an avalanche of red-hot volcanic ash, and followed this up with some even larger disasters.

A red-hot avalanche of flying volcanic ash: it's an impressive, not to say devastating, sight. The sliding pumice is itself exhaling hot gases; air swept into the flow is immediately heated to three times its volume; groundwater flashes into steam. The ash and the gases form a single, combination fluid. That fluid is almost as heavy as solid rock, with a tremendous downhill momentum. At the same time it is

ABOVE: Bwlch y Saethau, where according to legend King Arthur battled his nephew Mordred; behind, Y Lliwedd stands at the centre of a far greater act of violence, the Lower Rhyolite Tuff event.
BELOW: Ignimbrite rock, with the dark streaks called *fiamme* (flames), on the west ridge of Carnedd Llewelyn.

almost as mobile as flowing water. It's been named as a *nuée ardente*, a glowing (or, if you prefer, passionate) cloud-bank.

One from Mont Pelée in Martinique, in 1902, travelled down-slope a distance of 6 kilometres (4 miles) in two minutes, to surge through the town of St Pierre. Most of the town's buildings were undamaged, and wine bottles stood unbroken on the tables: but of its 28,000 inhabitants, there were just two survivors (one of them a prisoner in an underground dungeon).

The red-hot gases carried within the flow are what make it so lethal. The prisoner of St Pierre reported a sudden, searing blast of heat in the eddy of it which penetrated through his small cell window below street level. Death is caused by ash-suffocation, or by lung damage, or by shock following severe all-over burns.

What destroyed the people of St Pierre was actually a rather small *nuée ardente*. The rescuers, when they arrived, were amazed that the entire population had been killed by something that left only a few centimetres of ash in the streets. The passionate cloudburst which started off the Snowdonia cataclysms filled its own volcanic caldera 700m deep, and flowed over the edge to lie many metres thick down the slope of what is now Moel Hebog. It ran into the sea, but the sea didn't stop it; still red-hot it continued for 10km underwater to what are today the slopes of Snowdon, Y Garn of the Glyders, and the nose of Pen yr Ole Wen.

THE PITTS HEAD EVENT

Judging by a similar but smaller event at Novarupta in Alaska in 1912, the initial explosion can be heard around the world – or would be, if there were anyone around to hear it in the Ordovician period. And then the mountain simply boils over like a 10km-wide pot of porridge. A grey cloud rolls, or rather runs, down the mountainside, a cloud that winks red in its insides. Ash pours upwards, bunched and curved like grey broccoli; lightning flickers continuously in its grey edge. As the main ash avalanche hits the sea, steam explodes upwards, far above the mountaintops, with a roar that becomes continuous. Clouds of white steam and black ash now mingle, and the sea around is a froth of falling pumice. But already another stream of upward-bursting grey cloud rushes down the mountain's flank; and then a third.

There's a philosophical difficulty in describing all this in terms of a hypothetical observer. That hypothetical observer is now deaf. Very soon, they will be in thick darkness as clouds of ash block out the sun. And a few minutes after that, they're going to be dead . . .

This event, perhaps the most cataclysmic single day the UK has experienced so far and equivalent to a middle-sized nuclear war, takes its name from a small farm on the slopes of Snowdon above Rhyd-Ddu. The resulting rock, the distinctive Pitts Head Tuff, is of the sort called an ignimbrite – the name meaning fire-cloud-rock.

BOTTOM LEFT: Pitts Head Tuffs, in the cairn marking the top of Y Gribin ridge.
BOTTOM RIGHT: Scrambling the Pitts Head Tuffs, on Y Gribin of Glyder Fawr.

ABOVE: Nodules in the Pitts Head Tuff, Y Gribin: quartz has migrated through the rock and reformed itself into balls 2cm across. Y Gribin of Glyder Fawr.
BELOW: Classic climbing on the Lower Rhyolitic Tuff Formation: a climber confronts the twin cracks of Hope, on Idwal Slabs (V Diff). The climbing surface is a bed of ashfall tuff, originally horizontal, now tilted by the earth movements of the Idwal Syncline to an angle just too steep to walk up.

It's a volcanic tuff, made mostly of fine grains of ash; but a tuff of a particular and odd sort. Still red-hot as it comes to rest, it welds itself together in a compacted mass of volcanic glass. Lumps of pumice, still hot and soft, are compressed into flat discs. These appear within the rock as narrow dark streaks, called *fiamme*, the Italian for flames. A weathered outcrop of ignimbrite has a texture like a very old pile of damp newspapers. It's on a freshly broken piece that you see the strange streaky effect.

The Pitts Head Tuff is unusually pale – it's rich in feldspar – with the *fiamme* showing starkly in black or very dark green. It also has a particular habit, as it lies through the ages, of forming within itself spherical nodules of silica. The quartz chemicals assemble within the rock into balls the size of hazelnuts upwards.

This strange rock with streaks in can be found on Moel Hebog, and on Llechog above the Snowdon railway. It forms the summit of Y Garn in the Glyders. It's at the outflow of Llyn Idwal, and in the road cutting just below Llyn Ogwen outflow; it runs up the nose of Pen yr Ole Wen to the 400m contour. On the face of Moel Hebog, its silica-balls are grown to the size of melons. But the streaks are at their best and brightest on Y Gribin of Glyder Fach.

'Excuse me, but have you lost something?'

When you're standing immediately underneath Wales' most spectacular scene but looking intently downwards, then you have to have dropped your contact lens, or else your compass.

But the spectacular scene was actually obscured by cloud; the cloud was a showery one; and the rain had brought out all the colours and textures of the pitched stonework of the Idwal pathway. The wild rocks of the mountainside hid their natures behind grey chemical weathering and a layer of lichen.

However, the National Park pathbuilders have created, in effect, a museum display, a convenient 2 metres viewing distance below our eyes, all finely polished by the passing feet. Just a few paces above the information hut were beautiful swirly patterns fit to pave a palace. Volcaniclastic sandstone, if you want to be cumbersome: volcanic ashfalls rearranged by the tides and currents of a shallow sea.

'It's all right, I haven't lost my lenses, thanks – I'm just looking for the Pitts Head Tuff.'

ABOVE: The Idwal Syncline. Foreground, a Pitts Head Tuff boulder at the foot of Llyn Idwal. At the top, the Devil's Kitchen divides the dark basalts of the Bedded Pyroclastic Formation that form a shallow U-shape across the axis of the upward fold. Everything between is Lower Rhyolite Tuff.

Already, in the road cutting below Llyn Ogwen, I'd seen the black flames (*fiamme*) of the Pitts Head Tuff behind a half-century of weathering. But in every tenth or twentieth boulder of the stone-laid pathway, white rocks showed the black streaks of typical ignimbrite. The Pitts Head Tuff has been raised almost vertical here by the earth movements that, if the cloud only rises, will be extremely apparent in about 15 minutes time when I reach Llyn Idwal.

The narrow band of black-on-white ignimbrite follows quite closely the Idwal path. Sometimes the pathbuilders confuse us by bringing in rocks by helicopter, but surely not here, with so much suitable stone within wheelbarrow range. And so the streaky path stones will surely belong with the old-newspaper-textured bits of bedrock, and be small scraps of Snowdonia's first big disaster, the Pitt's Head.

But new rocks are appearing at the path side, and in the path itself; grey tuffs of the more normal sort described in the Lake District chapter, and lumpy tuffs with broken stones inside them. And more importantly – for the cloud has indeed gone up – here are 600m of crag and rockface around the head of Llyn Idwal.

After the haze of the Pitts Head disaster had covered the northern hemisphere for a decade or two, Snowdonia went quite quiet, with only minor eruptions. As the slow millennia passed, 200 metres of underwater sandstone and silt covered the pale streaky tuffs. Every century or so, an earthquake shook the big faultline along the Gwynant valley. And then, perhaps a million years after the Pitts Head event, there came the bigger cataclysm. Bigger, and in scrambling and mountaineering terms, much, much better.

THE LRTF EVENT

This time the outburst was centred on a volcanic caldera roughly where Y Lliwedd now rises. The Lower Rhyolitic Tuff Formation (LRTF) is a complex sequence of ashfalls, volcanic landslides, and ignimbrites. It can be recognised, right across the heart of Snowdonia, as a band of several hundred metres of first-class climbing.

Amphitheatre Buttress is the longest rock climb south of Scotland, all of it on the Lower Rhyolitic Tuff. Large parts of Clogwyn Du'r Arddu are LRTF, and the rest of it is rhyolite lava flows and intrusions out of the same volcanoes. Llyn Idwal flows out over Pitts Head Tuff; but almost everything we see onwards and upwards is from this first-class formation. Not just the varied tuffs in the pathway, but the Idwal Slabs are LRTF; as are all the rocks upwards to the summit of Glyder Fawr.

The LRTF was a mystery to geologists of 20 years ago; its hot-welded ash flows kept getting interrupted by sedimentary layers that seemed to be under the sea. Did Wales keep bobbing above the surface so as to fire off another layer of ignimbrite? Eventually the implausible became obvious; the LRTF consisted not simply of red-hot flying avalanches, but of red-hot flying *underwater* avalanches. This accounts for the way the good Welsh ignimbrite and ash, confined within its ocean basin, forms crag-size chunks quite close to Snowdon, rather than single-pitch climbs scattered as far away as Birmingham.

THE IDWAL SYNCLINE

The foot of Llyn Idwal is one of the classic standpoints, and there's a lot to look at. The ash flows of the Idwal Slabs lie in bedded layers, but those layers are not level. Instead they're tilted at an angle just too steep to walk up in boots, and hence make a set of delightfully not-too-difficult rock climbs. But further left, the beds of Glyder Fawr's Upper Face are tilted almost vertical; and on the opposite side of the cwm, the crags of Castell y Geifr tilt equally steeply the other way. This is the Idwal Syncline, a great upward-facing fold in the landscape. The faultline gully of the Devil's Kitchen marks the centre line.

On the right, careful survey shows the narrow band of the Pitts Head Tuff running up to the summit of Y Garn. On the other side of the fold, the PHT appears again, forming the ridgeline of Y Gribin. That PHT was laid down underneath, and before, the rocks of the Lower Rhyolite. But cradled in the top of the curve, on either side of the Devil's Kitchen, are slightly darker rocks that will tell us, when we get to them, about what happened above and afterwards.

ABOVE: Pillow lavas near the top of the Devil's Kitchen.
BELOW: Llyn y Cwn on Glyder Fawr, on the Bedded Pyroclastic Formation. Rocks here include basalt pillow lavas of gentle, underwater eruptions. The bedding-plane slabs at the lake side, left, indicate that the rocks ahead are rising more steeply than the slope they stick out from. Thus the lighter rocks above and left in the picture are the underlying, and older, LRTF. The colour change between dark basaltic rocks below and paler rhyolitic, above, is more obvious on unweathered small stones than when the crags are looked at as a whole.

This great U-fold constitutes the Idwal Syncline. Though we can't see it from here without a helicopter, the Idwal Syncline continues southwards, creating the bent shape of Clogwyn Du'r Arddu on the Llanberis flank of Snowdon. It also extends northwards but not quite so obviously, up the nose of Pen yr Ole Wen. It was created, 50 million years after the rocks were laid down, by the crunch of England–Wales into Scotland, the Caledonian Orogeny. That is described in Chapter 1, so I shan't talk about it again here. Because there is still more to see at this centre-point; the centre-point not just of the Idwal Syncline but of the entire lie of the intellectual landscape.

DARWIN'S DRUMLINS

In August 1831, the great geologist Adam Sedgwick (originally from Dent in the Yorkshire Dales) headed into Cwm Idwal with a student assistant: the young Charles Darwin. 'I cannot promise to teach you all geology,' said Sedgwick to his students; 'I can only fire your imaginations.' And he kept his word, not saying anything at all about the elongated hillocks and piles of rock rubble at Idwal's outflow, and again on either side of the lake's head.

RIGHT TOP: Twll Du, the Devil's Kitchen, above Llyn Idwal. Basalt isn't great climbing rock. But as its composition includes the darker feldspars based on calcium rather than sodium or potassium, it breaks down to a soil that's relatively rich in lime, and in wildflowers.
RIGHT CENTRE: Ripple marks in bedded basalt tuff, beside the path out of Cwm Idwal to Llyn y Cwn.
RIGHT BOTTOM: Thick basalt lava flows make up the crags of Clogwyn y Geifr.

Much later, having visited Patagonia on board the *Beagle* and seen ice in action, Darwin returned to Cwm Idwal and was astonished at the obviousness of the moraine remains.

I had a striking instance of how easy it is to overlook phenomena, however conspicuous, before they have been observed by any one. We spent many hours in Cwm Idwal, examining all the rocks with extreme care; . . . but we did not notice the plainly scored rocks, the perched boulders, the lateral and terminal moraines. Yet these phenomena are so conspicuous that . . . a house burnt down by fire did not tell its story more plainly than did this valley. If it had still been filled by a glacier, the phenomena would have been less distinct than they now are.
– Charles Darwin, *Autobiography* (1887)

While rain brings out the patterns in the path, the ice-dumped moraines are best seen in slanting sunlight. The set at the lake foot are from the end of the main Ice Age, 20,000 years ago. Those at the lake head record the brief cold snap of 12,000 years ago, the 'Loch Lomond re-advance' (from its classic location) or the 'younger Dryas' (from the associated fossil pollen which dates it).

The path crosses below the Idwal Slabs. As it climbs the cwm head, pitched paving gives way to loose stones, which are almost as good at displaying unweathered surfaces, and even handier to examine than the fixed paving. Among the rhyolite grey and speckles, some stones now appear of glassy black. We are climbing into the third of Snowdonia's distinctive disasters.

THE BPF EVENT

This third eruption episode will put the icing on Snowdonia's cake – except that unlike normal icing, the Bedded Pyroclastic Formation is basalt black. Basalt eruptions give a calmer sort of cataclysm. Much of this one takes place under water, blobs of lava squeezing out slowly to form the pillow lavas whose worn-down remains lie at the head of the Devil's Kitchen.

Black pointy islands of volcanic ash rise above the sea, the water around them a froth of falling ash. The shores of

The rhyolite tuffs of the Capel Curig Volcanic Formation give excellent grip when it comes to leaping onto ledges on Bristly Ridge (**TOP**), or above Tryfan's Heather Terrace (**BOTTOM**).

the new islands get washed away by tsunamis as chunks of other islands fall into the sea. Lava slides down and then runs level, to form black land made of glass. The glassy ground crackles as it cools, and then quickly weathers to orange shards and gravel. Showers of sharp-edged volcanic rubble fall into the sea, forming seabed layers 300m deep which will eventually be the summit of Snowdon itself.

Lava-lakes, crinkly like rhino hide, crack open to show their red-hot undercurrents. Occasionally there bursts up a fire fountain, a hundred metres high, like a really expensive sort of fireworks show.

The resulting Bedded Pyroclastic Series (BPS) rocks are black inside, though they weather to orange-grey. They lie bent-backed above the crags of Cwm Idwal, forming a flat U-shape bow of darker rocks split by Twll Du, the Devil's Kitchen. The northern aspect, and the dampness from above, bring out the satanic blackness of the crags. 'Pyroclastic' means solid fragments out of a volcano; but 'bedded' means laid down under water. And as you turn up the final stoneslope, a water-rippled surface of black ash stretches outwards into space.

The Bedded Pyroclasts form the summit of Snowdon and of Garnedd Uchaf (the Crib y Ddysgl Ridge) as well as the black lands around Llyn y Cwn. Elsewhere, on the principle of 'last in, first out', they've been eroded off the top. It's no great loss. The basalt is smooth, and also rather brittle, and makes for very bad climbing.

It has, however, one redeeming feature. Granite and its volcanic version rhyolite are made of quartz, mica and potash feldspar, and none of these three minerals contains any of the element calcium. But the darker minerals of basalt do, and as the BPS breaks up and weathers, small plants find scraps of lime-rich soil to grow in. So, for botanists with binoculars, the rare Snowdon Lily grows alongside Twll Du. Just don't ask any climber onto those loose and slippery crags to photograph it for you.

Underwater basalt disasters like those that formed the Bedded Pyroclastic Formation have been happening around Iceland in our lifetimes. Very small ignimbrite flows were observed by a lucky scholar of St Pierre who happened to be just out of range. The flying red-hot underwater avalanche has been observed by humans, since the start of written records, on precisely zero occasions. The account of what it was like was deduced from its results: the crags of Snowdon and its surroundings. We should be very relieved that it all happened 450 million years ago.

11. Walking the fault

11. WALKING THE FAULT

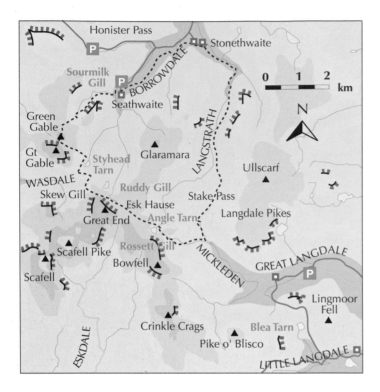

What happens when an irresistible force – in this case, a continent moving in from the north – meets an immovable object – the lumps of rock that are one day going to be Lakeland? There are two possible answers. The immovable rocks can bend: or else they can break.

The immovable rock lumps of the Lake District were, and still are, of two main sorts (described in Chapter 9). In the north, there is the compacted ocean sludge that's called the Skiddaw Slates. Further south, the main fells are the volcanic lavas and sediments of the Borrowdale Volcanic Series. And these two rocks reacted to the irresistible arrival of Scotland in the two different ways. The Skiddaw Slates are, as rocks go, flexible and bendy. They tended to fold up and squash down: their very slatiness is because they squeezed sideways.

The Borrowdale Volcanic behaved the other way. It bent a bit; but then it cracked apart and moved past itself. And these cracks, which we call faultlines, happened on every possible scale. Rockclimbers finds their rockface split by tiny cracks that they use for fingerholds, and slightly larger ones to jam hands and feet in; going up from that, there are fault-lines that form chimneys, and gullies. Faultlines running slantwise give us Lord's Rake, and Jack's Rake, and Pillar Rake on little Mellbreak.

The painter Heaton Cooper, who looked at these hills more attentively than most, said that their defining shape was the cube. The central fells, from Scafell to Helvellyn, come in chunks. This is, precisely, because they've been broken up by fault planes crossing one another in all directions. Lakeland is, in this very real sense, everything it's cracked up to be.

THE ROSSETT GILL FAULTLINE

One February, I set off up the Sourmilk Gill towards Green Gable. Lakeland's geology means that Lakeland scenery is just about perfect, but on this particular day I was determined to find fault. I found it first in the stones of the reconstructed path.

On a damp grey day, up inside the cloud, there's nowhere to look but down. At the same time, a coating of dampness brings out the colours and the textures of what's underfoot. Walking up a long steep path all rebuilt in jammed stones, under grey drizzle: this is not the best fun you can get on Lakeland fells. But see the swirly lava, how different it is from the stripy-layered volcanic ash. Spot the gritty lump of pink granite the helicopter brought over out of Ennerdale.

Trouble was, for this particular game the weather was all wrong. I'd hit a sunny winter's day, the ground like iron and the air like silver turning to turquoise. With immense discipline, I ignored the beauty of frosted Borrowdale below me for just long enough to spot a splendidly faulty boulder alongside the pitched path.

A faultline isn't simply a crack. The rock hasn't just broken, but has actually moved past itself. Along the UK's largest faultline, Scotland's Great Glen, the movement is 100 kilometres (60 miles); granite is on the left, you drive for an hour and a half, and you see the same granite on the right. In the boulder from below Dove Crag, pictured on the right, the movement has been about 10 centimetres.

I headed down Aaron Slack, and along past Styhead Tarn. Ice still hung on the shoreline, frosted with patterns that'd be gone in half an hour as the sun's warmth crept down Base Brown. At Sty Head, I was looking across the Napes face of Great Gable.

There was plenty there to find fault with. Every gully line, each chimney and ledge, the slot behind Nape's Needle and the Wasdale Crack in its front, all of these are part of the three-dimensional crazy paving created by the crunch of the continents. But the particular line I was looking for was bigger than cracks and gullies: so big as to be invisible.

Movement along a faultline can bring softer rock alongside a harder one. The softer side erodes away, leaving the

ABOVE: Faulted boulder beside path in Dovedale, Lake District. The sharp arrival of Scotland, 400 million years ago, has broken this bit of former lake bed in two places. The main faultline slants up slightly rightwards across the middle. The patterning on the right has moved about 10cm up the picture.
BELOW: The UK's largest faultline, the Great Glen, with Ben Nevis behind.

harder stuff upstanding. Just so is the Napes face of Great Gable. And the faultline which created this great hill face runs on across the central fells for 13 kilometres (8 miles).

My map for the day was no yellow-and-blue Explorer, no greeny-brown Harveys, but the pink and beige and green, the ochre and orange, and the seven sorts of purple of the British Geological Survey's Sheet 38. And my plan for the day was no ordinary ascent of Scafell Pike or wander around a lake. My plan was to follow that fault as far as I could find it.

Turning left, I didn't have to look very hard. Above the Corridor Route, the great slash of Skew Gill carves the side of Great End.

When two rock masses move past each other, the rock at the interface gets broken about and crushed. It's called faultline shattering. Faultline shattering is why gullies are much wider than just the crack between two moving lumps of mountain. Faultline shattering is why gully rocks have a texture like crushed and reassembled gravel. And faultline

shattering is why Skew Gill is one of the nastiest bits of hill-side anywhere.

Skew Gill makes footpath erosion look like a mere scratch on the surface. The water's got into Skew Gill and used the shattered state of the faultline rocks to rip the hill-side right open. I worked my way up, looking for the crushed gravel texture of the gully rocks that's called brecciation. But I didn't see it much because of all the boulders the stream had rolled over the top.

Early climbers felt safe in the gullies; and when, in about the 1880s, they came out onto the airy scary buttresses, they were surprised to find how easy they were. Gullies have streams in, and slime: but as well as that they have faultline shattering. Gravel coats the handholds, and when you've brushed the gravel off, the handhold comes away in your hand.

Outside, the face of Great Gable shone golden in the morning sun, allowing me to eye up how the line of the gully becomes the face plane of the Napes Buttresses. Inside, it was gloomy and cool; and the February day had bound up the gravel with ugly bulges of ice. Ice is nice, if you've got crampons and a couple of bent-end ice-axes. I hadn't, so I climbed around the ice.

At the top, a frozen waterfall lay over all the rubble. Lovely! Lovely . . . ? I'd expected to kick my way up that rubble to get out. It would be a long way back down the gully. So I set off up the side by a likely line – and discovered that faultline shattering can also take place within the human mind. After a moment of panicky scrambling among the gravel and slime, I emerged onto the firm fixed rock of the open hillside. And then I lay for a minute, my eyes resting on golden Gable, but my mind not considering at all the geological implications of it.

As the ground levels, water can no longer tear open the shattered rocks. As the fault crosses the ridgeline, it shows as just a small notch. In the foreground of the photo (page 110),

ABOVE LEFT: Breccia is rock formed of broken fragments of other rocks. Faultline shattering, followed by cementation with iron oxide, has formed this breccia on Arthur's Seat, Edinburgh.
ABOVE RIGHT: Strata which slide along faultlines without breaking up can form the scratches wonderfully named 'slickensides'. Marble in Glen Tilt, 300m downstream from Marble Lodge (NN896716).
BELOW: Ascending Skew Gill. It's the faultline shattering that makes this such a nasty place.

you can see that the notch is filled with broken stones. Frost action, that makes boulderfields on the exposed summit plateau, has here found rocks already shattered by the fault-line, and prised them all apart. Further on, the faultline has defined the face of Great End on the right; beyond that, a stream has exploited it to carve the upper part of Ruddy Gill.

Following faults gets you to interesting and little-visited corners. But on a really crisp, clear February afternoon, the well-visited corners do cry out to be visited once again. So I turned aside from my fault to trace some of Lakeland's perfection. The ridge to Great End is just rocky enough to be delightful, and I said I wasn't going up Scafell Pike but I changed my mind. Snow lay across the summit rocks, and the air was like blue champagne, and was that a bit of Wales showing away in the south? Not to mention that the path to Lingmell has uncommonly fine faultlines in some of its stony steps . . .

But several hours of diversion over the summit boulder-fields saw me back on the line again at Esk Hause. I faced back the other way along Ruddy Gill, raised my eye to the skyline notch above Skew Gill, and looked through the notch to the face of Gable where it all began. Esk Hause itself is another notch defined by my faultline. Behind it, the fault is the back of the sheltered shelf that carries the path east-wards under Hanging Knotts. The corrie glacier found the pre-existing faultline a help when carving Angle Tarn. The faultline next defines the pass at Rossett Hause; and down the slope beyond, it carves out the gill that gives it its name: the Rossett Gill Fault.

Ahead now, Mickleden is a U-shaped glaciated valley. But where does the ice first slide downhill but in the dip of an existing stream? And the stream carved the ground along the convenient pre-existing faultline. Thus the Rossett Fault, only 5 metres wide, has amplified itself by a factor of a hundred to define the Mickleden valley. At the end of that, the fault gives us the gap of Blea Tarn, carves two little valleys (one up, one down) into the shoulder of Lingmoor Fell, and plunges into Little Langdale. There it finds itself end-stopped by an even bigger break, the one from Eskdale that runs through Hardknott and Wrynose to end at Elterwater.

The Rossett Fault may indeed run on up to Blea Tarn; but my car was away at Seathwaite, and it was time for me to turn aside. Another handy faultline has carved its line up Stake Gill, and through the notch at the top. All the way up, a little light still lingered on Lingmoor Fell.

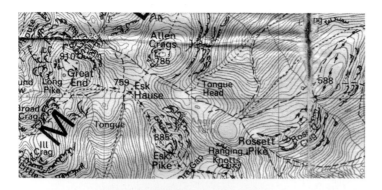

LEFT: The same eight grid squares, as seen by the Ordnance Survey (**ABOVE**) and the British Geological Survey. All the dashed lines on the geological map mark faults. The purplish colours represent intrusive igneous rocks squeezed out from a huge lump of buried granite magma under Esk Pike and the Scafells. Esk Pike itself is the crushed remains of a volcanic vent. The other colours are various forms of volcanic debris of the Borrowdale Volcanic Series. In Rossett Gill itself, the Pavey Ark Member (olive-green), a pebbly volcanic sandstone, has been displaced 200m by movement along the fault. Extract from well-used OS Landranager 89 © Crown Copyright. Extract from BGS 1:50,000 Sheet 38 Ambleside (Solid & Drift Edition) © NERC.

BELOW: From above Skew Gill, east along the fault to Esk Hause.

OPPOSITE: West along the fault from Esk Hause. Just below the skyline, a gully runs up to the faultline notch, viewpoint of the previous photo.

At Stake Pass, the world had gone grey, and by the time I was down in Langstrath the stars were shining on the snow-fields above. Lumps of ice on the path show up nicely in the torchlight, except that it's much nicer to switch off the torch, and see the black hillsides on either side and the gleam of the river – and never mind the occasional sudden slide as the foot hits the ice-lump: it's better than the usual squelch into the bog.

ABOVE: Looking from close to the top of Rossett Gill along Mickleden to the head of Great Langdale. The glacier has used the faultline as its initial incision for the carving of Mickleden. The line continues through the gap of Blea Tarn (middle distance, hidden) and across the shoulder of Lingmoor Fell before being cut off by the transverse faultline that runs along Little Langdale. The hummocks in Mickleden are drumlins, moraine waste left by the glacier.

BOTTOM RIGHT: Small-scale faultlines in three different directions decorate a slab on the side of Glyder Fawr, Snowdonia.

Langstrath is Lakeland's second-emptiest valley. The thousand stars above were echoed by not a gleam from the surrounding country. Cam Crag blocked out a few hundred of the stars, and then the Intake Ridge did the same. An hour later I came around the corner, and distant headlights flickered down the valley, and eventually a swag of white fairy lights amidst the black was the Stonethwaite Inn. It was a Sunday night, in the off-season, and the notice on the door said the inn was closed.

But the fairy lights said it was open, and the fairy lights didn't lie. At the bar, the talk was of survival in the wild. 'Does he really only eat those insects and things? He's quite chubby . . .'

I leaned back and enjoyed the outrageous suggestion that Ray Mears, the professional survivalist, pinches the cameraman's crisps. I also enjoyed, even better than Mears' beetles and barbequed bunnyrabbit, the Stonethwaite's sticky toffee. The toffee sits warm in the stomach for the walk round the end of Bessyboot to Seathwaite. It's a shame to switch on the car headlights and head out again along the road; at the end of another weekend, and another way of looking at Lakeland.

12. Andesite and rhyolite

12. ANDESITE AND RHYOLITE
Glen Coe and Ben Nevis: the subsided cauldrons

ABOVE: Looking across the recently formed caldera which forms the top of Tenerife island. Just out of picture on the right, the dormant volcano Teide rises from the caldera's centre to form the summit of Spain.

Granite underground, as we'll see in Chapter 13, quite often means volcanic eruptions on top. And volcanic eruptions mean the best of rocks for climbers and for connoisseurs of fine scenery alike. The Scottish Highlands have granite bursting out all over, from Cruachan to the Cairngorms, from Strontian to Galloway in the far south. So where are the lavas and tuffs on top: the blocky knobbly volcanic mountains that reproduce, on a bigger scale, the delights of Snowdonia and Borrowdale?

The sad fact is that almost every crag, every pebble of these one-time wonderful mountains has been eroded away. Now, if you'd only been here in your climbing boots in the

late Devonian . . . But two fragments of Scotland's Snowdonia did, by a happy accident, manage to survive. Those remaining bits are Ben Nevis, and the central section of Glen Coe. In each case, they escaped from erosion, rather like rabbits escaping the bulldozer, by burrowing into the ground beforehand.

CAULDRON SUBSIDENCE
As ocean crust hauls itself downwards under the edge of a continent, great blobs of molten ocean floor drift upwards. They melt their way into the continental crust, creating a mix which, after long cooling, will become granite. Or else they melt their way right up into the open air, and emerge as volcanoes. When this latter happens, the magma chamber underground can sometimes empty itself right out, so that the existing rocks collapse into the empty space provided.

The resulting hole is called a caldera, the Latin word for a cooking pot. It is, typically, a dozen kilometres or more in width. It is not the same as a crater, which is the hole at the very top of a volcano where the magma pipe which feeds it emerges. A crater occupies the summit of a single volcano, is typically a kilometre or two wide, and comes from a Greek word meaning – ahem – a slightly different sort of cooking pot. (And, just to complete the confusion, a quite different sort of hole scooped in the side of a Scottish mountain by ice is called a corrie, meaning cooking pot in Gaelic rather than Greek.)

The first caldera recognised was easy enough to spot. When Santorini, in the eastern Mediterranean, collapsed into its magma chamber around 1600 BC, seawater flowed onto red-hot magma and created the explosion which blew away all but the edges of the island. That the second caldera recognised was the rather more subtle Glen Coe one is tribute to the sharp eyes of the Scottish geologists of 1909.

At Glen Coe, a patch of land some 8 km by 13 (5 miles by 8) has sunk into the magma chamber. Such an event is called 'cauldron subsidence'. As the chamber roof collapsed, magma squished up at the edges. At Ben Nevis, the sinking land-patch was rather smaller. In each case, the result, after 400 million years of erosion, is a small but intensive area of classic climbing; but the foreground, as you look up at it from the surrounding ground, will be granite.

Head up towards the great north face of Nevis, and the granite surrounding the collapsed cauldron will give you rounded boulders and loose stones in the path – but also, a fine granite waterslide in the Allt a' Mhuilinn. Opposite the Nevis crags, Carn Mor Dearg is just outside the cauldron subsidence. So it too has pink granite scree, and tottering granite towers which give scrambling routes of only moderate quality.

The Carn Mor Dearg Arete, the best walkers' way onto the Ben, is a succession of rounded granite boulders, all scratched about with crampons. Big drops are on either side, and ahead you look at the volcanic lava. That andesite (the darker sort of lava) makes 3 km (2 miles) of crag, about 600m (2000ft) in height. A patriotic Scot might point out that here is almost as much rock as the whole of Snowdonia, just more conve-

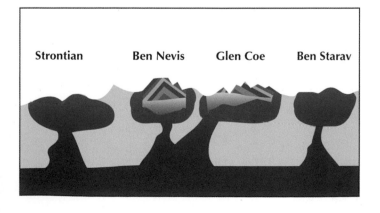

Strontian   Ben Nevis   Glen Coe   Ben Starav

niently assembled on a single site.

The narrow granite along the arete gives half an hour of easy but exciting scrambling. Then, as the ridge end runs into the mountain, the boulders become less rounded, and darken: you have stepped onto the andesite. And you'll continue to step on it for nearly another hour, up steep loose rocks, to the summit plateau with its various ugly structures. Turn and peer over the northern edge, for a closer look at the top of Tower Ridge, where lava makes the UK's longest rock climb.

As you turn downhill from the summit, the great north face accompanies you at first, until cairns and the scoured Pony Path lead down the steep zigzags of the mountain's north-western slope. At about the 900m (3000ft) contour, the stones below turn back to granite, well-displayed where the path crosses the Red Burn. After more rounded granite stones than you really wanted, you reach the junction above the Youth Hostel. From here to any of the car parks, you may spot small outcrops of the country rocks, limestones and schists, all altered to brittle hornfels by the heat of the granite.

Glen Coe's caldera is obvious only as having lowered the grand volcanics by 600m to preserve them as part of today's landscape, and thus giving us Bidean nam Bian and the Buachaille to play about on rather than another granite Ben Starav. The actual caldera structure, however, is not so easy to see. Instead of a surrounding bath of granite (as around Ben Nevis), there is a narrow 'ring-fault intrusion' of pale, uniform-coloured microgranite. Even this has been overwhelmed, in the south-west, by a later granite lump expanding out of Glen Etive. And inside the ring-fault, some country rocks of quartzite and schist have sunk alongside the volcanics, further confusing things.

Quite likely, though, you'll be stopping at the track end of Achtriochtan, if only to take that ever-familiar photo looking up to Stob Coire nam Beith. From there a two-minute wander down the old road towards Clachaig Inn will show you the pinkish ring-fault granite as it crosses the riverbed (NN138566). It then heads southwards up the flank of An t-Sron as a faultline gully, andesite to left of it and granite to the right.

Up the main glen, roadside pulloffs give you a grand view of the volcanic rocks, only slightly obscured by the foreground bagpiper. A change to a paler colour, at roughly half height on the Three Sisters, shows (better in some lights than others) that the rocks here are of two different kinds. Nobody, to my knowledge, complains about the Ben Nevis andesite. But here in Glen Coe, it is topped, both metaphor-

A ring of granite surrounds the volcanic rocks of Ben Nevis.

LEFT: Waterslide in Allt a' Mhuilinn, below the Nevis Hut.

ABOVE: On Carn Mor Dearg Arete.

BELOW: If Carn Mor Dearg Arete is the walkers' way up Nevis, the way for scramblers is the Ledge Route. This gives good andesite under foot and hand for 500m of height gain, and great views of the rest of the great north face. Behind on the left: the granite slopes of Carn Mor Dearg.

ically and up the actual mountain, by the rhyolite which is the first of Scotland's truly great climbing media. (Or the second, if your sophisticated fingertips have learnt to love the Lewisian.)

In the Lake District and in Snowdonia, we distinguished the rhyolite from the andesite by its being rather lighter in colour. Here in Glen Coe, the rhyolite is again lighter-coloured; it is also somewhat pinkly tinged.

But there is also the difference you feel through your feet. You might be scrambling the andesite, finding it rocky enough, by no means holdless, perhaps a little more lichenous than you'd like. And then you walk up a short grassy terrace and place your hands on something paler, slightly pink, and altogether better. The rhyolite is compact and clean, rough, and well covered in small useful holds for climbing up. On Bidean nam Bian, and over the whole of Buachaille Etive Mor, it rises steep and magnificent for hundreds of metres.

BELOW: Buried treasure: The wonderful andesite and rhyolite of Bidean nam Bian were preserved for today's climbers by having sunk into a volcanic caldera 400 million years ago.

THE VIEW FROM BEN NEVIS

Bidean is big – but so are the surrounding hills. So let us return now to Nevis, as (if the cloud's not down) it's a useful place to look around at where this book has already been, and what rocks are still to scramble over.

Looking outwards from Nevis' scruffy summit, first we see the ring of granite that seeped up the edges of the cauldron subsidence. That granite extends over Carn Mor Dearg and also the ridge beyond, Aonach Mor and Beag. Beyond it, and all around, stretch the schist hills of the Dalradian (Chapter 6). Those hills are decorated with incidents of metamorphic quartzite; that quartzite is most noticeable in the white capping of Sgurr a' Mhaim just across Glen Nevis, but also runs westwards along the Grey Corries.

Further west, Mullach nan Coirean of the Mamores is again granite, but a separate intrusion not part of the Nevis caldera. Southwards Ben Cruachan, and away in the northeast the plateau of the Cairngorms, remind us that this important and very recognisable rock has yet to be walked over in this book: it's going to be the next chapter.

OPPOSITE: The Aonach Eagach ridge runs just inside the Glen Coe cauldron subsidence. The block tuff being scrambled over could be an avalanche that tumbled inwards down the caldera's rim slope.

ABOVE LEFT: Pathbuilders have brought together rhyolite and darker andesite on the way up to the Lost Valley, Glencoe.

ABOVE RIGHT: Aonach Dubh, the westernmost of the three sisters of Glen Coe, from the west. Of its three rock tiers, the lowest is darker, more vegetated, andesite lava. The upper two tiers are the paler rhyolite, offering dozens of attractive routes for rock climbers.

LEFT: Barn Wall, on Bidean nam Bian, shows the pinkish tinge of the Glencoe rhyolite. When you get to grips with it, this intimidating face offers a multitude of square-cut footholds.

If the day is very clear, or if you're carrying a computer-generated panorama, you can look back across the Dalradian shales at the three rocks that were Chapters 3 to 5. In the north-west, faint shadows along the horizon are the Western Isles with their Lewisian Gneiss, 150km (90 miles) away. Just west of north, Liathach stands in jagged Torridonian Sandstone, with Beinn Eighe's Cambrian quartzite on its right.

Far away to the south, you can't quite see Chapter 8, the sedimentary greywackes of the Southern Uplands. (Maybe no human eye can see it, but from Bidean nam Bian the computer can view a single Southern Upland hill, Blackcraig in South Ayrshire.)

All those stand as reminders, back beyond several chapters of volcanoes, that the metamorphic rocks and the sediments can also make great mountains. But we're not finished with the volcanoes quite yet. Look away to the south-east, just to left of Ben Vorlich and Stuc a' Chroin.

ABOVE: On the rhyolite of Stob Coire nan Lochan, part of the Bidean massif. Columnar jointing (see Chapter 14) can be made out below the walkers. The flat surface they stand on suggests the top surface of an intrusive sill, rather than of a lava flow.

LEFT: Rhyolite at its finest, in the climbing ground of Buachaille Etive Mor. Crowberry Ridge runs up the centre to the silhouetted Crowberry Tower. The left-hand face of the ridge is the celebrated Rannoch Wall.

There you (or at least, the computer) can glimpse the Ochils, in Scotland's so-called Lowlands. The volcanoes thereabouts are of the same Devonian age as Ben Nevis; and their rocks have been similarly dropped to preserve them for posterity. Not, however, by any subsiding cauldron, but by the sinking of the rift valley that makes up Scotland's Central Belt. Those Ochils are Old Red Sandstone, covered in Chapter 15. The volcanic rocks of central Scotland rise to the 2000-foot contour only in northern England – which will be investigated in the chapter after next.

Finally in this verbal panorama, and finally in this book, across the sea to the west are even more volcanoes. After several chapters which mostly peruse the Pennines, it will be back northwards for the black and jagged scenery of the Skye Cuillin.

But for now, there's 1344m (4409ft) of steep and stony descent, over those stones first of andesite, then granite, to get us off Ben Nevis . . .

13. GRANITE LANDS

In the Beginning God created the heaven and the earth. And the earth was without form, and void; and darkness was upon the face of the deep . . . And God said, Let the waters under the heaven be gathered together unto one place, and let the dry land appear: and it was so . . . and God saw that it was good.

Genesis 1, verses 1, 2, 9

ABOVE: Pebbles of Eskdale Granite in Greathall Gill at the foot of Wastwater.
OPPOSITE: Half Dome, Yosemite valley, California. The scrambling route with the fixed cables runs up the near face. As the huge lump of underground granite was uncovered by erosion it expanded, and cracked away in sheets. Each cracked-off sheet edge makes an awkward moment on the way up.

Granite is the epic simplicity of Yosemite, where a quite young lump of solidified magma has been dug out by erosion and axe-hacked by glaciers into huge blank walls. Half Dome is, as its name implies, a hemisphere, where you spend an hour between two fixed cables walking up the curve of a single granite lump. Or else you climb the steep side, and spend two days on one flat face of rock. California's Sierra Nevada goes on being granite for 14 more days – unless you happen to get torn to bits by a bear.

Americans tend to overdo things. UK granite is less overbearingly huge, but it is still not small – not even on Dartmoor. Granite comes in many styles: the dark cones of Mourne or Arran, the wide flat lines of the Cairngorm plateau, the gleaming slabs of Glen Etive. Many styles, but a single unifying mood. That mood is not 'cheerful'.

Granite is grim. Granite is great sweeps of moorland, or steep uniform slopes. It is yellow malnourished grass, black peat, and heather. Here is no intricate play of knobbed outcrop and grassy corner. Here is no delicacy. Indeed, the one decorative feature, the plateau tor, could be considered particularly indelicate – Cac Carn Beag, the summit rockpile of Lochnagar, whose appropriate Gaelic name means Small Pile of Poo.

Granite lands, in the UK at least, do feel like the first, primitive places hand-crafted by the Prime Mover on Day Three of the Creation. Is granite indeed the first of all rocks, of which everything else is the crumbled and reconstituted remains? Or is it actually an afterthought, squeezed in after everything else was finished? At the very start of geology, the great argument was about the granite, and how it got here. In the 1880s, James Hutton of Edinburgh used his head and his eyes, but also a less dignified organ: 'Lord pity the arse that's clagged to a head that will hunt stones . . .'

GRANITE AND THE GEOLOGISTS

With our five-day working week, and our motor cars to carry us to the hills, today's hillwalkers probably spend as much time in the presence of rocks as Hutton on his long-suffering horseborne arse. That is not to say that we'll put our time to such effective use as he did. Having spent impressionable years in Torridon with its three very different kinds of crag, I passed the next decade not looking at the rocks of the Lake District because they were boringly all the same. Well, the works of J.S. Bach are all boringly the same – at least until you actually listen to them.

But this is the other advantage we as hillwalkers share with Hutton on his horse: our ignorance. Geology is not just a body of more-or-less incomprehensible information, any more than Bach means memorising the BWV numbers of all the Cantatas. What that composer is actually about probably cannot be expressed in words, or he would have written words rather than musical notes, wouldn't he?

But the game or artform we call Science is less mysterious than Baroque counterpoint. Geology is about the imagination to understand the world around us; the sceptical intelligence to prove or disprove those understandings; and the eyes and the feet to find out more. A blind geologist is possible; an immobile geologist would be harder to accept. Geologists lacking imagination have been, sadly, not uncommon; and as a result every interesting bit of geology has taken 50 years longer than it should have done.

Then there are geologists who are imaginative and lively,

ABOVE: Cac Carn Mor, where the rock gods took a dump on Lochnagar. (Mor means 'large', though it's actually rather smaller than Cac Carn Beag alongside.)

but wrong. Wrong ideas, like those of Abraham Werner the Neptunist, are crucial if we're to get any right ideas at all. We who go up mountains for fun, being (with luck) almost as ignorant as James Hutton, are offered the chance to exercise not just our legs and lungs but our eyes, imagination, and sceptical intelligence as well.

How come this ground we walk on is made of so many different sorts of stuff? The facts, as they appeared around 1780 in Edinburgh to James Hutton, his colleagues and enemies, were as follows.

Firstly: many rocks, the ones we call sedimentary, are made out of gravel and sand. At first glance, sandstone appears to be a compressed version of a beach or a sand dune. First impressions often deceive, but not this time. The closer you look, the more sandy the sandstone looks. The ripple marks and mud cracks illustrated on page 148 in Chapter 15 were both found within the city limits of Edinburgh.

Next: while some sediments lie in respectable flat layers, even those around Edinburgh are tilted slightly sideways. And on the Galloway or Berwickshire coast, where Southern Upland greywacke reaches the sea, the sedimentary beds run almost vertical, and are curved. (To call them 'bent' or 'folded' implies that they were formerly flat and straight. That is part of what we're going to be arguing over.)

Third: fossil seashells are found on the tops of mountains. Those mountains include Snowdon and, as it happens, Everest. This fact about seashells had already surprised Aristotle and Leonardo da Vinci. Unless God put them there just to tease us, there can really only be two explanations: the sea was once much higher or the mountains were once much lower down.

Finally: sandstone is made of sand and conglomerate is made of pebbles, but there are rocks that are not apparently made out of the remains of other, earlier rocks. Basalt is one such, and also granite. Looked at through a lens, these rocks are crystalline.

To explain these four facts, two theories arose, based on the two ways the seashells could have got onto Snowdon. Plutonism said the land had been much lower down, and then been raised by subterranean heat. The rival theory,

FAR LEFT: Sandstone is made of sand – as is shown at Sanday, Orkney. The sea has picked out from the rock some 400-million-year-old ripples resembling those in the beach sand below.
LEFT: Fossil seashell and coral 500m above sea level, Cross Fell.
BELOW: Sediments don't stay flat: folded greywacke at Balcary Bay, Galloway.
BOTTOM: The Alps are founded on granite. The granite of Piz Badile rises above the darker shale and schist of the Bregaglia valley, southern Switzerland. Verifying that the granite really does emerge from underneath might require a prolonged stay in Soglio (foot of picture).

known as Neptunism, said the sea had once been much higher up; and that the very first rocks crystallised out of the ocean like limescale on a saucepan. This required the ocean to have covered the entire surface of the earth, so as to drop its granite onto the top of Ben Macdui; but that's exactly what it did do, as described in the Bible, with Noah's Ark floating on top.

Each of these theories has a glaring gap. Neptunism: where did all that water go? Plutonism: where did all that heat come from?

The Neptunist question is being asked again on Mars at the moment. The northern plains of Mars appear to have once been an ocean: they have an eroded shoreline, and level sedimentary beds. Leaving aside the big unanswerable question of where the ocean went, Mars-ologists are wondering what other effects that sea would have had, and then trying to find funding for a spaceship to see if those effects are there.

It is legitimate, at least to start with, to leave the big picture and focus in on the details. Granite is easy to recognise, and fairly easy to find, even on horseback. It is formed of three minerals: black biotite, translucent quartz, white or pink feldspar. Each of these minerals is chemically quite simple. Quartz in particular is a compound of just two common elements, silicon and oxygen. Understand the granite, and the sediments will drop into place by the simple natural process of broken-up granite sliding to the seabed.

Buried in eroded mountain chains, one frequently finds a heart of granite. The Galloway Highlands, and Arran, are just two examples of granite surfacing like a whale out of sedimentary rocks. The pink granite of Eskdale and Ennerdale lies underneath the Lake District hills, though so far erosion has only exposed it at the edge. The Mont Blanc granite rises from surrounding shale and limestone.

This tor (**ABOVE**) on Slieve Binnian, in the Mountains of Mourne, does seem to have been laid in level strata like sandstone. One up to the Neptunists. But rocks on Slieve Commedagh (**BELOW**), 8km to the north, are more blocky-looking.

For the Neptunists, granite with its simple structure was the very first rock that dropped to the ocean floor. This does explain why it's found now in the middles of mountains, with the layers of schisty sediment stirred up by Noah's Flood lying all over the top. For James Hutton, the schisty sediments came first, and it was the granite bulging upwards from underneath that made the mountains. Both of the theories explain those known facts about granite. Now comes the interesting bit. What will the two theories predict in the way of new, *unknown* facts?

Is granite laid down in beds? Because according to Hutton and the Plutonist theory, it isn't. But the crags and tors of the Cairngorms do show horizontal layering: one point to the Neptunists. Though the layering in granite isn't quite the same as the strata in sandstone: it's more of a tendency to break up into rectangular blocks.

Granite, as a fundamental stone in both theories, should not contain bits of other stuff. But it does, as the beach stone in my picture opposite shows. Such foreign fragments are actually quite common in the granite kerbstones of city pavements.

NEPTUNISM vs PLUTONISM

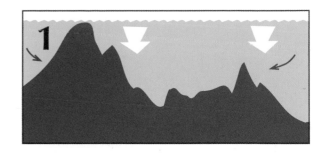

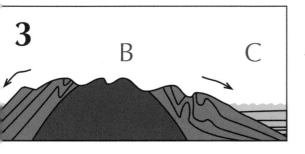

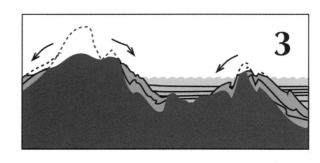

¹LUTONISM

Sediments erode off an existing continent.

Granite rises under the sediments, compressing and folding them to form Alpine Schistus.

Granite and schistus erode to form Lowland Sediments. Now return to 1 and start again.

A represents a Hutton-type unconformity. B to C represents the section up North Glen Sannox, Arran, towards Goatfell.

NEPTUNISM

1. Granite and other crystalline rocks precipitate from the Universal Ocean.
2. The Universal Ocean sinks. Eroded material forms sloping and folded sediments on the side slopes.
3. The Universal Ocean sinks further. Eroded material forms level strata, the Lowland Sediments. Then the Universal Ocean drains away. In later versions of the theory, the ocean makes a temporary return to precipitate crystalline basalt on top of Lowland Sediments.

LEFT: Beach granite with xenolith: Airds Point, Dumfriesshire.

BELOW: In close-up, the granite 'includes' (wraps around) fragments of the surrounding schist.

BOTTOM: Hutton's Riverbank, 250m downstream from Marble Lodge in Glen Tilt (NN897716). The granite 'interjection' shown in the upper picture is arrowed.

Edinburgh, however, is paved with dark brown basalt from Arthur's Seat, so Hutton didn't get involved in this particular discussion.

The Neptunists would have that grey bit in the granite as a fragment of the original nucleus or understuff, the pre-primary rocks placed by God underneath the primordial ocean on Day One. The grey fragment would have to have been a stone on the seabed as the granite precipitated around it. Hutton would explain it as part of the original overlay, breaking off and being engulfed by the rising hot rock.

The beach pebble opposite is made of Criffel granite, which meets the sea a few kilometres away. The rocks behind the pebble's beach are greywacke sediments; they are the ones shown as 'folded greywacke' earlier in this chapter. The fragment in the granite is similarly grey. But those greywacke rocks are layered and gritty, which this fragment is not. If we looked more closely at the beach stone, would the two theories make different predictions about what we ought to see? This being a chapter celebrating scepticism and ignorance, see what you think of the pebble before studying its caption.

ABOVE: Xenolith in Criffel granite. The country rock is gritty greywacke (pictured page 125). For Neptunists, that's irrelevant: the grey bit in the granite is a fragment of God's original ocean floor, embraced in granite precipitated from a cold ocean. For James Hutton, however, this is a fragment of that surrounding greywacke, severely cooked by the hot granite but not actually dissolved. The fuzzy, crystalline edges of the grey xenolith are quite convincing in favour of James Hutton.
BELOW AND RIGHT: Granite lands: Vixen Tor, Dartmoor (**BELOW LEFT**); Lochnagar on Deeside (**BELOW CENTRE**); Mountains of Mourne from Slieve Bearnagh (**BELOW RIGHT**); Hen Hole on the Cheviot (**RIGHT**).

Hutton's evidence that basalt erupts hot from underneath was based on a classic Edinburgh hill, Arthur's Seat: that will be in the next chapter. When it came to granite, he examined not beach pebbles, but the Cairngorms. The middle of the Cairngorm granite doesn't contain many clues as to whether it came upwards from underground or downwards out of the sea. But its edges do. Hutton went for a walk along Glen Tilt, and in the riverbed there he saw intrusions of pale pink granite. At Dail-an-eas Bridge, near Marble Lodge, he noticed that 'the granite is here found breaking and displacing the strata in every conceivable manner, including the fragments of the broken strata, and interjected in every possible direction among the strata which appear.' (*Theory of the Earth,* 1795)

The Neptunists had granite as the first rock of all. But in the River Tilt, granite had squeezed into the cracks and gaps in the surrounding rocks. This implied that the other rocks were already there for the granite to squeeze itself

into. Specifically, if the granite was there first, it couldn't have formed itself around ('included') any chunks of something else.

From Glen Tilt Hutton continued to Arran. The rocks up the stream in North Glen Sannox towards Cir Mhor corresponded exactly with the left-hand side of Part 3 in the diagram (see page 127). Lowland rocks, and below them the

grey 'Alpine Schistus', had been tilted upwards by the arrival of the granite. The right-hand profile of Part 1 matches the Hutton Unconformity described in the Introduction, which so convincingly demonstrated the great age of the earth. And for good measure, at Newton Point on the way back to the ferry, he came across just another such unconformity, also called 'Hutton's Unconformity'.

Hutton's Unconformity at Siccar Point had shown that the earth has had many cycles of erosion and sediments, with the land somehow arising in between. Hutton's Riverbank in Glen Tilt shows that granite arrives hot, from below; and in Glen Sannox the land has been bowed upwards by its arrival.

This granite-arrival Hutton then identified as the uplift force that his theory needed. However, in this he was incorrect. The force that makes mountains is not hot rocks rising, but continents coming sideways and colliding.

THE HOLISTIC CRYSTAL KIT

New Age culture: it's a religion with even less in the way of actual beliefs than old-style Anglicanism. Still, its devotees do go into great detail as to how chalcedony promotes inner spirituality, while amethyst creates harmony in testing business situations. Even if it were all so, I find it considerably more exciting that three simple crystals – quartz, feldspar and mica – create the entire granite style of landscape. For this rock at any rate, it is all determined by the birthsign crystals . . .

A roughly half-and-half mix of quartz and feldspar has a lower melting point than any other rock. As magma cools, the other minerals crystallise out. Granite is in this sense the natural endpoint. Any gathering in a European mountain hut tends to speak some sort of German, wherever they actually come from. And any rock melt of continental crust tends in the general direction of granite.

Quartzite, perhaps the simplest sort of rock, is made of very tough quartz crystals bonded together with more tough quartz. Granite, the second simplest, is the same tough quartz, binding together two other crystals, biotite mica and feldspar. Mica supplies the black specks. Feldspar is pink or white, depending on its exact chemical composition; and the granite follows the colour of the feldspar.

More importantly, mica and feldspar are in a sense soft. They respond to rain and other forms of chemical attack by breaking down into clay minerals and, eventually, to soil. This combination, of tough quartz bound up with two decomposable companions, is what determines the specific and individual character of granite.

TOP: Waterworn granite, Airds Point. Black biotite mica, pinkish feldspar, translucent white quartz. Crystals are about 2mm across.
ABOVE: Dwarf azalea has small, succulent leaves to resist drying out on the coarse granite gravels.

Granite, in huge rounded underground lumps, resists deformation, and is even tougher than quartzite because less brittle. Stonewallers hate it because the best you can do with a hammer is to knock small lumps off.

But when granite breaks up into boulders, the mica and feldspar rot away at the corners. This gives the characteristic roundedness of granite. Crystals of tough quartz stay sticking out of the eroded surface; and this gives granite its characteristic roughness and grip.

The quartz eventually drops out, to make granite ground that's composed of sharp-cornered quartz gravel. It makes for comfortable walking between the boulders, or as the surface of a path. But it doesn't hold moisture, and any soil that starts to form is quickly washed away. Plant life on the Cairngorm plateau has a particular problem, at any time when it isn't actually raining, of drought. And so, while they hunch low out of the cold winds, they also adopt desert strategies for water conservation, with small but fat and shiny leaves.

Lower down the hill, where soils do form, they are based on the same quartz gravel. When the vegetation mat is broken, such soils wash away; and granite lands, where they're at all steep, suffer badly from path erosion. Arran and the Mountains of Mourne take a lot of path maintenance, by comparison with more heavily used mountains that have more robust sorts of soil.

THE WAY IT BREAKS

Granite cools under pressure in the deep underground, several (or several dozen) kilometres down. As erosion lifts off the load, the granite expands. Expanding, it cracks away in sheets parallel to the eroding ground surface. The layers that the Neptunists interpreted, incorrectly, as bedding from when the rock was laid down: are actually expansion cracks from where it was dug up.

So the rounded granite ridges of Galloway Glen Etive are topped with slab ground, almost as walkable as city pavements – albeit with better smells and more interesting views, not to mention, in Galloway in particular, intervals of black bog.

Where glacier carves into granite already so shattered, the result is the 'cyclopean masonry' effect. This is named after the massive ruins left around the Mediterranean by the Mycenaeans but attributed to a one-eyed giant called Cyclops encountered in Homer's *Odyssey*. In Cairn Gorm's cyclopean northern corries, Pygmy Ridge has holds that may be rounded, but are also plentiful, flat-topped, and roughly grippy.

Where on the other hand the granite has expanded sideways parallel to a valley wall, it splits away not level but following the slope. The result is great featureless slabs, evil-gleaming when wet or in the haze of a summer afternoon. Even though the slope may not be particularly steep, such ground makes a supremely untempting way of getting uphill.

Streams come down the slabby granite in long white waterslides. At Buttermere's Sourmilk Gill, and at the Allt Coire Eoghainn behind Ben Nevis, the damp streamside slabs are notorious for people slipping down a very long way indeed. And yet, where granite slabs are clean, stream-free, and not too steep, they can give delightful easy climbing. When it comes to getting a grip on it, the large-scale smoothness means vegetation doesn't: the small-scale roughness means the climber's fingers do.

But as the granite steepens, actual handholds are uncommon, and the climber makes a way with cracks. On what we may call epic granite, there aren't any cracks. And then, at the head of a long sea loch just south of Glen Coe, there are the Etive Slabs.

Etive Slabs are unique in the UK. Five degrees less steep and you could simply walk up them. Ten degrees steeper and they'd be impossible.

Granite resists the power of moving ice, of mountain-building episodes; and also the human hammer. The Pict who sculpted the Maiden Stone (**LEFT**), near Inverurie, understood about strength through simplicity. The builders of Balmoral Castle (**RIGHT**) did not.

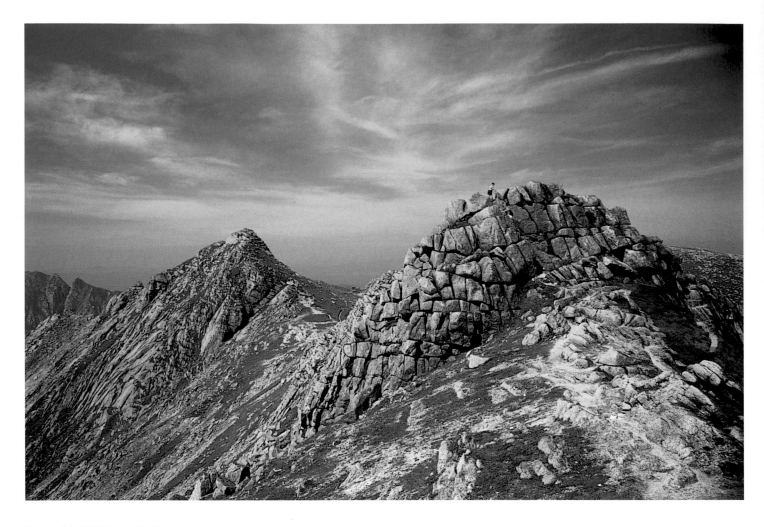

THE CAUSE OF TORS

Big bare slabs; wide gravel plateau; high slopes of black heather. Granite country is strength through simplicity – an effect, though, that's somewhat spoilt when there's a silly little tor on top. The existence of these tors presents a bit of a mystery, especially in the Cairngorms. There has, after all, just been an ice age over here.

The Cairngorm plateau was glaciated a mere 20,000 years ago. These delicate structures could scarcely have survived under an ice age. But then again, they could scarcely have been created or excavated in the short period since. Did the ice scour the side-slopes but not actually cover the Cairngorm plateau, which is where the tors are all to be found?

And what combination of wind, rain, rivers, ice, or eruptions creates such striking shapes anyway? Two hundred years ago, natural historians interpreted the Dartmoor tors as built structures, sophisticated abstract versions of Stonehenge. They even worked out specific Druidic rituals to explain and account for various holes, pits and tunnels.

ABOVE: Cyclopean rock walls, rounded corners, and serious path erosion: Stacach Pinnacles of Goat Fell, on Arran's granite lands.
BELOW: Slab shine on Stob Coir' an Albannaich, Glen Etive.
OPPOSITE ABOVE: Two easy Cairngorm climbs in the two different granite styles. (**LEFT**) Cyclopean masonry on Pygmy Ridge; (**RIGHT**) slab land at the foot of Domed Ridge, Coire Bhrochain.
OPPOSITE BELOW: 'Climbing on the Etive Slabs is in my opinion unique, as unique as gritstone climbing in England or hard ice in Scotland; each requires its own grading system and is a specialist section of the sport of mountaineering.' Brian Robertson in the *Scottish Mountaineering Club Journal*, 1967.

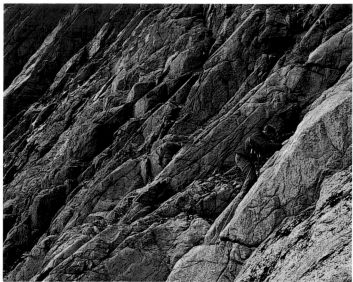

The actual explanation is every bit as weird, even if it doesn't involve human sacrifice. Tors formed underground, in the hot tropics. But it took an ice age to dig them out.

Granite splits in sheets, as the countryside overhead erodes away. But to break up further, into blocks, it must crack in two perpendicular directions as well. This 'jointing' may simply be reopening cracks and weaknesses formed by the rock's original cooling of 400 million years previously. The jointing will make the rectangular lines of the cyclopean crags, and be the blockwork of the eventual tors.

During the Tertiary, the geological period immediately before the Ice Ages, Britain was moving northwards through a hot, humid climate. Groundwater, brown and soupy with plant juices, seeped downwards into the granite bedrock. It penetrated along the joint-lines to dissolve the feldspar and the mica. Where the granite was well-broken by joints, the plant juices turned it all to quartz gravel and rotten orange clay. Where the granite joints were spaced more widely, rock remained as upright lumps within the underground gravel. Such still-buried tors have been found in Dartmoor quarries.

Next we need a way of unburying them. On a frosty morning, your lawn heaves up and you have to go and roll it down again with a roller. (At least you do if you're a particularly lawn-proud person.) The same happens to hilltops, especially in the warmer spells of an ice age. Ground moisture expands to ice during the night. In the morning it melts, and any stones that have been slightly lifted slump down again. But where they slump to is a millimetre downhill from where they started. Over quite short periods, millennia or even centuries, this process can transport earth and stones right off the hilltop. The ground creeps downhill in lumps called solufluction lobes.

In the intervals of the Ice Age, then, solufluction can uncover the tors. This still leaves the question: how do they survive the ice itself? One clue here is that the tors of Dartmoor are even more implausible and tottery than the Cairngorm ones: Dartmoor was never iced over. Another clue is the low rockpiles and plinths that are the knocked-over tors that didn't survive the ice: one such forms the summit of Cairn Gorm itself.

We're told about – and if we're fortunate we even tread on – the awesome power of the moving glacier. The ice down in the Lairig Ghru was like that: but the ice on the Cairngorm plateau wasn't.

There's ice that's wet at its base, and ice that's frozen on. Wet-bottom ice is lubricated, and starts to slide. The sliding creates friction heat, and melts some more lubricating water; so that ice that's once started to slide begins to make it a habit.

The ice-slide may have started down some landscape dip. But sliding ice, with its frozen-in boulders, is an awesome grinder. Soon the dip becomes a valley. Snow blowing across the plateau ends up in the valley, adding itself to the sliding ice at the expense of the ice of the plateau. The sliding ice deepens, its grind becomes more powerful. And its valley floor, now hundreds of metres down, gets a milder climate than the plateau above, and even more meltwater to lubricate the glacier base.

So it is with glaciers, as with human morality. Once you start to slide, it gets ever harder to regain the chilly stability of the high ground. Let your bottom once get damp, and in no time at all you're down in Gleann Einich all covered in unsightly moraine . . .

Up on the plateau, on the other hand, ice flows as a solid. Its base is frozen down, its top moves outwards at a metre or two in the year. And so the plateau ground is gently rolling, with the little River Dee running down the same shallow valley it had before the ice came, and tors only slightly battered about. And then you come suddenly to the plateau edge, and look down 600m into the deep 'U' of the Lairig Ghru, erratic boulders and drumlin humps in its bottom. Beside you, the Dee leaps down a crag of ice-chewed granite. Plateau (dry-bottom ice) and chasm (wet-bottom ice): the combination of the two is the Cairngorms.

Tors can also form in at least six other sorts of stone. Stiperstones, pictured in Chapter 5, is a quartzite tor, and (as Chapter 16 will describe) tors also make themselves out of the Millstone Grit. But the true tor is the pile of granite blocks, overhanging at the sides and with quartz gravel in the gaps: the tor that provides the moment of fantasy at the crest of the wide bleak heather and boulder of Dartmoor, or the Mountains of Mourne, or the Cairngorms.

ABOVE: Plateau of Cairn Gorm, above Coire an t-Sneachda. Outlined on the right, the Grade 1 scramble of Fiacaill Ridge.
BELOW: East of Cairn Gorm, the Little Barns of Bynack stand on a rounded ridge crest where the flow of the icecap would have been particularly slow.

14. Stone arriving sideways: dolerite intrusions

14. STONE ARRIVING SIDEWAYS: DOLERITE INTRUSIONS

For two years, between 1825 and 1827, Charles Darwin was studying at Edinburgh University. In his autobiography 40 years later, he looked back with astonished amusement at his geology lectures. 'Equally striking is the fact that I, though now only sixty-seven years old, heard Professor Jameson, in a field lecture at Salisbury Craigs . . . with volcanic rocks all around us . . . say that it was a fissure filled with sediment from above, adding with a sneer that there were men who maintained that it had been injected from beneath in a molten condition.'

ABOVE: Dolerite is a featureless rock, usually black or dark grey on a freshly-broken piece. Occasionally it's enlivened by greyish or pinkish feldspar crystals, as in this fragment from a dyke on the north face of Tryfan, Snowdonia.

Why are there seashells at the summit of Snowdon, and pillow lavas on Cadair Idris? How come Ingleborough is made of remains of sea creatures? As detailed in the last chapter, the theory known as Neptunism believed that it was not the land that has risen, but the sea: on many occasions, with Noah's Flood merely the most recent and well-documented (well, it is in the Bible). For the Neptunists, every rock was a sedimentary one. What makes Darwin's being taught this theory on Arthur's Seat itself so poignant is that it was there, 50 years earlier, that James Hutton had found utterly clear evidence that Salisbury Crags has been squeezed in sideways in a molten condition. Jameson, while misinforming the young Darwin, may even have been standing in front of the celebrated Hutton's Section, the rocks silently giving him the lie.

In the centuries since Hutton, the tough dolerite of Salisbury Crags has been quarried to pave the streets of Edinburgh, and Hutton's Section has got smaller. On the other hand, it's easier to find, as there's now an interpretation board in front of it. And unless my photo has come out very badly, I hope it's altogether obvious that the dolerite, above, has forced itself, under pressure, in between the beds of the sandstone. The bottom edge of the dolerite, next to the sandstone, is blackened: this is where it has cooled extra-fast into a glassy state. The top edge of the dolerite contains little bubbles, formed by gas coming out of solution as the rock crystallised. It's hard to see how bubble-holes could get into a sediment.

LEFT: Arthur's Seat from Edinburgh Castle. The dolerite sill has been accentuated by quarrying to build Edinburgh's Old Town.
BELOW: The dolerite sill of Salisbury Crags, Edinburgh. The interpretation board, middle distance, stands in front of Hutton's Section.

TOP: Hutton's Section at Salisbury Crags. The dolerite (above) has forced its way downwards and then outwards between the sandstone beds. The bottom of the sill is blackened, where rapid cooling of the magma has made it go glassy.
ABOVE: The smoothness of the top edge of Salisbury Crags also indicates it as an intrusive sill rather than a lava flow. Gas bubbles (vesicles) have risen towards the top of the melt, but not penetrated the very top edge, which had already solidified.
RIGHT: Small dolerite sill, tilted by later earth movements, at Gullet Quarry in the Malverns.

Despite having been so bored by Professor Jameson that he'd resolved 'never as long as I lived to read a book on Geology,' Darwin took with him on board the *Beagle* Lyell's lucid account of Hutton's theory. And the young naturalist must have found it most frustrating: where worse to have one's geological ideas thrown into turmoil than on a small ship surrounded by seawater? At the very first stop, St Jago in the Cape Verde islands, he leapt ashore to look at some stones. And within an hour, he had found a band of white shells running through rocks 45 feet above the current level of the sea. The land, it was apparent, really did move itself up and down. Learned lecturers could indeed be quite, quite wrong: and to show them so, all you needed to do was look. A useful lesson for the future author of the *Origin of Species*.

Dolerite is the underground version of the basalt that flows from certain sorts of volcanoes. When basalt lava squeezes sideways to form a sill such as Salisbury Crags between existing strata, it cools slowly enough to form crystals: the result is dolerite. Dolerite is compact, and shows its crystalline nature only under a powerful lens. Its usual colour is very dark grey, or black; sometimes it has crystals of feldspar. The feldspar isn't the alkali feldspar found in granite, which is white; it is the feldspar that uses sodium or calcium rather than potassium, and is greyish, or greyish pink. The darker crystals (which in dolerite are too small to see individually) contain iron. Centuries of dew and rain can turn the iron orange, so that the weathered surface of dolerite is often orangey-grey rather than the black it is inside.

Dolerite, as it cools, must shrink. Shrinking in the up-down direction is no problem, with the great weight of rock on top. But shrinking in sideways, it has to crack. The most efficient way of cracking is in hexagonal columns. Dolerite rarely shows the perfect 'columnar jointing' of the basalt at the Giant's Causeway in Antrim or Fingal's Cave on Staffa in the Hebrides – and for the matter of that, neither does basalt itself. However, if it's dolerite, it ought to show columnar jointing. That said, any thinnish layer of hot rocks will cool in the same sort of way, so that columnar jointing is also sometimes shown by lava flows and even ignimbrites (welded ashflow tuffs).

Dolerite comes in sideways, insinuating itself between two already-existing beds. On the small sill at Gullet Quarry in the Malverns, the intruding magma has even taken a cast of the ripple marks off the limestone it squeezed into. Stand at High Cup Nick and look at the Great Whin Sill and it certainly appears as a single layer squeezed in between the limestone underneath and the exactly similar limestone above: indeed, it occupies the space between two beds.

And yet at the same time, how could it possibly? Especially when you've walked round to Hadrian's Wall, and seen the same rock-layer still there 65km (40 miles) away. Arthur's Seat is a fairly obvious volcano: it has lava flows, and a volcanic vent plugged with welded-together lava chunks. But the northern Pennines have no volcanoes, no tuffs, no lava flows anywhere closer than the Lake District or Edinburgh. Just how does the dolerite do it?

The rich are different; the Royal Family don't behave like ordinary people. And the unchanging laws of physics work in different ways for a pebble and the Great Whin Sill. Thus, a hot saucepan off the stove cools down in a few minutes. A house with thick stone walls can take 24 hours to heat up when you come back from Tenerife and switch the central heating back on. But a sill of molten dolerite stays hot and molten for years and decades. Basic physics is that ten times as thick means staying hot for one hundred times as long. A dyke or sill 100 metres thick takes 80 years to cool from 1600°C to 800°C; one that's 1km thick takes 8000 years. Even after 40,000 years, that 1000m intrusion would still be hot enough to roast potatoes.

Chunky andesite (pictured at Dow Crag at the end of this chapter) was thick and sticky, and flowed rather more reluctantly than toothpaste. But dolerite is comparatively runny. At 1600°C, the temperature of the Salisbury Crags intrusion, dolerite magma is about as mobile as a very stiff honey, or a fairly free-flowing peanut butter.

Dolerite sills are big and thick; dolerite flows like chocolate sauce. So dolerite can travel remarkable distances. The particular dolerite of the Great Whin Sill has travelled, indeed, from the area around Arthur's Seat.

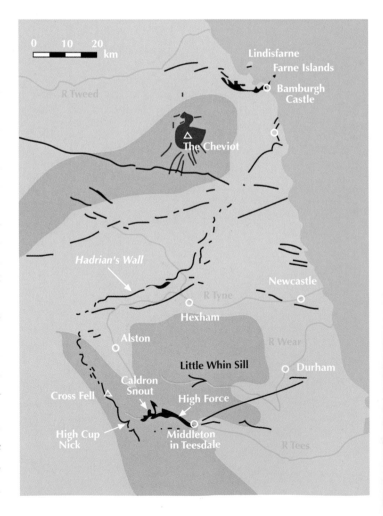

THE EDINBURGH ERUPTIONS

The small volcanic mountains of Scotland's central valley don't anywhere rise to 600m (2000ft); the Ochils do, but the Ochils are Old Red Sandstone. However, the fact that the Great Whin Sill rises to 750m (2500ft) on the flanks of Great Dun Fell gives an excuse for including Dumgoyne, Bass Rock, and Arthur's Seat in this book anyway. This is just as well. Arthur's Seat is the most exciting miniature mountain in Britain, even better than Side Pike above Langdale or Dduallt in mid-Wales. And the volcanoes of the Scottish Lowlands are a rather different sort of eruption from Lakeland or Ben Nevis. Between the Highlands and the Southern Uplands, this is the UK's rift valley.

The Highlands of Scotland, the Southern Uplands, and the mountains of Cumbria have all been formed from crushed continental crust, from landscape under compression. But the natural state for landscape is actually the opposite: scenery is, on the whole, suffering from being stretched.

At this point, we need to think a bit about the huge convection currents in the Earth's mantle: the forces that drive the expanding oceans and the moving continents on top (diagram on page 16). When porridge boils in a pot, we naturally think of the seething motion as being driven by the gas flame underneath, and powered by the upward push. But equally, the air-cooled porridge is sinking at the sides, in a process that will keep the oatmeal on the move for a few seconds after you switch off the flame. The rising of the hot, and the sinking of the cold: these two together drive the convective circuit of the cauldron. (Thick but spoonable porridge has viscosity around 10 Pascal seconds, comparable with honey, peanut butter, and basalt magma at 1600°C.)

The first idea of continental drift had the process driven by upwelling hot magma. A more mature understanding combines this with the downward pull of sinking cold ocean crust. And an understanding more mature even than that realises that only the second process is the important one. The shape of the mid-ocean ridge, as shown in the diagram, makes sense if we see the ocean not as being

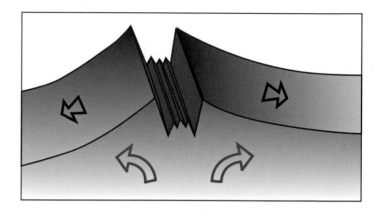

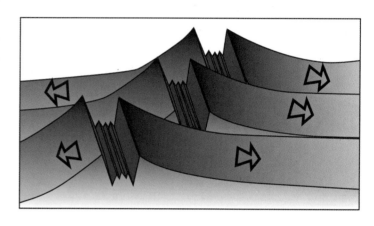

ABOVE: The mid-ocean ridge was originally understood as an upwelling of magma from the earth's mantle (top). However, the way it's offset in the South Pacific, and elsewhere, makes sense only if we see the ocean floor as being pulled apart from the sides, rather than pushed up at the middle.

BELOW: The Scottish Lowlands are under tension, with faults forming a rift valley. Sandstone (yellow) has eroded from above the dark-grey Highland schist and light-grey Southern Upland greywacke, and disappeared out of the diagram. Where the fault has brought softer rock down opposite the harder schist and greywacke, erosion produces a faultline scarp.

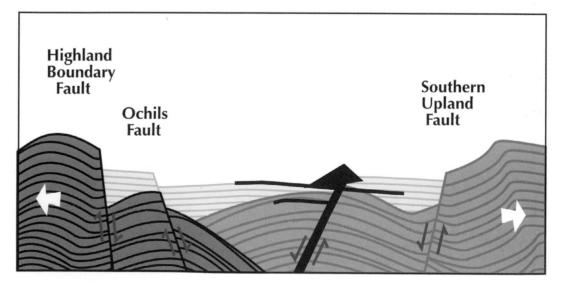

Highland Boundary Fault

Ochils Fault

Southern Upland Fault

pushed apart by upwelling magma, but as being pulled apart by distant subduction zones. And with this realisation, it also becomes less mysterious that a new division of the plates has started happening in Africa, and then just faltered to a stop, leaving the Red Sea anxiously wondering whether it's ever going to expand into an ocean . . .

So, in the diagram of continental drift on page 16, we need to remove the two red arrows pointing upwards under Point A. And, while the continents at D and B are being crushed and crumpled, the continent at C is being pulled by its right-hand edge, and as a consequence is being stretched apart.

ABOVE: Volcanic plugs, lava flows, and dolerite sills form the small but rather rocky hills of Scotland's so-called Lowlands. Volcanic lavas on East Kip, in the Pentlands.
BELOW: Dolerite under Stirling Castle.

The result can be the kind of faulting shown on the previous page, and the formation of a rift valley. Scotland's Midland Valley is supposed to have formed in this way during the late Carboniferous, as the UK was tugged towards the subduction zone at the far-away north-western edge of the Old Red Sandstone continent, at the edge of the Panthalassic ocean (map page 21). Thus Arthur's Seat would be a rift valley volcano, similar to Kilimanjaro today.

An alternative theory suggests that the UK passed across a mantle hot-spot (Point E in the diagram already referred to, page 16). Some instability at the base of the Earth's mantle, far below any tectonic activity, sends a plume of hot lava upwards, eventually to punch through the crust above. The plume persists for tens of millions of years, while the continents and oceans drift past overhead. The result is a

chain of volcanic islands quite independent of tectonic plates, and with a slightly different, deep-mantle, sort of lava. Present day examples include the Emperor Seamount chain, with the hot-spot currently driving the volcanoes of Hawaii. The only hot-spot currently below a continent is firing itself up at the underneath of the Yellowstone National Park in the Rocky Mountains of the USA.

The two theories – continental split, and deep-mantle hot-spot – could both be true. The line of holes punched, sewing-machine style, by a hot-spot plume may define an initial break-line for a rift system or even an ocean. Iceland,

for example, is over a hot-spot that lies exactly on the line where the Atlantic Ocean is currently splitting apart. But whether copying Kilimanjaro or Yellowstone, volcanic plugs do form a noticeable line across the Scottish Lowlands, from Arthur's Seat, to Bass Rock and North Berwick Law. The ones at Edinburgh and Dumbarton are crowned with castles. Other castles, such as at Stirling, stand on associated dolerite sills. Dolerite sills and basalt lava flows make low but craggy outcrops across the Campsie Fells, the Gargunnock hills, and the Lomonds of Fife.

BLACK LADDERS

Dolerite is obvious enough when it's squeezed itself from somewhere in Scotland to emerge between beds of pale limestone. Dolerite does, however, intrude itself most massively when it's still close to its home volcanoes. In the eastern part of Snowdonia, dolerite sills hundreds of metres thick form actual mountain masses.

ABOVE: The Black Ladders of Carnedd Dafydd, seen from Carnedd Llewelyn. Roughly level bedding, above and below, is at odds with the strongly vertical lines of the crags between. The upright tiers are caused by columnar jointing.
LEFT: A dolerite column eroded out on the east ridge of Carnedd Llewelyn. Black when broken, this dolerite shows an orange tinge when weathered. That and the smoother texture are a warning to tread slightly more carefully on rocks that are less grippy than most of Snowdonia.

Rather than being obvious, these dolerites are at first sight pretty perplexing. Here appear to be some roughly level beds of grey sandstone. Or else – we are looking at them from right across the valley – some roughly level lava flows (the level-lying rocks above and below the Black Ladders, pictured, are in fact grey sandstones). Up on top, there are more of the horizontal strata. But in between are strata which appear to be at right angles, running straight up and down the mountain.

This all makes sense once the upright 'strata' are reinterpreted as columnar jointing, the crag in question being a thick sill of dolerite. Go closer, and the sill may reveal its nature by having a surprisingly smooth top or bottom surface: it starts and ends in the straight break where it opened up the rocks. Or if the original top surface has weathered, it may have formed blocky steps, like a badly made version of the Giant's Causeway. The Crib Goch ridge of Snowdon, an intrusion of sticky rhyolite, betrays its nature in just such blocky breakage, giving the scrambler a surface that consists almost entirely of footholds.

Those footholds, though, are flat: and the handholds to go with them are often absent. Dolerite rocks are smooth and solid. Scramble over them, on the ridges of Moel Siabod say, and find them less deliciously grippy than the rest of Snowdonia. So if you spot the slightly orange tone of the weathered rocks, or notice the tell-tale black showing at a broken corner, it's a sign to tread a little more carefully. And

the Black Ladders, at the back of Carnedd Dafydd, are ignored by rock climbers not just for being three hours in from the car park. They are also, in a world of rough grey rhyolite, a rock that's a whole lot less satisfying to climb about on.

ABOVE: Dow Crag, in the southern Lake District. Intrusions aren't usually as obvious as the Great Whin Sill or Salisbury Crags. Dow Crag formed as an underground intrusion of andesite magma, which is stickier than dolerite; so Dow Crag is thick and chunky, and doesn't show the obvious columnar jointing of lavas that flow out into a shallow layer before cooling. Furthermore, it hasn't travelled far from its source, so is still surrounded by volcanic rocks similar to itself.
BELOW: Climber on Murray's Route, Dow Crag. The massive andesite shows no particular structure or texture, apart from a trace of columnar jointing.

15. THE SANDS OF TIME
The Big Red Edge of South Wales

ABOVE: Shrinkage cracks in Carboniferous sandstone: Camstone Quarry, Arthur's Seat.
RIGHT: Current ripples in sandstone: Arthur's Seat.

How is sandstone formed, and what is it made of? It's obvious enough: it's made, as the name implies, from sand.

It's also obvious that the sun goes round the earth; that a slow-worm is a sort of snake; and that the continents don't shift around the surface of the earth. So it's instructive to put ourselves back into the 18th century and pretend once more to be Mr James Hutton of Edinburgh. If sandstone is really a compressed old beach or lake bottom, then the more we look at sandstone, the more signs we should see of its original beach or bed.

Hutton was lucky: he lived in Edinburgh. On his doorstep he had the splendidly intelligible basalt and dolerite of Arthur's Seat. (Indeed, they weren't just on his doorstep: they were his doorstep – and the rest of his house as well.) But at the back of Salisbury Crags, in the Camstone quarry, there was also sandstone. And when he looked closely at that sandstone, here and there he could see ripples exactly the same as on beaches and riverbeds. He could also see a strange pattern of dark bands, shown in the illustration on page 150. These can be interpreted as the cracks formed in muddy sand as it dries under the sun. The cracks happen to have been refilled with a different sediment, a harder one containing iron. Thus the former cracks end up standing proud of the rock surface.

In still water, sandstone, like other sediments, is laid down in flat horizontal layers. But underneath an active current, sand builds up on the downstream sides of sandbanks, so that the layers are tilted. If the current moves away to another part of the river, a horizontal layer may follow: the horizontal layer perhaps made of the finer sediments

dropped out of still waters. Such a structure, called cross-bedding, is the rule rather than the exception in sandstone formed from desert dunes.

Not everything that's obvious turns out to be untrue. Looking harder at sandstone simply reinforces the original conclusion. Geologists before Hutton didn't look at rocks all that much, and consequently got a lot of things wrong. But even they correctly deduced that sandstone is, indeed, made of sand.

We'll see that the UK's southern half has been covered kilometres deep in sandstone, twice over.

OPPOSITE: Cross-bedding in Millstone Grit, on Hargreaves' Original Route (Very Severe), Stanage Edge, Peak District. The climber gains foothold in a layer that formed in water flowing strongly from left to right. The climb is considered one of the best on gritstone for its delicate balance and friction moves.

THE ROMANCE OF THE OLD RED SANDSTONE

ABOVE: Old Red Sandstone in the Town House, Dunbar, showing what a mere four centuries of erosion can do to this soft stone.

Hugh Miller of Cromarty in north-west Scotland was an original 'lad o' pairts' – a self-made intellectual from the working class. His trade was stone-breaking in the quarries around his village. Thus he was particularly well-skilled, in his Lowland black-and-white plaid, at bashing apart the Old Red Sandstone (ORS) of Easter Ross and finding fossil fish.

There's more ORS in South Wales, and indeed in north Devon, the Scottish Lowlands, and elsewhere. With its rich red colour and interesting fish it inspires such affection that they named a geological era after it. That was a bad idea. The rocks of the Old Red Sandstone are indeed old; but not all of them are red; and even some that are red aren't sandstone. Rather a lot of them are conglomerates, which is to say, sandstones that also contain larger lumpy bits. There are two lumps of ORS conglomerate in Lakeland –

the Great and Little Mell Fells. But the period's main representative is a whole lot of volcanic rocks in Scotland. So it's less vivid but also less confusing to name the period of the ORS as the Devonian.

Where does all the old red sand come from? Its red colour indicates a dry desert. Its coarse nature, and conglomerate pebbles, imply a nearby mountain range. We now know that during the Devonian period, the UK was passing through the southern arid zone, the part of the world that currently contains the Kalahari desert. And the source of the sand was the huge Caledonian mountain range along the Scottish border, formed in the previous Silurian period and now rapidly eroding.

Sandstone is soft; especially the Old Red, as people who live in houses made of it know to their cost. So the ORS is mostly a stone of the low country. In only one place does it rise above the 2000ft contour so as to be noticed by this book.

THE BIG RED EDGE

Along the edges of the Caledonian mountains, over all the lands that would be southern Britain, the Old Red Sandstone lay. The Caledonian mountains were worn down almost flat; the sandstone debris lay buried and forgotten under a shallow sea, and under an ever-thickening layer of limestone, and later of gritstone and coal. It lay there undisturbed for 200 million years.

Then the arrival of Africa at the far corner of Spain (the Variscan Orogeny, described in Chapter 3) raised some of it back into the open air, in a long band across what would shortly be becoming Wales. Happily for hillwalkers, that band was facing north. And so the Ice Age, when it came, piled snowfields against it, gnawed into it with many small glaciers, and created a hill scarp that stretches for 80km (50 miles). Four separate ranges – the Black Mountain or Mynydd Du, Fforest Fawr, the Brecon Beacons and the Black Mountains or Mynyddoedd Duon – carry the Big Red Edge from Ammanford across to the English border.

For any long-distance hillwalker with a small scale map, the thing is irresistible.

LEFT: From bottom to top (or left to right): Silurian shales and slates; Old Red Sandstone; carboniferous limestone; coal measures.

TOP: The Old Red Sandstone escarpment: Picws Du and Llyn y Fan Fach, Brecon Beacons. Picture by John Gillham.

ABOVE: First sign of the sandstone: Old Red Sandstone conglomerate on Pentir Blaencennen moor.

I came along it first as an unwinding exercise after university exams. The sun shone, and for three days I walked westwards, looking north over green lowlands to the rounded brown hills beyond. Just once I dropped into an early-morning village to enjoy fresh fruit and liquid milk and to buy more muesli. The rest of the time I walked with the dawn dew on my boots, and the midday sun on my neck, and the brown hills fading to mauve and grey at dusk. After three days, with 30km (20 miles) of the range still ahead of me, I found that I'd unwound enough, and needed some human company; so I dropped off at the Sennybridge road and hitch-hiked home.

Many years later I returned in support of an equally map-struck friend who was attempting the scarp in its entirety over 48 hours as a charity fundraiser. As for me, I was now aware of the Devonian System (of rocks) and Period (of time – 45 million years of it). I was aware of its typical rock, the Old Red Sandstone, and knew that this, for

151

ABOVE: This sandstone (actually from the Carboniferous Period) has been formed by shifting currents in the bed of a stream. A pebble as pretty as this takes some finding, but who minds spending time on a beach? This one was on Barns Ness beach, near Dunbar, which also has more crinoid fossils than you ever really needed.

hillwalkers, was it. I was looking forward to remaking its acquaintance.

We approached from the north-west, out of a village called Bethlehem. The Big Red Edge, which stretched away to our left for a tough two days of walking, was hidden in mist. But it was reassuring to find, on a preliminary hill called Trichrug, the familiar Silurian greywackes of mid-Wales and the Southern Uplands. As the diagram on page 150 shows, these older underlying rocks ought to outcrop below, and consequently to north of, the Big Red Edge. And here they were.

Within a few miles, the stones underfoot changed from sharp-edged grey to softly rounded brown. The next real rocks, however, were limestone. The sandstone at this extreme western end is shallow, and we'd already passed up the entire Devonian Era onto the Carboniferous on top. The challenge of covering 160 km (100 miles) meant that we

were in too much of a hurry to puzzle over this. There was just time to appreciate the magnificent limestone scarp standing to support Carreg Cennen Castle – the castle itself is also worth a glance. And in path-side rocks I found fossil coral and seashells absolutely the same as ones I'd last been looking at on Cross Fell, away at the other end of England.

Mist made the scarp itself invisible. Pentir Blaencennen was limestone grassland, broken with typical limestone scarps, which I was trying to ignore as I was thinking about the Old Red. Happily, the glaciers had brought down mountain samples across the moorland below, and we could look at these as we walked. The ORS sediments were washed out of the very high mountains to the north by flash floods and vigorous river systems. Often the end result is conglomerate, a rock of pebble-beds bound together with the reddish sand. Handsome boulders scattered across the limestone moor were just such conglomerate, mostly of tough quartz pebbles, but with orange fragments which must have come out of some intrusion. I was pleased to see a few broken fragments of Silurian grey also swept into the mix.

The mist slowly rose. Evening light played across the

ABOVE: Fossil sand dune reveals itself in cross-bedding of New Red Sandstone, at an old Dumfriesshire quarry.

rounded hills and green fields to the north. But cloud still covered the Big Red Edge above us; more interestingly, it was now becoming night time. We weren't going to see much of the Big Red Edge in these conditions, were we?

Well, there was the stone underfoot, grey rather than red by torchlight, but comfortingly rough for not slipping over in the darkness. Gradually we became aware of the great hollow of blackness on our left: a place that swallowed up the torchlight, as the grassland tilted abruptly over and sprouted lumps of rock. And then, getting towards midnight, as we paused on the final climb to Bannau Brycheiniog, the cloud sank away. The great scarp behind us seemed to float in the starlight, tall and black, cut by narrow bands of snow. A new moon gave just enough light to pick out the horizontal strata of it, following the spurs and curves back along the 5 km (3 miles) we'd just groped our way along.

The cloud came down again; and stayed down through the following day, along the more popular part of the scarp that's the Brecon Beacons. But right on that range's high point, foot erosion has worn the top of Pen y Fan to bare red slabs. And there, even tired and hurried long-distance types are able to spot two separate sets of ripple marks from the floor of a long-ago Devonian ocean.

THE NEW RED SANDSTONE

Geologically, any fine particles can get packed together to make a sandstone: so that greywacke, and some sorts of quartzite, can be counted as sorts of sandstone. But the normally recognised sandstone is made of grains of quartz, which is ordinary beach sand, cemented together with iron oxide. Iron oxide is rust, and gives sandstone its reddish or yellowish colour. As anyone who's attempted to repair an old car will know, rust makes a fairly effective cement.

Iron oxide dissolves in water, and is taken up and out of circulation by plants. So the reddish sort of sandstone forms mainly in dry, desert lands; or, in the case of the Torridonian, in the early world before the plants started.

Sand washes out three ways. It can be carried in streams

and rivers and dropped out in freshwater lakes. It can be carried out into shallow seas – but not into deep seas, as sand cannot travel far from land. Thirdly, it can drift around as desert dunes. The UK's three main sorts of sandstone show each of these ways of getting laid. The Torridonian was deposited on dry land by streams and flash floods. The Old Red Sandstone is mainly the remains of river deltas emerging into a shallow sea. And the New Red Sandstone is desert dunes.

The New Red nowhere makes mountains, so could be omitted from this book altogether. But it deserves a mention for two reasons. Firstly, it's what I live on myself, and my house is made of it. Secondly, there's an odd and to me amusing correspondence between the New Red and the Old.

The ORS sediments are the eroded-down rubble of the huge Caledonian mountain range to the north, caused by the collision of Scotland with England. The New Red Sandstone is the eroded-down rubble of the huge Variscan mountain range to the south, caused (200 million years later) by the sudden arrival of Africa. The ORS sediments are red because the UK was then passing through the southern tropical zones, the band of climate that today contains the deserts of Namibia and central Australia. The NRS ones are red because the UK was then passing through the northern tropical zones, the climate band of the Sahara.

In between the Old Red Sandstone and the New Red Sandstone, we passed across the Equator, and the UK grew lush tropical forests of tree fern. Or else it was under water, and grew lush tropical coral reefs. The reefs became limestone: the tree ferns turned into coal. Welcome to the Carboniferous.

BELOW: Fine-grained, well-bedded sandstone is one of the easiest stones there is for carving. Areas with such sandstones experience a flowering of graveyard sculpture: The rapid weathering of the sandstone can even be a bonus. Seventeenth-century tombstone made from the New Red Sandstone at Durisdeer, Dumfriesshire.

16. Mountain Limestone, Millstone Grit

16. MOUNTAIN LIMESTONE, MILLSTONE GRIT
Yorkshire and the Peak District

Yorkshire, as any Yorkshireman will tell you, is not like other places. Elsewhere, hills rise out of the boggy lowlands, up to high cragged sides and sharp rocky summits. In Yorkshire, the rivers run underground, while the hills rise in flat layers like a pile of pancakes. And the crags instead of going up, go sideways. Take a traditional huge crag, cracked and water-worn; turn it over and lay it flat; plant ferns and little flowers in all the spaces – and you have the limestone pavement.

The difference is in the Yorkshire landscape; it is in the Yorkshire temperament. But underneath all that, it's a different sort of rock. Normal rock breaks down, over millions of years, into soil; soil grows plants, insects, and so-called intelligent life such as ourselves. Limestone starts off alive, and runs the clock in reverse, from biology backwards to geology.

WALKING ON DEAD SEASHELLS

The green layer of scum across the planet's surface, the layer we call life, has already (in Chapter 4) created 20 per cent of the air we breathe: being responsible for the oxygen in it. So it shouldn't be too surprising that it's also caused a large, yellowish-coloured 4 per cent chunk of the ground we walk about on. It shouldn't be surprising; but, when I walk up Ingleborough, on crushed coral and tiny seashells all the way, surprised is what I am.

About 500 million years ago, at the start of the Cambrian Period, life came up with one simple new trick. It found out how to combine calcium, from the clay minerals around it, with carbon dioxide (CO_2) out of the atmosphere, to make a hard material called calcite. (Conveniently, it found the two components already dissolved together in the sea.) Calcite, as shell, protected you from being eaten by other life. Much later, during the fish-era of the Devonian, calcite toughened with protein would form skeletons to hold you together, and useful teeth for you to eat other life with yourself.

Calcite shells, bones and teeth form fossils; and fossils mark out the rock strata almost like barcodes in the supermarket. So, from that small chemical discovery, we reckon the start of the geological periods all over the ocean. For within an eyeblink of geological time, a few tens of millions of years, the seashells had taken over the sea. Or at least they appear to have done so. We can't tell how many of the soft squishy sort of creatures lived on, and how many became extinct as horrifying hard-shelled lifeforms invaded their ecological space and ate them.

Calcite is slightly soluble in water. So it not only falls to

ABOVE: Calcite, which is pure calcium carbonate, is a hard mineral suitable for making shells and teeth out of; but it also dissolves in water. If that water evaporates, the calcite reforms, as in these stalagmites in Cheddar Cave.

the seabed in hard heaps, but also dissolves, and precipitates out again to cement the hard heaps together. Indeed, calcite is used by humans to cement together our buildings: calcite is the lime used in lime mortar.

The UK's first rock made out of dead seashells – the Durness limestone – is already found in the Cambrian period. The first English limestone is the Coniston one, at the very top of the Ordovician rocks. In the Carboniferous period, the sea-level happened to be high because of new mid-ocean ridges elsewhere in the world, and because CO_2 in the atmosphere was ensuring a warm globe with no icecaps.

At this point the UK, now combined within a single continent, happened to be drifting across the Equator. The result was warm tropic seas, vigorous seashells and coral, and a lot of limestone. It covered England, and the low Midland Valley of Scotland, many kilometres thick: and over most of that territory it's still there, buried under younger rocks. At the end of the Carboniferous period, the distant collision of Africa with Spain raised the Pennine range gently upwards. So it's in the Pennines – in Yorkshire, but also in the White Peak – that limestone is displayed today up in the open air.

Limestone means green grass (in Scotland and even Lakeland, grass is brown or biscuit-coloured), light grey rock, and mud slightly paler than the usual mud colour. The path south out of Castleton is a gulch between grey cliffs: not at all like the Lake District. Limestone mud is both stickier and more slippery than the normal sort. It's jolly good exercise, that White Peak mud, more strenuous even than deep heather.

What's odd about the White Peak is that it's actually upside-down. The bogs, that belong on the valley bottoms, are up on the tops, and so are all the farmhouses and the fields. All the interesting stony bits, and the steep-sided hill country, are in the valleys. Or, in the words of the Victorian author and mountain-lover John Ruskin: 'The whole gift of the country is in its glens. The wide acreage of field or moor above is wholly without interest; it is only in the clefts of it,

ABOVE: Ingleborough gives about 200 million years of Yorkshire history. Below, not in the picture but quarried for roadstone 500m down the road, are hard grey-black shales and greywackes that belong with the Skiddaw Slates of Lakeland and the shales of the Howgill Fells to the north. Next up, the Great Scar Limestone forms the wonderful pavements around Ingleborough's base. Alternating shale/limestone/gritstone make the main body of the mountain: the stepped Yoredale Series. A hard cap of Millstone Grit forms the flat summit.

LEFT: Thornton Force, below Ingleborough, on the Ingleton Waterfalls Walk. Great Scar Limestone above, Ordovician slates below. The slates are strongly tilted, with the limestone lying across the eroded-off ends of the strata; so this is an unconformity, exactly like Hutton's Unconformity described on page 11. Here, the entire Silurian and Devonian periods are missing.

BELOW: Boulders of grey slate contained within the limestone under the lip of the waterfall. These represent the beach formed as the Carboniferous sea invaded the already old grey continent.

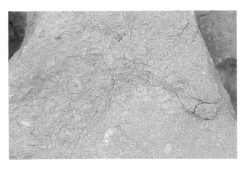

ABOVE: Fossil coral (the oval blob with rays) and shells (sliced, to form white curves) are found in the mountain limestone all over the UK. The samples making such a satisfying match with each other are from Cross Fell (**LEFT**), Ingleborough (**CENTRE**) and Carmarthenshire (**RIGHT**). Fossils will only be found in fresh, unweathered rocks. These three came from a cliff exposed by track excavations, a clean stone out of a fallen wall, and a quarried block.

BELOW: Limestone pavement on Hutton Roof Crag, Cumbria. It's uncommon in the rest of the world outside Yorkshire, the result of Yorkshire's level-lying limestone beds being scraped bare by ice and then washed into by rain.

and the dingles, that the traveller finds his joy.' I find my joy in Dovedale, whose trees grow one on top of the other, and sticking out above the trees are towers and walls and arches of limestone. It's not like real rock, it's like glacier ice that's been gouged into holes by the hot sun.

There are indeed mountains in Derbyshire and Staffordshire. Only they're all down in the valleys. In Yorkshire, on the other hand, some of the very finest mountains are actually underground. And if you think Ingleborough looks odd from on top, down in Great Douk Cave you see the whole limestone pavement effect, as it were, inside-out.

Had there been any humans, we might have greatly enjoyed the 70 million years of that hot tropical sea – England's Caribbean. And in fact we still can, as it formed the Great Scar Limestone, 200m thick, and gave us the limestone pavements of Ingleborough and Malham Tarn. Great Scar Limestone knobs, and the same stuff scattered: these make the high moor of Craven, where the path runs away playfully into green hollows and hides in the mist. Froth blows off Malham Tarn in lumps, displaying the soapy nature of limestone. And finally at Attermire, you walk below that same limestone upright, or overhanging, or in caves and screes and tottering towers. Down, down green grass and a last stony lane between high limestone walls, to the market square of Settle, whose buildings are limestone tamed into pubs and information offices and fish and chip shops.

ABOVE: Yorkshire's underground mountains: Calf Holes in Ribblesdale (**LEFT**) and the Kingsdale Master Cavern (**RIGHT**).
BELOW LEFT: The Howgills seen along Dentdale. Limestone in level beds forms the Yorkshire landscape of flat tops and wide, low scars in the middle distance; Ordovician shales and sandstones make the steep-sided Howgills behind.
BELOW RIGHT: Limestone, raised into mountains by continental collisions, forms many of the world's most spectacular ranges, including the Pyrenees, Everest, and parts of the Alps. Yorkshire rose gently, its limestone beds remaining level; but this could be the early life of the Mendips. It's actually the Picos de Europa, in northern Spain.

LIMESTONE, GRITSTONE, SHALE: THE YOREDALE SERIES

The invasion, when it came, was not of package holidaymakers with tubes of sunscreen. What finally overran the warm blue tropic sea was a great river delta, bringing grit and gravel from high lands to the north. When the river outlet is far away, only a thin silt drifts out to the sea and settles gently to

the bottom: the end result will be a mudstone or shale. Then the river shifts its channel, and a rush of sand and gravel suddenly covers the seabed. And so, on top of the shale, will eventually form coarse gritstone. The river shifts again, and nothing at all arrives: just the occasional dead seashell, the slowly rising limestone precipitate.

The massive sediments piling on the seabed caused the seabed to sink; the mountains, by see-saw action, rose up; and the whole thing started all over again. In parts of Yorkshire, the shale-grit-lime cycle took place eight times over.

The shale is soft, and erodes away, leaving the harder limestone rocks standing as the long low cliffs called 'scars'. Two sets of shale-grit-lime have given a stepped southern end to both Ingleborough and Pen-y-ghent. And in the Yorkshire

valleys, the scars run along the valley sides, separated by broad platforms of almost level land. This effect gives a step-sided appearance to Wensleydale in particular. Wensleydale's river is the Ure; the old name for Wensleydale is Yoredale; and the stepped rocks are called the Yoredale Series.

The Yorkshire character has its gentler limestone side – an aspect that could be called sentimental, even, decorating the lids of biscuit tins with lumpy grassland and stone farmhouses the colour of winter sun. But it also has a sharp admixture of grit. The two sides of Yorkshire, the grit and the biscuit-tin, should not be confused, as they were when one TV company set Emily Brontë's *Wuthering Heights* on pale-coloured pretty limestone. Indeed, do Catherine Earnshaw's two lovers correspond in some half-recognised way to the two sorts of Yorkshire landscape? Edgar Linton is mild and gentle, but lacking in warmth: while Heathcliff's very name suggests the gritstone moorland. 'My love for Heathcliff resembles the eternal rocks beneath: a source of little visible delight, but necessary,' says Cathy in Chapter 9.

Whatever you may think of its application to literary criticism, the difference between limestone and grit is very obvious when you're walking over it. I was made well aware of it even in the middle of the night, when crossing between Pen-y-ghent and Whernside in the course of a Yorkshire Three Peaks walk. The path showed as a dark streak of trampled peat across the heather, and every few steps we'd sink unexpectedly knee-deep in it. Above us, Ingleborough squatted like a frog in the moonlight, a frog with just its back and shoulders sticking up out of a puddle of mist. We crossed a stile, and found a field of short grass with a few thin rushes. The path, so wide and trampled, had simply vanished. And we didn't need the scattered pale boulders to tell us we'd walked onto the other sort of rock.

At the end of the Carboniferous period, the limestone/gritstone alternation was finally decided, when one huge river delta covered Yorkshire and the northern Peak District. The resulting coarse pebbly sediments give boggy tops to hills from Ingleborough south to the edge of Sheffield.

BELOW: Yoredale walling: the alternation of gritstone (**TOP**) and limestone (**BOTTOM**) can be followed in the walls. At the same time the ground underfoot shifts from tussocks and peat to gentler grass – the lower picture is on aptly named Green Hill. (By the top of the upper wall, the waller was wheeling his barrow across the geological boundary into some nearby limestone.)
ABOVE RIGHT: Sometimes the sandy river delta rose above sea level and grew a swamp forest of tree ferns. The eventual rock result was coal, seen here on the Berwickshire coast. As coal makes no mountains, it is not discussed in this book.

MILLSTONE GRIT

'The granite hills of Arran . . . present distinctive problems met with, in some degree, only in the Cairngorms and on the gritstone outcrops of the Midlands.' So says the old climbers' guide to Arran. The Cairngorms are also granite, and could be expected to present Arran-like distinctive difficulties. But what's this with the English Midlands?

Arran granite and English Millstone Grit are about as different as two rocks can be. Granite is igneous, the slow solidifying of kilometres-wide blobs of underground magma. Gritstone is sedimentary, laid in grains across the sea bottom. Granite is speckly black-and-white; gritstone is grey or beige. Granite makes huge crags, and flat plateaux with tors on top. Gritstone is a crag that's several kilometres wide but only a single pitch of climbing high, all the way along the moorland edge. Granite has tors, whereas gritstone… Here the opposition breaks down, for are there not some grey, sandy-textured tors above the Derwent Reservoir?

There are indeed; and this is the first clue that granite and gritstone do indeed match together despite their very different natures.

RIGHT: Millstone Grit with waterworn quartz pebbles, Stanage.
BELOW: Stanage Edge, in the Peak District.

The typical minerals of granite, as described in the granite chapter above, are the hard quartz, the softer feldspar that's liable to rot and decompose, and the black specks of biotite mica. The starting point for sandstone is sand, which is to say, quartz again. The Millstone Grit is a particular sort of sandstone where the sand fragments have knocked about in the world for only a short time before being made back into rock. The sand fragments in a gritstone are still sharp-edged, and still contain relatively large gritty bits. More significantly, they still contain some feldspar.

It's the combination of the still-sharp quartz with the softer feldspar that makes Millstone Grit just right for making millstones. The quartz gets ground down, but the feldspar crumbles away, and fresh sharp quartz is exposed. Thus the millstone never loses its bite. All of the worn-down quartz grains simply trickle into the flour, where they get sold on to the customer.

Granite cracks apart vertically as it cools down, deep underground; and then, as it emerges under erosion, cracks again parallel to the land surface above. Gritstone has the same cracks, but in the opposite order. The horizontal cracks are simply bedding, separate layers laid down on the seabed. The vertical joints form afterwards, as water is driven out under pressure and the stone shrinks. More joints will form, in the same way as crevasses in a glacier, if the strata are bent in later earth movements.

The same quartz and feldspar mix, and a similar system of joints: so the gritstone forms tors in the same way as granite does, albeit in a strikingly different colour scheme. (And in parts of the USA, where there isn't any Millstone Grit, they make their millstones out of granite.)

So what are the distinctive problems met with on the gritstone (as well as on the granite)? I found out at the age of 18, as I stood at Stanage Edge below a climb called Buttonhook Crack. Buttonhook Crack is V Diff, which is one of the easier grades and should certainly have been easy enough for me. But Stanage Edge was near-enough vertical: and Buttonhook Crack had smoothly rounded footholds and nothing at all for the hands.

In the 1950s came the first of the working-class climbers; the most famous of them being Joe Brown and Don Whillans, two plumbers from Manchester. Finding the Lake District too far away and infested with university students and Old Etonians, they took the bus out to Stanage Edge. And there, not knowing any better, they taught themselves to climb up smooth, holdless Stanage using a special sort of grip, the hand-jam. Instead of your hand gripping the rock, this consists of getting the rock to grip your hand. Place the hand deep inside the crack: turn it sideways, and clench it to a fist, pressed between the crack's two sides. Now step up.

And in the absence of rock-spikes to suspend a sling, they threaded ropes through ordinary plumbing nuts, the ones they used on weekdays to connect up bath taps and toilets, but now wedged into the narrower cracks to protect themselves as they ascended. And so I worked my way up the Buttonhook Crack, one fist above the other, feet on each of the round-lipped ledges as they occurred.

An uncomfortable distance above the ground, the Button-

TOP LEFT: Millstone (in Jurassic gritstone) on the North York Moors.
TOP RIGHT: Gritstone imitates granite, forming a gritstone tor – Wheel Stones, above the Upper Derwent Valley.
RIGHT: The hand-jam hold, not quite so painful as it looks.

hook crack runs up to a wide, horizontal gap; and starts again, some 2 metres to the left. The main trick here is, never put the knees on any horizontal foothold: for you can't step up off a knee.

Knowing I shouldn't, but it was only going to be for a moment, I put my knees onto the ledge gap; I wriggled; and found myself lying along the incut ledge, flat, snugly tucked below the overhang half a metre higher up. I was quite comfortable, my right cheek resting against the rough rough rock. I looked out at the world, and wondered what I should do next.

Those like myself brought up on Lakeland volcanics are often wrong-footed on Stanage. We find gritstone disconcerting, and complain of the arrogant Midlanders who set all the climbing grades too low. And the same complaint is made about the uncouth Aberdonians who graded the granite climbs of the Cairngorms. But if you're raised on the Millstone Grit, a holdless smooth-edged crack is a handy ladder, straight up the face, and no fiddling around for footholds or little ledges. Just jam in a hand, the other hand higher up, and then jam in the toes. What could be more straight-up than that? And provided you do the hand-jams right, they hardly hurt at all.

LEFT: Climbing Narrow Buttress (Very Severe) on Stanage Edge.
BELOW: Pym Chair to Swine's Back: a single hard gritstone layer forms the flat top of Kinder Scout in the Peak District.

17. The black magic of gabbro

THE TERTIARY VOLCANIC PROVINCE

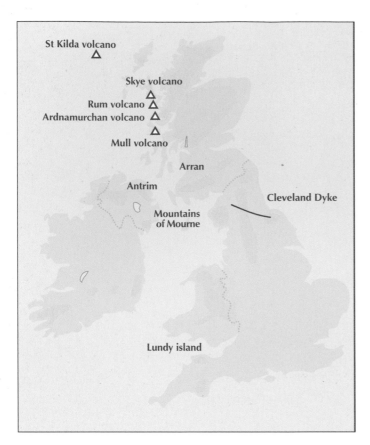

St Kilda volcano

Skye volcano

Rum volcano

Ardnamurchan volcano

Mull volcano

Arran

Antrim

Cleveland Dyke

Mountains
of Mourne

Lundy island

Everywhere else, the really good rock is also really old. Yorkshire limestone is likeable, but the seriously craggy crags of Lakeland and Snowdonia are stuff from the Ordovician, the third of the 11 geological periods. Scotland's mountain rocks are mostly Precambrian, and older than life itself.

Then, a mere 65 million years ago, came a burst of tectonic creativity unseen since the England–Scotland crunch. As the Atlantic Ocean cracked open, unzipping from the Azores northwards towards Iceland, volcanoes rose and black lavas poured along what's now the UK's north-west coast, from Northern Ireland to the Hebrides.

The counties of the Tertiary Volcanic Province are all uncompromisingly rocky, but at the same time rocky in wonderfully different ways; from the granite cones of Arran and the Mountains of Mourne, to the black basalt of Antrim and Mull, and the broken cauldron of Ardnamurchan. The Province has even mounted a small invasion of England, establishing an outpost at Lundy Island. In a blitzkrieg that makes the German tanks of 1939 seem rather slow, it also sent an armoured column of red-hot basalt all the way across Northumberland into eastern Yorkshire. The Cleveland Dyke, which squirted southwards from the Mull volcano, is supposed to have reached the North Yorks Moors in only a few days.

Of the various provinces of the United Kingdom, which is the best for a walker or mountaineer? You might consider Northern Ireland; or decide it's obviously Scotland. Wales has a balanced combination of clean, steep crags and shaggy back country. But actually, it's not any of the political areas defined for purely human convenience. The hill-people part of Britain is the Tertiary Volcanic Province.

The Tertiary Volcanic Province: to paraphrase a slogan originally intended for Heineken beer, it's a great state to be in. Where is the capital and chief resort of this exotic holiday destination? If asked for the best dozen hills in all the UK, many would simply start at Sgurr nan Gillean and list the 12 summits, dark, jagged, and incomprehensibly Gaelic, that make the Black Cuillin on the island of Skye.

OPPOSITE LEFT: Ben Crom Reservoir from Slievenaglough,
Mountains of Mourne.
OPPOSITE RIGHT: Cir Mhor from Goatfell, Arran.
ABOVE TOP: Granite of the Red Cuillin, Skye.
ABOVE LEFT: Ailsa Craig, off Scotland's south-west coast,
is the vent-plug of a rhyolite volcano.
ABOVE RIGHT: Carsaig Arches, carved by the sea out of basalt,
Isle of Mull.

17. THE BLACK MAGIC OF GABBRO
Gabbro lands: the Skye Cuillin

ABOVE: Dark-coloured, crystalline, and very, very rough, gabbro is the outstanding rock for clambering about on.
BELOW: The so-called Tourist Route on Sgurr nan Gillean.

A book on the Lake District remarks casually that 'any dark-coloured crystalline rock gets labelled as being gabbro.' The 1300-page *Principles of Physical Geology* by Arthur Holmes (1965 edition) gives gabbro a single picture, taken through a microscope, and just one sentence: 'A thick dolerite sill may become progressively coarser towards the middle until the rock is a gabbro.'

Walkers and climbers know better. Gabbro is not like other rocks. Gabbro is special, inspiring terror and inspiring joy, often both at the same time. Other rocks are brown, beige or greyish: gabbro is black. Other rocks are smooth, slimy, or in the best of cases tolerably rough: gabbro grips the boot like Velcro and tears the skin off the fingertips. Other rocks you can walk around and go up the grassy way: gabbro makes ridges that you have to climb, or else not get up the mountain at all.

The Cuillin of Skye are simple jaggy mountains, as drawn by a five year old with a fisted crayon: one line up, one line down, one line up, one line down, break the lead and tear a hole in the paper. The black gabbro forms towers and pinnacles and steep sharp ridges, all jagged and notched to make them more entertaining to mountaineers. At the crag foot in a jumble of massive boulders is the beautiful, blue-green, rock-fringed Loch Coir' a' Ghrunnda.

A CLOUDY SKYE

As we stood on the rim of Coir' a' Ghrunnda, leaning into the maritime airstream, it was like being molested by an over-friendly St Bernard. In between slobbering us with wet kisses, the clouds gambolled among the ridges and crags. One minute we saw a great deal of grey nothing; the next, a tunnel opened for 10 seconds to show a boulder balanced like an egg on a distant ledge. And 10 seconds after that, the rags of cloud flew past our ears and we were looking down long, black, glacier-scratched boiler plates to the shoreline, the wide Atlantic, and a gleam of yellow sunset.

Steep sides make for a sheltered bottom. Fifty metres back, our bivvybags were unrolled at the base of a sheltering crag beside a lochan whose water was barely shaken by the nearby gale. With a Sligachan bar meal already inside us, there was no need for cookery. So we spent the dusk hour in a wander round the water. The wander was slow and careful – any slip and we'd rip our waterproofs on the super-abrasive black rocks. Loch Coir' a' Ghrunnda was silvery grey with a subtle hint of pink. The wet rocks shone like seals. Glacier boulders on the corrie rim made striking shapes against the sky, and behind them the daylight slowly sank into the Atlantic.

Back at the bivvybags, the lochan chuckled and rippled between the stones; 150 metres above us, the gale was hissing through the ridges. A day on Collie's Ledge and a two-hour stint of Skye bog after supper meant that we weren't going to really appreciate these soporific sound effects: we were asleep in seconds.

Coir' a' Ghrunnda in mist is all very well: indeed, as we had discovered, it's a great deal better than that. However, there are good reasons for not going any higher than its 700m (2,300ft) altitude. Take a bad bearing on the mainland of Scotland and you end up in the wrong valley with an afternoon of peat hags. Take a bad bearing on Skye and you could die. And a bad bearing is easily taken: gabbro attracts climbers and scramblers, but also the needle of the compass, as part of the rock's colour is due to magnetite, the dark oxide of iron. Paths don't show on bare rock and boulder. And Skye's sharp ridges aren't obvious to follow because of the equally sharp subsidiary ridges and side-ribs.

So when dawn slid over the rim of Coir' a' Ghrunnda as greyly damp as a bunkhouse blanket, there were good reasons for not going up.

But there were also good reasons for not going down. On a bad day, ground-level Skye is grim. You can put on your waterproofs and go to the beach, where the sea is grey and the sand is gabbro black, and it's raining. You can hang around in the camp site feeding the midges. Or you can go for a low-level walk. The stiffness of the damp clothes and the waterproofs, together with Skye's low-level ground of peat and bare boulder, means that the walk will be a slow one. The midges won't have any trouble keeping up . . .

Given good reasons for not going down, and good reasons for not going up, we went up. Ghrunnda to Sgurr nan Eag is one of the less tricky bits of the Skye ridge. But misty Skye is never going to be simple. A trace of path leads to a rock wall. Is this rock wall a small step leading to the next path trace, or is it a climb graded Severe leading nowhere? Does the scree ledge on the right lead around the obstacle, or only onto a loose face of monster gullies? If an obvious foothold has lichen on, then it's a foothold on a wrong route. Scree turned over by people is paler than primordial scree. And we do have an altimeter.

And so we travel along this less-tricky bit of the ridge – try up this way, no; round here, could be, check the altimeter, check the map, check the compass; compass not quite right, on another 10 metres, compass again, look over the shoulder to remember what it looks like for when we're coming back.

ABOVE LEFT: Coir' a' Ghrunnda.
LEFT: Gabbro, like basalt, contains calcium, and any soil that gathers in the cracks of it is fertile. The northern rock cress occurs only in the high corries of the Cuillin.

'Up here?' wonders Colin.

'Hmmm . . .' I reply, and take another bearing.

Slow it may be, but what it reminds me of is a fellrunning descent, one where foot hits bog, next foot hits scree 3 metres further down. This misted rock ridge has the same thin line between disasters on either side, the same feeling of the brain clenched tight like a fist.

Some scenery gets boring when you can't see it. Not the Cuillin ridge. The grey backdrop brings out the dripping pinnacles, outlines an interesting boulder that we might not have noticed, encourages us to spot the rare northern rock cress growing in a crack.

Two days of grey weather on the challenging Black Cuillin have left us with one bleeding shin from a stone that turned on Sgurr Alasdair, and ripped trousers from a casual lump of gabbro. The succession of weird rock-shapes, one behind the other out of the mist, means we're starting to suffer from sensory overload.

A little chimney leads down to a cave where they shelter while they're queuing for the Thearlaich-Dubh Gap. Below the cave, the cloud-wall is a simple grey nothingness. The pinnacles we can see are impressive, but it's the even bigger and wetter ones we can't see that create the real drama. Or do they? I've a feeling that the T-D Gap is one of those spots that's even worse when you can see it than it looks to the misted eye of the imagination.

Damp rock and no rope is reason enough for not doing the T-D Gap today. But an even better reason is that the Gap is not the proper gabbro at all. It's trap rock, as it used to be called. In today's terms, the Gap is basalt.

BASALT LANDS

Gabbro gives superb grip, even in the wet: but basalt is slippery. Gabbro is rich in holds: basalt is smooth. Gabbro is mostly firm and sound; basalt is loose, with little flowers of wild thyme growing in the cracks.

And below the misted mountains, at the bottom edge of the supremely steep-angled gabbro screes, basalt stretches across the island in a landscape of level grassy terraces and short crags, crags whose slightly orange tint clashes deliciously with the wildflowers. North of Portree, you can walk for 30km (20 miles) along mountaintops made of short, lawn-like grass, bog-free because drained through the cracks of the basalt, wildflowered because the basalt decomposes into lime-rich ground. The Skye gabbro is weird and wonderful; the basalt of northern Skye is, quite simply, weird. It forms hexagonal pillars, tottering pinnacles, and crumbly orange crags; and then an unexpected flat place that'd make a truly exciting croquet lawn.

What's odd is that two such different rocks, giving such opposite sorts of good walking, can co-exist on the one island. What's even odder is that two such different rocks are, chemically, actually exactly the same.

Black pyroxenes, greenish olivine, and the greyish or pinkish sorts of feldspar: these minerals are the stuff from under the continent, the material of the Earth's mantle; and between them they make basalt. Meanwhile the gabbro is olivine, pyroxenes, and greyish pinkish feldspar. The makings are the same: the difference is in the crystals. Basalt has flowed out as lava, cooling almost immediately into a glassy flat slab. It's a mixture of microscopic crystals and volcanic glass; but over the ages the glass devitrifies and weathers away. Gabbro is the same stuff, but crystallised very, very slowly in the deep magma chamber underneath that basalt volcano. Carved out by ice, exposed to the open air, the feldspar and olivine start to decompose: but this just gives the gabbro its wonderful porous texture and fearsome grip.

A very late lunch at the Sligachan Inn, and our socks are making their steamy contribution to the Sligachan's very special atmosphere. And then the windows suddenly go all

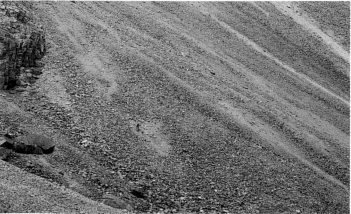

bright and sunlit. We look up at a ridge whose walkers are experiencing the simple colour scheme of jaggy black on blue, rather than romantic shady grey. Up there, the sun is bringing out the mauve tints hidden in the black rock, that rock will be becoming warm under the hand, and the air will be clear right across the Atlantic to the Outer Hebrides . . .

Damp socks be damned. Let's get our boots back on, and up there onto Sgurr nan Gillean.

ABOVE: The face of Clach Glas, seen from Marsco. The notched skyline and black gully slashes are dykes of 'trap rock' or basalt.
BELOW: The two sides of Skye: the Cuillin (**LEFT**) and the Quiraing (**RIGHT**). The odd thing is that these two rocks, the gabbro and the basalt, are exactly the same, apart from the small matter of crystal size.

18. Basalt lands and the opening of the Atlantic

18. BASALT LANDS AND THE OPENING OF THE ATLANTIC

At the end of the Permian, over a period of at most some hundreds of thousands of years, 95 per cent of all known species were extinguished. Even those that made it through – these included cockroaches and ginkgo trees – were presumably reduced to a few, small, scattered populations. Life in the sea died along with land life and the plants. The soil died, and rivers that had flowed through fertile plains became multichannelled gravel torrents. The sea-bottom filled with unoxygenated black sludge, indicating that the ocean currents had shut down. With a stagnant ocean and soil-free lands, the world's self-sustaining cycles had simply stopped. Gaia was dead.

The Permian-Triassic boundary where all this happened is best seen in places currently inconvenient or dangerous, such as Afghanistan and China. It happens that during the Permian, the world was a single continent, Pangaea. Much of the world's land, including most of Europe, was continental interior far from ocean and so was a lifeless sandy desert anyway. So it was less noticeable that at the start of the Triassic, suddenly, *everywhere* was devoid of life.

ABOVE: Basalt lava is dark, blocky, and fine-grained: Clutter's Cave, Malvern Hills.
BELOW: Massive basalt lava flow on the shore of Loch Scridain, on Mull, where the flood basalts are up to 600m deep. The goats' cave, slightly above the present-day sea level, is 50m east of Mull's celebrated fossil tree.

No meteorite traces have been found dating from this particular time. (It's the slightly milder cataclysm at the end of the Cretaceous that was caused by a comet.) What did happen over the half-million-year period was an eruption of basalt. Black basalt is the form taken by the rocks of the Earth's underlying mantle wherever they erupt onto the surface. Basalt is actually the commonest rock of all, but most of it is underwater as the oceanic crust. Being denser, it slides away underneath the lightweight, lighter coloured continental crust.

Basalt emerges into the upper world at the mid-ocean ridges. But it arrives more spectacularly at mantle hot-spots; and most spectacularly of all when a new hot-spot is just starting up. (The hot-spot diagram is in Chapter 1, page 16.) So we get the Deccan Traps, a flood of basalt covering much of northern India, whose hot-spot currently finds itself underneath Réunion Island. We get the Columbia River basalt which covers much of Oregon in the USA, and whose hot-spot has machine-gunned a line of extinct volcanoes across the moving continent. That hot-spot now fires up into the underside of the Yellowstone National Park, with its hot geysers, mud lakes and 60-km (40-mile) caldera.

And, over the same half-million years as the Permian/Triassic extinctions, we get the Siberian Traps. Around the city of Irkutsk, an area the size of Western Europe has been covered several kilometres deep in black lava.

A book from 20 years ago notes the coincidence of dates, and sketches an explanation in terms of the then-fashionable Nuclear Winter; that dust and sulphur particles in the upper atmosphere might shut out the sun and cool the entire world. The problem was that, as discussed later in this chapter, basalt eruptions are comparatively tame events and don't throw stuff into the stratosphere.

Today's explanation is the opposite. The carbon dioxide exhaled along with the lavas could have caused global warming beyond the earth's ability to convert the gas to forests, coal measures, and limestone. At a certain point as the ocean warmed, methane hydrate emerged from its lurking place on the seabed to make the global warming much, much worse. Some such 'runaway greenhouse' seems to have happened, permanently, on the planet Venus next door to us.

This theory, in its current form, speculates that a temperature rise of 6°C was enough to eliminate virtually all living things and shut down the circulation of the ocean. Recovery was not quick. For 5 million years, no coal measures were laid down. For 20 million, there was no coral.

Normal engineering practice is a safety margin of 10 per cent. If a bridge is expected to break at 100 tons, we don't load it beyond 10. In terms of human-induced temperature rise, we have already passed 0.6°C. Our hope is to limit our temperature rise to 2°C – just one third of the level that made the Earth uninhabitable even for plants for 5 million years. Then again, to avoid excessive despair, much larger temperature jumps have been survived by us lifeforms during the current Ice Age.

What does all this have to do with the hillwalker on the Isle of Skye?

In about the year 63,000,000 BC, a mantle hot-spot seems to have arrived at the surface to the north-east of these islands. It was rather a small one, covering what are now the sea areas Hebrides, Faeroes and Bailey, together with, at the other side of the opening Atlantic, the east coast of Greenland.

BELOW TOP: A'a lava, the Hawaiian name referring to what it's like to walk over in bare feet. Raise, Helvellyn range.

BELOW BOTTOM: The pinnacle is shaped from a basalt lava flow; below are bedded strata of a sedimentary tuffite where volcanic ash has been washed into standing water. Carboniferous lava at St Abbs Head, Berwickshire.

A single pinprick can burst open a rubber balloon – or rather, the balloon, already under tension, bursts itself, once the pin has opened the first tiny hole. Below the Atlantic, the ocean crust was already under tension and unzipping northwards between Spain and Mexico. The rather large pinprick of the Hebrides hot-spot may have been what defined the line of the North Atlantic Ridge, so that Greenland moved west with the USA rather than remaining on the European side.

The basalt lava flooded an area under the north Atlantic no larger than the present British Isles, to a depth of 500m: less than a tenth of the volume of the Siberian Traps lava. It did not extinguish most of the Earth's life. It did create, as mere pimples on its eastern edge, a line of 3000m (10,000ft) volcanoes on Mull, Ardnamurchan, Rum, Skye and St Kilda.

BASALT LANDS

Basalt may be the earth's commonest rock, but it's mostly underwater. It emerges at mid-ocean ridges, then slides sideways as the oceanic crust until it hits a continental edge. In that subduction zone, it's the basalt ocean floor that gets dragged back down into the Earth's mantle. Until the hotspot plume, and the opening of the Atlantic Ocean 63 million years ago, the UK was basically basalt-free.

In the English Lake District, on the other hand, things are seldom that simple. Lakeland has eruptions of pale rhyolite lavas; of mid-grey andesite ones; but also of black basalt. How come?

When ocean crust is dragged downwards at a subduction zone, the friction generates heat. The pale-coloured, quartz-rich crust above can get melted, rise, and emerge as a pale-coloured rhyolite lava. But just as often, the melted crust is mixed with melted basalt from below. The result, now, is an eruption of mid-grey andesite. The Andes stand above the

subduction zone where the Pacific is being dragged down under America; and the Andes, accordingly, are made of andesite.

But sometimes, molten basalt rises through the continental crust undiluted, and emerges as black basalt lava. In the Lake District (as in the Andes) andesite lavas predominate, but all three sorts are common, often on the same hill. In Snowdonia, the final lavas of the long cataclysm emerged as almost undiluted black basalt – the Bedded Pyroclastic Formation which forms the dark forbidding walls of the Devil's Kitchen.

Basalt eruptions, as seen and studied most intensively today in Hawaii, are rather non-violent affairs. The crucial fact about basalt is its low viscosity: it is runny rather than stiff. As it rises towards the surface, the hot gases can emerge and bubble away without causing huge explosions and columns of volcanic ash. Instead, lava lies in black stony-looking lakes which crack to show their red-hot insides to the tourists on walkways and purpose-built hotels along the banks. Basalt emerges not from tall impressive volcanoes, but from cracks in the ground.

But once out, its low viscosity means it can really move. Basalt magma moving within the ground forms dolerite intrusions like the Great Whin Sill (Chapter 14), squeezing across England in a matter of weeks or days. Out in the open, it moves like spilt milk.

That statement needs a little qualification. The viscosity of basalt lava of the painful A'a sort, at 1600°C, is 10–100 Pascal seconds. The viscosity of milk is about 0.003 Pa s, so it's 1000 times runnier. However, lava flows are larger than milk jugs. A'a lava 20m deep flows down a 10 per cent slope at about walking speed. Spilt milk 2mm deep flows at the same speed, and in much the same style. You'd have to dye the milk black, though.

Unlike milk, the basalt cools down and comes to a stop. The result is a particular sort of flat-topped lava landscape. Gas bubbles float upwards within the cooling lava, so that the top part of each individual flow is crumbly and tends to erode away. This means that the next lava flow above gets undercut, and breaks off in an abrupt steep step. Such formations are called 'trap', not because the small slippery

FAR LEFT: Basalt lava flow at summit of Dove Crag, Lake District.
LEFT: The near-black basalt colour shows only on unweathered surfaces.

ABOVE: The landscape called trap: flat-topped, steep-ended lava flows above the path to the Quiraing, Skye.

OPPOSITE: Basalt cooling in a shallow, uniform layer forms hexagon-jointed columns, as at the Giant's Causeway and the island of Staffa. A clump of such columns has collapsed outwards to form this 'black rose' at Loch Scridain on the coast of Mull.

crags are awkward to climb down, although they are, but from the Scandinavian word for a step.

Having flowed into a flat layer and cooled as a unit, the lava will show columnar jointing described in the dolerite of Chapter 14. Where the flow has pooled in a particularly uniform layer, perfect hexagonal columns can form. The same single lava flow may have given us the Giant's Causeway in Antrim and the island of Staffa in the Hebrides.

Staffa resembles London's Barbican Centre but with barnacles on. Black geometric columns rise straight out of the water and the spray. Green sea bangs in and out of the massively cantilevered Fingal's Cave. Fingal is out, hunting the speedy deer from mountain top to mountain top across Mull's main island, so you can sneak in and take photos of his interior décor: his heavily textured ceiling, his Jacuzzi-style open-plan bathing arrangements, his stark but effective black wallcovering. You do your sneaking along a narrow concrete ledge protected by a wire handrail. The ledge is a wet one and the handrail rather loose; so all in all, a visit to Fingal's Cave is pretty much a must.

The Quiraing, in northern Skye, is that island's most magnificent basalt viewing point. All along the Trotternish peninsula runs a single ridgeline of gentle grass. Tilting of the island since the time when the basalt actually flowed means that the western slope, that should be a level lava-flow top, now slopes gently downwards to the coast a half-day's walk away. On the eastern side, where it would be convenient to make a way off the ridge to the coast road immediately below, that way is barred by an almost continuous black crag.

This basalt lava has flowed out onto the sandstones and shales that were Skye's tranquil landscape before the eruptions. Those softer rocks are eroding away, undercutting the basalt; and this gives rise to a rather special landscape effect.

Most rocks have planes of weakness that are roughly horizontal: the bedding in sedimentary rocks, the joints

in granite. Columnar jointing, described above, means that basalt has its planes of weakness running up and down. As a consequence of this, it has a particular tendency to break off in crag-size chunks that slide towards the sea. At the north top of Sron Vourlinn (NG452713), there's a crevasse a few metres in from the cliff edge where another chunk of the mountain is just setting off downhill towards the coast road.

These landslips have created green valleys which run along, rather than up-and-down, the slope; and a fine collection of weird gothic pinnacles. Further fine landslips have created the Old Man of Storr, a tall pinecone-shaped pinnacle 20km (12 miles) down the coast. With its undercut base and smooth yet crumbly basalt rock, it was an irresistible temptation to the fearsome rock climber Don Whillans, who made its first ascent in 1955. It's rumoured that the coin he left at the summit is still unclaimed.

BACK TO BASALT

In the Middle Ages, alchemists sought the *Prima Materia*, the First Matter that everything else was made of. First Matter was without properties and qualities, the Chaos out of which God constructed the Universe. Reduce anything – lead, buttercups, or ordinary garden soil – to a black formless lump of First Matter, and then rebuild it into anything else in the Universe – gold, for preference.

Half a millennium later, the geological school called the Neptunists identified the fundamental rocks: every rock there is, is formed from eroded sand out of either basalt or granite. From then on they started introducing errors to explain how come basalt so often ended up on top. But right at the beginning, they were pretty much correct. Basalt is indeed basic.

Melt down continental crust, and you'll start a new rock out of crystalline underground granite, or its lava-flow equivalent, rhyolite. But tap the Earth's mantle, or melt down oceanic crust, and you make a new rock that'll be basalt, or its crystalline underground equivalent, gabbro. This book started at the beginning, back at the mangled complexity of the Lewisian Gneiss. Finally, 2000 million years later, it's arrived at the primitive simplicity of the original magma melts.

SNOWDONIA TO THE SOUTH COAST

A popular backpacking trip wends its way north to south through Wales. It starts in Cambrian slates, but before the first lunchtime reaches Aber Falls, where the Afon Goch falls off the edge of the Ordovician volcanics into those softer, older rocks. On the second day, the walk works its way up through the sequence of Chapter 10, and stops to eat its lunch (as it were) on the black basalt at the summit of Snowdon itself.

On the fourth day, with the rucksack straps sore on the shoulders and the first blister plasters on the battered feet, the walker passes across the wild boulderfields of the Rhinogs: the centre of the Harlech Dome, ancient underwater mud avalanches now forming heathery beds of greywacke. Then it's back up through the geological periods, across Cadair Idris, with pillow lavas of the underwater volcanoes seen on the very summit.

Increasing fitness, and the Ordovician giving way to the gentler Silurian mudstones, means fast striding across Plynlimon and the paths of central Wales, yellow grasses stretching to the horizon, skylarks overhead, and a strange beehive cairn on lonely Drygarn Fawr.

The pinkish tiers of the Brecon Beacons rise ahead, grey-green pools at their foot, seawater ripples across their slabby Old Red Sandstone tops. Then there's limestone, with its short, comfortable turf, its awkward ankle-twisting boulders. After a brief (and perhaps slightly sordid) interlude of coalfields and the suburbs of Swansea, the route reaches the Bristol Channel, with limestone again rising in great folds out of the sea.

But the walk ends, like all walks, in the warmth of home – a fireside if you've got the older sort of home – feet just about healed, a pile of very nasty washing unloaded thankfully into the machine, and a memory vivid with conflicting pictures of 200 miles of hill: hill made out of slates, lava and tuffs, greywacke, Silurian mudstone, sandstone, limestone and coal.

It's been a long, and sometimes tough, journey over all the rocks of Britain: through 2 billion years, and at least 17 sorts of stone, each creating its own sort of scenery to walk, climb or scramble across. As the long walk ends at the fireside of home, the story ends with the igneous rocks, the granite and basalt where it also all begins.

ABOVE: Aber Falls (Rhaeadr Fawr), northern Snowdonia. Slates, compressed out of ocean muds, lie below and between the volcanic rocks of Snowdonia, just as the Skiddaw Slates lie below the volcanic rocks of the Lake District. **TOP:** The contact of heat-altered slates, below, with microgranite, near the top of Aber Falls.

LAVA LORE

ABOVE: Black basalt (left) and two pieces of rhyolite from Dale Head, Lake District. Failing an expensive microscope test, any dark-coloured volcanic rock is labelled as basalt. The backs of the samples (right) look much alike, all showing weathered surfaces of pale grey.

FAR LEFT: Red steam-oxidised basalt from St Abbs Head, Berwickshire, with the gas bubble holes called vesicles.
LEFT: The same St Abbs Basalt with the vesicles filled by minerals migrating within the rock. Mineral-filled vesicles are called amygdales (meaning almonds).

FAR LEFT: Flow-folding: sticky rhyolite lava has flowed over itself as it cooled. Cerreg Cochion, Snowdonia.
LEFT: Rhyolite above Llyn yr Cwn, Snowdonia. Gas bubbling upwards has been frozen in place as the lava solidified.

ABOVE: Rhyolite, with vesicles (gas bubbles), from Glencoyne, above Ullswater.
ABOVE RIGHT: Andesite lava is dark grey. This one, from Dow Crag in Lakeland, has pink feldspar that will have crystallised in the magma chamber before eruption.
RIGHT: Fairly recent lava flows on Tenerife, Canary Islands.

THE MAGNIFICENT SEVEN
Understanding the igneous

Basalt is formed from lava that erupts and cools quickly, with crystals much too small to see. Basalt magma that crystallises deep underground forms gabbro. The intermediate form, in small intrusions close to the surface, is dolerite, which has crystals too small to see without a magnifying glass.

Similar differences in crystallisation give plutonic granite with its big visible crystals; intrusive microgranite; and volcanic rhyolite lava. The bottom line of the table below has the big-crystal plutonic rocks; the top line has the same rocks in their fine-grained volcanic forms.

Looking left to right across the table – from deep underground granite to deep underground gabbro; from eruptive rhyolite to eruptive basalt – the differences are of colour and of chemistry. The granite-rhyolite rocks are rich in silica compounds, including quartz, the mineral that's pure silica; this makes them pale. The basalt-gabbro rocks are low in silica and entirely without quartz, and are very dark or black. The terms 'acid' (for the granite side) and 'basic' (for the basalt side) were formerly used, referring to the proportion of 'silicic acid' the different rocks would contain if there were such stuff as silicic acid.

Geologists have been happy with dolerite being quite different stuff from dolomite, or with chlorite (in metamorphosed slates) containing absolutely no chlorine; but the 'acid-basic' usage, quite at cross purposes to how the terms are used in chemistry, was finally too confusing. The granite side is now 'felsic', for feldspar and silica, the main constituents. The basalt side is 'mafic', for magnesium and Fe, which is iron.

The difference between the two rock types goes deep. Indeed, it goes 50km deep – this being the thickness of the continental crust, formed out of the lighter silica minerals. Basalt is heavier in the hand than rhyolite, and forms the denser ocean-type crust. Lavas formed at the mid-ocean ridge are pure basalt.

At subduction zones, such as the Andes, the descending ocean crust is melted by friction, then rises through and mixes with the continental crust above. (The subduction diagram was on page 16.) The intermediate-type lavas that result are, typically, andesites. The hole in the diagram would be filled by diorite, the crystalline version of andesite. But in the UK at least, diorite is uncommon, greyish, and nondescript, so I've left it unmentioned.

But the differences between the three sorts of lava are not just about shades of grey. Silica is extremely sticky stuff, while mafic lavas are much more free-flowing. The scenery of northern Skye shows the way basalt runs across the land in level steps that end in small crags. Rhyolite crags, on the other hand, are big and lumpy.

That's if the rhyolite gets to flow over the crater rim at all. As the magma approaches the open air, the gases that fizz out of the sticky solution find it difficult to seethe upwards in an orderly fashion. Instead, the rhyolite volcano forms explosions, and columns of hot gas mixed with volcanic ash. And while the rhyolite lavas may flow slow, the ash-column when it eventually comes to collapse will produce red-hot ash-clouds and *nuées ardentes* that are the most dangerous volcanic events of all.

The difference between tourism on the brink of Hawaii's lava lakes, and total extinction in the town of St Pierre, turns out to be a simple matter of silica content.

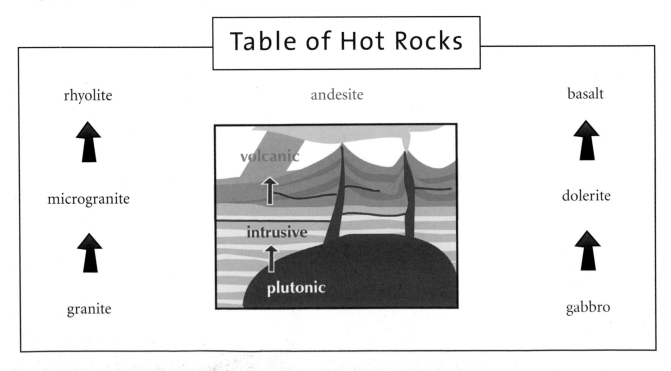

Table of Hot Rocks

rhyolite   andesite   basalt

microgranite   dolerite

granite   gabbro

volcanic

intrusive

plutonic

19. A 200-million-year walk over Dufton Pike

19. A 200-MILLION-YEAR WALK OVER DUFTON PIKE

Lakeland rocks are excellent to climb up and to walk over. But they are not the easiest rocks to read. They are very varied, between tuffs and lavas, sediments and slates; but at the same time they are uniformly grey, and the all-important textures are subtle. The same goes for Snowdonia, and even for Glen Coe.

Better, as a start-point, are the Yorkshire Dales. The shales and greywackes are altogether different from the limestone and gritstone which lie on top; the lime and grit are pretty different from each other; and Thornton Force is obvious enough for anybody. In Scotland, the Mamores are tri-coloured like the Italian flag, or at least like an Italian flag that's been washed a bit too often: grey schist, pink granite, and pale yellow quartzite. Even better is Torridon, where the three rocks form a simple scheme: gneiss underneath, then 900m of red-purple sandstone, and a quartzite cap on top. And then, eastwards, you can trace the same scheme tangled by the Moine Thrust.

Experienced geologists go wild over Assynt because it's so deliciously mixed up. I make no apology for devoting three whole chapters instead to Loch Torridon, where everything is, at least to start with, so deliciously simple. Also, it is among the UK's most rewarding mountain walking.

However, my sample walk here is back in England, up a small hill called Dufton Pike. On this edge of Cross Fell are not three pretty easily distinguished sorts of stone, but seven. Of the mystic crystals that make up the rocks, two – feldspar and mica – are seen in centimetre sizes. There are fossils that will need neither faith nor a microscope. Everything's intriguingly mixed up, but not beyond all disentangling.

And because it's all so interesting, there's an existing guidebook to keep you right. The walk starts by following

BELOW: Dufton Pike may not look like a Lakeland fell, but under the grass it's made of good Borrowdale Volcanics.

LEFT: Lime kiln, Great Rundale. Any unweathered surface in the crags above should show coral fossils.

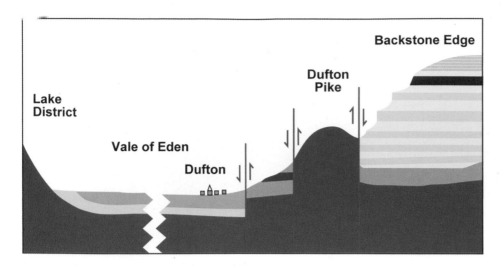

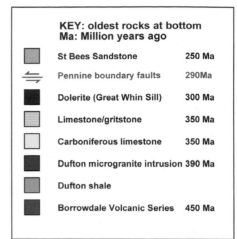

KEY: oldest rocks at bottom
Ma: Million years ago

	St Bees Sandstone	250 Ma
	Pennine boundary faults	290Ma
	Dolerite (Great Whin Sill)	300 Ma
	Limestone/gritstone	350 Ma
	Carboniferous limestone	350 Ma
	Dufton microgranite intrusion	390 Ma
	Dufton shale	
	Borrowdale Volcanic Series	450 Ma

BELOW: Limestone scarp and pavement on Backstone Edge, above the Great Whin Sill.

BOTTOM: On Dufton Pike, looking where the walk will shortly be going – up Great Rundale onto Backstone Edge. Despite being so grassy, the hills reveal seven different sorts of rock.

Lakeland Rocks and Landscape, the field guide published by the Cumberland Geological Society; where that book turns back, just keep on up the hill.

Heading uphill from Dufton, you start on red-coloured sandstone and cross 350 million years before tea-time. And at the top you find yourself once again on sandstone, although of a slightly different sort: this time it's limey and yellow.

To help make sense of all this, the Law of Superposition states: 'What's underneath is older than what's on top.' This may be obvious, but it's still surprisingly helpful. Well, it would be, except that almost everywhere that's interesting disobeys this obvious truth. The slope heading up from Dufton manages to break the Law three times over. It turns out that the red sandstone I stand on at the bottom, in Dufton village, is 100 million years younger than the yellow sandstone 600m higher up, on the top of Backstone Edge. So much for your Law!

Superposition can in fact fail in three different ways. The rocks can be faulted, bringing older up alongside, or even over the top of, younger. The Moine Thrust (Chapter 5) was an example of that. The rocks can be folded: both folding and faulting confused the timescale in the Southern Uplands of Chapter 8. Finally, an intrusion can squeeze in sideways: the intrusion will necessarily be younger than both the rock below it and the same rock lying above it. On Cross Fell, the rocks will be disordered by both faulting and intrusion.

And it's not just time that's upside-down. Space is also a bit bent. On this side-slope of the Pennines, Dufton Pike is made of Borrowdale Volcanics, and yes, that's Borrowdale as in the Lake District. The rocks of Rundale Beck are from the Skiddaw Slates, and that's Skiddaw in Lakeland as well. The sandstone at the start is St Bees sandstone, and St Bees is way over beyond Lakeland on the west coast. Only after

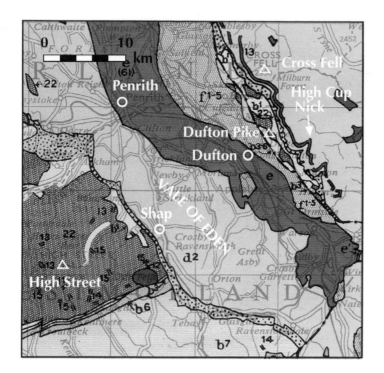

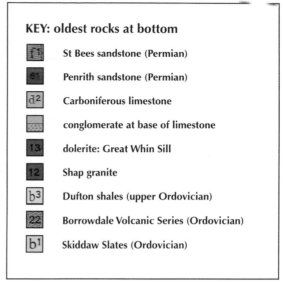

KEY: oldest rocks at bottom

f1	St Bees sandstone (Permian)
s1	Penrith sandstone (Permian)
d2	Carboniferous limestone
	conglomerate at base of limestone
13	dolerite: Great Whin Sill
12	Shap granite
b3	Dufton shales (upper Ordovician)
22	Borrowdale Volcanic Series (Ordovician)
b1	Skiddaw Slates (Ordovician)

LEFT: Geological map of the Vale of Eden, the North Pennines, and the edge of the Lake District. The western Pennine scarp is complicated both by faulting and by the Great Whin Sill intrusion.

several hours of, in effect, a squashed-up version of Lakeland, was I going to emerge onto the Pennines above.

Dufton Pike itself is a splendidly pointy grass summit, whose proud stance comes from its awareness that, underneath the grass, it's made of those real Borrowdale rocks. Here and there, that pale-grey rock pokes out, with the bubble holes (vesicles) to show that it did indeed come out of a volcano.

Back westwards, the slope with the grey rocks on plunges steeply, to disappear underneath a wide plain of gentle sandstone country. The Vale of Eden was looking lovely, pastel green where the frost lay on the fields, the ploughland showing the red colour of the underlying rocks. A puff of chimney smoke marked the odd farmhouse or the village of Dufton. And beyond those 25 kilometres (15 miles) of flat sandstone, faint against a blue sky, the grey rocks I stood on emerged again at the other side, in the shapes of Kidsty Pike and High Street and the distant ridge of Helvellyn.

By this time, although it was only 10 o'clock in the morning, I'd walked through 200 million years and was seeing and being on my third geological system. Having started on sandstone of a mere 250 million years ago, the path had crossed the Outer Pennine Fault, thus breaking for the first time the Principal of Superposition, and suddenly found itself much earlier on, much lower down, in Earth's history.

Specifically, stepping up across the Pennine Fault meant stepping down 170 million years into the Upper Ordovician strata: the Dufton shales. One Upper Ordovician boulder, of grey deepwater sandstone, has been hauled out of the ditch to stand mid-track; presumably it will get moved next time a tractor passes.

Above the Ordovician boulder the track bends left a bit; and now a wall alongside it is neither red nor grey, but a strident blackish orange. Crystals of mica twinkle out from

BELOW LEFT: St Bees sandstone in Dufton Ghyll. White flakes are early-morning water ice.
BELOW MIDDLE: Dufton shales, belonging to the middle Ordovician. Rocks later in the walk won't be this nondescript. (White splodges are lichen.)
BELOW RIGHT: Dufton microgranite, a 'porphyry' in that it contains big visible crystals of white mica.

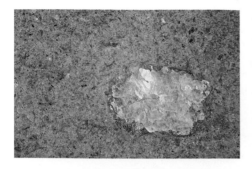

ABOVE LEFT: The white mica is called Muscovite. A 2cm crystal in Dufton micro-granite.

ABOVE MIDDLE: Shap granite erratic by Rundale Beck. Pink feldspar crystals, 1cm wide, would be much showier in a polished piece.

ABOVE RIGHT: Rhyolite lava of the Borrowdale Volcanic Series on Dufton Pike. It shows vesicles, gas bubble holes.

under greenish algae – for the orange wall stands under tree shade. It's the Dufton microgranite: a small intrusion squeezed out as a hot offshoot of the Shap granite 25 kilometres (15 miles) away across the Vale of Eden.

What's underneath comes first. And considered as story-tellers, geologists have a problem. Well, they have two problems, actually – the first and most obvious being that the characters in their story, though involved in plenty of conflict, don't actually get to have sex or even to sit down and talk it all over: the plot, it has to be admitted, is somewhat slow. But the deeper problem is the way that the beginning is also at the bottom. Should the story be explained upwards, with the lower, earlier rocks supporting the newer? Or should it start with what the people can see, which is what's on top; and then have the rock-reader look deeper?

But on the edge of Cross Fell, neither way works; and what we end up with is a thoroughly modern novel, with flashbacks and flashes forward and everything explaining everything else. The difference between a walk and a work of literature is that when you reach the last page of a book, you don't get the chance to turn round and read it all over again, backwards, in the downhill direction.

And so I came down off Dufton Pike, travelling also forwards (or as geologists would put it, 'upwards') in time. From here to the top of Backstone Edge, the rocks are in roughly the right order. However, the faultline marking out the back gap of Dufton Pike, one of the set of them which raised the Pennines, has also skipped us across an entire geological era, the age called the Devonian. Just so's not to miss out, a handy glacier has brought Devonian rocks to us, across the Vale of Eden, to a point alongside the path. They're at Rundale Beck, on the north bank 200 metres below the track crossing (NY691273). Recognise them as granite by their rounded shape, then peer through the lichen and the grey surface weathering to see the big pink crystals.

TOP LEFT: Fossil coral in limestone, Great Rundale.

TOP RIGHT: Barites lump in Great Rundale. Image shows area 5cm high.

BOTTOM LEFT: Tufa, formed as dissolved calcite precipitates out again. Not the same as tuff! Trackside, Great Rundale.

BOTTOM RIGHT: Limestone breccia, trackside, Great Rundale.

OPPOSITE: Limestone in Maize Beck.
Did the stream make these ripple marks, or has it uncovered a rippled stream bed of 200 million years ago?

The Shap granite is a small blob of melted rock which rose into the eastern edge of the Lake District. Its position is just right for being carried away in all directions by Lakeland glaciers. Also, its large crystals of pink feldspar make it an easy one to spot, so that geologists can say 'fancy meeting you here' not just on the eastern side of Eden, but as far away as Whitby on the North Sea coast.

At the back of Dufton Pike, though, I step off the Ordovician downslope, right across the absent Devonian Period, and onto the Carboniferous. Carboniferous means mountain limestone, and the slope above rises in scars of yellowish-grey limestone and grassy shelves. And limestone, of course, means fossils.

Fossils are a fabrication. Photographed in books they look terrifically convincing, and there are plenty of splendid ones in the Natural History Museum. But anything in an actual crag or boulder turns out to be a faint smudge requiring an act of faith to be believed in. The reason I'd gone up Great Rundale was, in fact, the Great Whin Sill. The Great Whin Sill as it crosses Great Rundale is actually rather small and implausible. But the fossils certainly weren't moss stains or smudges of iron. They were little whiskery creatures and stripy oval blobs that once basked on the reefs, half the world away from today's crisp-frozen bogs of the high Pennines. (Well, quarter of a world – during the Carboniferous period, the UK was drifting north across the Equator.) You can find real, believable fossils in the unweathered rock freshly exposed by the track works (NY714275).

A small coral creature, a slightly livelier version of a clump of moss, fell off the side of its stone into some silty sludge, and got buried. Minerals in the water filled its little cavities with calcite. The whole lot hardened, turned into rock, and lay for 200 million years. Then a bulldozer came to dig a track, and the coral chappie emerged into the air as a little picture for me to look at. Really, does this seem at all a likely story? It's easier to believe that the Good Lord, with an indulgent smile behind His big beard, has painted in the fossils, just so that us poor people can unscramble all this complicated Upper Carboniferous and Permian.

The mines in this valley were worked for lead for 50 years in the 19th century. Eight years after they closed, they were reopened for the sake of barite. This mineral yields barium, which had suddenly found use as a filler or stiffener for rubber, and bicycles were requiring a lot of rubber. In the 1980s the mine dumps were worked over, again for barite, but this time for use in drilling muds in the oil industry. Barite looks like a flaky sort of quartz but is actually barium sulphate: it is notably heavy in the hand.

Meanwhile, chunks of rock at the track side are revealing the power of calcite, the limestone sort of cement, here making the chunky concrete called breccia. Calcite dissolves in water, then undissolves again, to make the spongy stone called tufa; this too is on display, before the track slips up through a gap in the scars, the land flattens, and the view of four geological periods vanishes behind a tuft of heather. I've suddenly stepped up over the edge of Cumbria into the heart of the Pennines. Great Rundale Tarn stretches silvery-grey under a pale winter sky, and most of what I can see is peat.

The easy way through peat is by the stream; it drains the ground a bit, or washes it away altogether to bare rocks. The high Pennines are yellow limestone, and brownish grit.

ABOVE: The Great Whin Sill at High Cup Nick.

And all of this is off the top edge of the guidebook, so there's original observation to be done here. And it's tricky. Limestone and gritstone ought to be different: one's made of grit and the other's made of dead seashells. But is what I'm walking over a gritty sort of limestone, or a limey sort of grit? It seems to be some of each, alternating with softer bands of dark shale. That combination, gritstone-shale-limestone, is not implausible. It's what made the Yoredale Series, the stepped landscape of Wensleydale and Pen-y-ghent back in Chapter 16. Something of the same sort could have been happening up here.

Just as I'm feeling I've got a grip on things, the beck runs across a slab of weird ripply limestone. Good, this isn't in my book: I can try applying logic to work out what's what. Did these rock ripples (see page 189) form recently, or are they seabed ripples from 350 million years ago?

The rippling of the rock has left a fossil seashell standing half-exposed, which suggests that this might be a seabed from 350 million years ago. But a closer look further downstream shows that the ripples run not only across the top of the lime-stone layer, but also down into the joints; and this means that the ripples must be later than the layer. Keep walking across it, thinking about it, and looking at it. Where a gorge forms lower down, the rippling has happened only at the level of the present-day Maize Beck. These are recent ripples.

But what a busy day this is turning out to be. Having visited a displaced lump of Lakeland, and then the high peaty Pennines, the path bends right and enters limestone country. Limestone means bright grassland and blocky scree, and long low scars of yellow rock; and the winter sunlight is like pastel-yellow paint across a small limestone pavement.

Arrive from above, across the little limestone pavement, and come upon it suddenly: this is the way to approach the Great Whin Sill. When you reach it this way, the Whin Sill is indeed as great as King Alfred or the Egyptian Pyramids or the lakes in the middle of America or anything else that's unarguably great. On a winter afternoon, sunlight picks out the columns of the dolerite under your foot, and the rest of it stretching around the valley, in both directions, like an ancient temple or colonnade, followed by another one alongside, and then a few dozen more shrinking into the distance.

ABOVE: Limestone gorge of the frozen Maize Beck, just below the footbridge of the Pennine Way. It is now clear that the rock ripples aren't ancient but have been made by the stream current of the current stream.

This dolerite rock layer, as thin in landscape terms as a sheet of clingfilm, stretches through the mountains as far as Hadrian's Wall and the Farne Islands off the Durham coast. It was squeezed out by volcanoes in the Edinburgh area. Think about it and it's as unlikely as fossils. But see it suddenly on a sunlit winter evening, and it is obviously so. Oh, and between the two valley walls, away past the ends of the Whin Sill, there's another rather lovely view of the Vale of Eden. Just when you're ready to start looking at it.

I made my way down the actual nick of High Cup Nick; because I'd noticed a small gully cutting the sill and exposing a little of the limestone that's underneath it. How, I wondered, has the limestone reacted to the rather hot and heavy intrusion overhead? And the interesting thing is, it hasn't. A smooth level line is the top of the limestone and the foot of the columnar dolerite (see page 190). The 30m layer of molten lava has slipped in between the limestone as neat and easy as the knife blade of an old-time Pennine bandit.

The wide, well-rounded valley is floored with dolerite boulders fallen off the Whin Sill, then limestone boulders, then gentle limestone grassland. Then grass turns to tussocks and bog, and I don't need the beck emerging suddenly from underground to tell me I'm back on top of gritstone.

A farm track runs down a ridge and rejoins the stream. Up right, a meltwater river once ran around the edge of the Eden Valley glacier, and has carved me a convenient slot through the back of Keisley Bank. Grey rock pokes out of the channel sides: grey not just because it's getting late in the evening, but also because we're back on the Borrowdale Volcanic.

The last of the daylight sees me on the tarmac track of the Pennine Way, walking down towards the scattered lights of Dufton. On the wall alongside, my hand trails along the warm roughness of Permian sandstone. According to the book, the sandstone gorge of Dufton Ghyll shows level bedding of the sea-bottom sort. Dufton Ghyll in the dark is admirably atmospheric; high crag walls, oak branches against the stars – but it does stop you seeing any sea-bottom sandstone.

Dufton's pub, the Stag, doesn't do food on weekday winter evenings. But it has an open coal fire; and on the wall alongside it, a handy geological map. I'd spent the late morning looking for the quarry of the Dufton micro-granite on the side of Dufton Pike, and failing to find it, but it wasn't my fault. It was, in fact, the Outer Pennine Fault. The orange stuff with the big crystals lies only on slopes lower down, under glacier rubble and access restriction. But up across the Pennine moorland, what's this they've written? 'Yoredale Series'! Trying to work it all out is fun enough. But what a bonus to get a bit of it actually right . . .

Conclusion

CONCLUSION
My country: your country

LEFT: Permian sandstone in the author's garden. There are no obvious bedding planes. The bedding is there, and the rock can be conveniently cracked apart into slabs and blocks; but it doesn't split up of its own accord. This makes it very suitable for building the brownstones of New York.

BELOW: Cone of Dumfriesshire sandstone by Andy Goldsworthy. Behind is Tynron Doon, Southern Upland greywacke shaped by glaciers and with an iron age settlement on top.

Not many of us can say that the house we live in was dug out of its own back garden. My village lies on Permian sandstone, laid down when Britain was not far north of the Equator in the position now occupied by the Sahara. We have four old quarries, one of which is currently used as a rubbish dump; and a fifth one still in occasional use. The village even has its own geological legend. We tell visitors that Dumfriesshire sandstone forms the base of the Statue of Liberty as well as many of the brownstone buildings of New York. But even geologists (so our geo-joke continues) have trouble telling whether New York brownstone is from nearby New Jersey, or from across the Atlantic – because of course there isn't any difference. Dumfriesshire moved eastwards, with the opening Atlantic, at 2cm a year for 50 million years: then got loaded onto ships at Glasgow and carried all the way back again.

Permian sandstone is a handsome brownish red, easy to split, cut and carve. It's given us a village centre of grace and good proportions, neat field walls, and deeply-cut little streams, plus a habit of going slightly too far, artistically speaking, on gravestones. But the stream bottoms are grey, not red, with pebbles of the Southern Upland whinstone or greywacke that crops out across the valley floor 3 kilometres upstream. The grey-red unconformity, representing about 150 million missing years, lies somewhere under the upper fields; in one stream bed it's possible to stand with one foot on the red rocks and the other on the grey.

Ten minutes away, at the edge of a barley field, lies a granite erratic that's travelled 50km by glacier out of the Galloway Hills. Down the valley, my friend Max lives on a tiny outcrop of limestone, not at all common in southern Scotland. Max builds drystone walls, and knows the sandstone and the whin with his strong scarred hands better than

I know them with my feet. Carry on to the coast, and Criffel rises as a great rounded lump of granite.

Up-valley, there's a small coalfield. On either side are the hills; and on a day when I merely meant to take pictures of some greywacke, I came across a delightfully clear example of a meltwater channel. Next valley west, another friend has just constructed a small hydro-power plant. With justified pride he showed me his pipe-run, cut through not just the Southern Upland greywacke and shale, but also some Southern Upland conglomerate. That's a pudding stone, made up of small pebbles, and it's unusual because pebbles don't normally make it off the edge of the continental shelf and down into the deep ocean abyss.

Then again, what'll they make, in 20 million years' time, of that landfill site? A truly original rockform, containing the perfectly preserved fossil of the old mechanical typewriter I chucked out a few years back: we just have to hope they won't be using it as a marker horizon as they try to unravel the sixth of the Earth's great mass extinctions . . .

Southern Dumfriesshire isn't even all that special. Live in Shropshire, say, or Edinburgh or Arran, buy a bicycle, and enjoy five or more geological periods and a dozen different rockforms in one day. Britain has a more varied geology than any other country in the world. Of the 10 major divisions of time, three take their names from Wales (Cambrian means Welsh, while the Ordovices and Silures were mid-Welsh tribesmen) and another is from Devon. The rest of the world is represented only by the Jurassic (from the French mountain range not the Scottish island) and the Permian, from Perm which is in the Urals. Scotland (Caledonia) supplies a major mountain-building episode. Yosemite is granite; Spain has limestone; the Andes

obvious; but to see the volcanic fragments in a lump of pale grey tuff, you'll need to stand and peer at it for a minute or two. A walk where you're really looking at the rocks will take longer than you expect.

All rocks are grey, before you look at them. Start the habit of seeing what's there, and get to know them – and even so, quite a few of them will remain, unhelpfully, featureless and grey. Lavas, hornfels, and greywacke sandstone in particular take a lot of looking at.

So it's good to start off with rocks where you already know the answer. I've given grid references for many of the outcrops pictured here. There are also geological guidebooks,

FAR LEFT: Erratic granite at the edge of a barley field.
LEFT: Sometimes, even an amateur can make a stunning discovery. This fossil fern, found by the author in the Torridonian sandstone, caused a fundamental revision of the entire geological sequence. At least, it would have done if it really had been a fossil fern from 500 million years before the beginning of life on land . . . Actually, it's iron-rich surface water creeping into a crack.

have their andesite. Britain's hills have gneiss, sandstone, quartzite, schist, greywacke, shale, slate, rhyolite, andesite, ignimbrite, tuff, granite, dolerite, mountain limestone, grit-stone, gabbro, basalt. Let's enjoy them all.

READING THE ROCKS

It took you several years to learn to read the English language. Reading the rocks is easier than that – but that doesn't mean it's easy. In fact, I'd compare reading the rocks to reading a map. At first it's a bit of a mystery; quite quickly, quite a lot of it starts to make sense; but you'll never know it all.

And to read the rocks, sometimes you'll need your glasses – or, even better, a strong magnifying glass, such as you can get in a photographic shop. They will call it a 'loupe'; in a geological shop it will be a 'hand lens'. Ten times magnification is good for seeing crystals, sand grains, and glassy shards in the tuffs of Lakeland. What you probably don't need is a hammer: the aim is to appreciate the rocks and outcrops, not to bash them to bits and spoil them for those who come later. But most of all, you need quietness and time. The difference between sandstone and granite may be

listed as Field Guides below. These walk you up the hills, stop you alongside some interesting rock, and show you things. Some of the things shown are obvious to the point where they leap up and poke you in the eye; such as the landslide tuffs at the foot of Goats Water, or Hutton's Unconformity. Others are so subtle as to be invisible to the inexperienced.

Geology books are written by geologists, to whom all of it is obvious. So don't expect to see everything the author does. Also, any book (including this one) will go to a lot of trouble to show a nice, clear, typical example. We don't show you the fossil you actually see, which isn't much more than a suggestive smudge. We don't show you the rock that might be a welded tuff but is perhaps a lava flow. Right from the start, you'll see some things you can understand, and one or two that are stunning. Just don't expect to understand it all. There are stones that puzzle even long-standing geologists – especially in the Borrowdale Volcanic.

The next stage may be a geological map. It could be for an area you often visit (though again, the Lakeland tuffs really are tough . . .) or for where you live. The mapping of the British Geological Survey (BGS) is based on the Ordnance

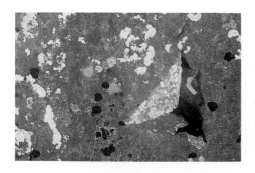

ABOVE: Some rocks are less easy to read (though a hand lens can help). Of the three nondescript grey rocks above, one is sedimentary, one is metamorphic, and one is out of a volcano. Even if you find a lichen-free, unweathered surface, some stones just don't have much to communicate. But the more you look at and identify the easy rocks, the easier become the difficult ones!

FROM LEFT: Greywacke from Queensberry, Southern Uplands, unforthcoming even without all the lichen on it; hornfels, a Skiddaw Slate sediment altered by the heat of the nearby Ennerdale Granite, on Red Pike Buttermere; andesite lava on Carnedd Uchaf – its one fairly distinctive feature, the dark grey colour, shows only on the unweathered interior.

BELOW: Wind turbines, environmentalists sometimes tell us, are handsome noble structures that encourage tourism. But CO_2 reduction may be better served, in the long run, by resolutely believing only what is actually true. (This windfarm, on Windy Standard, in Kirkcudbrightshire, combats global warming. It has also wrecked the mountaintop.)

Survey 1:50,000 Landranger, and it's best to read the two maps alongside each other, to tie the rocks in the BGS one with the contour lines in the other. The best geological map is classed 'Solid & Drift'; it shows 'Solid', the underlying rocks, where these are exposed or are under soil; but 'Drift' (glacie rubble, along with river gravel, peat, etc), where the bedrock is covered up and there's no hope of seeing it.

The cleanest and clearest rocks are indoors out of the rain. Your local museum will probably have a well-labelled collection of your local stones. The Natural History Museum in London has a fine set of glass cabinets, hidden away behind all the audio-visual displays and simulated earthquakes. No doubt they are correct in labelling all their quartzite as sandstone, though I wish they didn't.

The Internet is also tremendously valuable. Even the reader-compiled Wikipedia has, in my experience, slightly fewer errors than the average textbook. Confronted on a geological map with 'lamprophyre' or 'hyaloclastite', just plug it into the search engine.

The more you look, the more you see. And the more you see, the more interesting it all is. That, at any rate, is the hope of this book. Even when walking uphill in a thick low cloud, there is a lot to look at in the path under your feet: clean, exposed stones, hand-sized for picking up; boulders whose subtle textures have been polished by a thousand boots and subtly emphasised by the rainwater.

But my ambitions go further. I hope to infect you with the idea that what's actually the case is not only truer, but also a lot more interesting and amusing, than what isn't. The world as you start to understand it gets more, rather than less, wonderful. It also, paradoxically, just keeps getting more mysterious. Continental drift, and red-hot underwater avalanches: you couldn't have made this stuff up.

ABOVE: Borrowdale is made even a bit more wonderful by understanding what it is, and how it got there.

Science isn't always right. The study of mantle plumes is in a state of flux, metaphorically speaking as well as literally. Some of what's currently accepted and is in this book is going to get disproved. But science is a way of looking at the world that, done right, is uniquely good at finding out when it's got it wrong.

To try and believe in things that are indeed the case, rather than the Loch Ness monster, is absurdly ambitious, very tough, and in the end actually impossible. The Loch Ness monster is an amusing creature; but there's only so much to be said about something that doesn't exist. Whereas the Caledonian crunch, the mountain building which created Loch Ness, can be examined in the quartz vein under your foot. This tough discipline, of believing what actually is, can make you a bit of a bore in conversation. But it can also reveal a new and very deep-seated sort of beauty, in the world seen clearly.

Mostly, we form our beliefs to suit the beliefs of our social group; and confronted with an inconvenient fact, we simply disbelieve it. Astrology hardly ever does anyone any harm. The Loch Ness monster may not exist, but it does a lot of good for the tourist industry in Drumnadrochit.

But comfort thinking is like comfort eating. It's bad for us, and in the end could even shorten our life on the planet. If this business of Global Warming is to get sorted out, and the Earth to continue as a habitable planet, we people on it are going to have to be clear-sighted, imaginative and yet sceptical; absurdly ambitious, and at the same time hard-working and humble. A bit like those early geologists James Hutton, Adam Sedgwick, Charles Lapworth or William 'Strata' Smith. It can be done. And we really do have to do it.

READING ABOUT THE ROCKS

LEAFLETS AND BOOKLETS

Booklets produced for tourists are almost always well explained and well illustrated. They can, however, be frustratingly brief. Beinn Eighe and the Ingleton waterfalls are particularly recommended as they combine a helpful booklet with a fine walk and some really interesting rocks.

Yorkshire Dales National Park

Ingleton waterfall walks – good rocks and a good leaflet
Geology by Albert Wilson – 32 pages, covering all of the YDNP

Scottish Natural Heritage with British Geological Survey

Cairngorms: a Landscape fashioned by Geology
(also Edinburgh; Loch Lomond; Skye; Arran; and an increasing list)
Excellent photos and diagrams. The Skye volume is particularly valuable.

Scottish Natural Heritage

Beinn Eighe Mountain Trail – a good walk in itself and also for its rocks and landforms.
Lochaber Geotrails: Road to the Isles; Glen Nevis; Glen Coe; Glen Roy
Quite a lot in each leaflet, though the 'trails' are actually visits to car parks.

FIELD GUIDES

Snowdonia Rocky Rambles
(Sigma, 1996) ISBN 1 85058 469 9
Lakeland Rocky Rambles (Sigma,1995) ISBN 1 85058 396 X
both by Bryan Lynas, both currently out of print but available second-hand
Extremely useful and lucid field guides, where almost everything explained is understandable and almost everything revealed is visible. The outings, unusually, are right away from the car parks and across the summits.

Lakeland Rocks and Landscapes: a Field Guide
Cumberland Geological Society ISBN 1 873551 03 7
(and similar field guides found on the BGS website)
Some chapters good, others less so. Don't be too discouraged if you fail to find the 'very clear' exposure described. The next chapter will be by someone else who will have done it better.

Geology Explained in the Lake District by Robert Prosser, pb (Fineleaf reprint, 1977) ISBN 978 0 9534437 7 2
Good landscape diagrams and plenty of grid refs of visitable outcrops. As it's rather old, there's no colour illustration and no plate tectonics.

The Highland Geology Trail by John Roberts, pb (Luath, revised edition, 1998) ISBN 0 946487 36 7
Covers all the west and north-west Highlands, a huge area of fascinating ground, so can be frustratingly brisk in its coverage. Aimed mostly at the car-borne, but does have some foot excursions.

Yorkshire Rock: a journey through time by Richard Bell, (Earthwise, BGS, 1996) ISBN 0 85272 269 9
Aimed at school children, but I found it lucid and by no means shallow. Very attractive watercolour illustrations. No actual excursions, but grid references for many outcrops to visit.

Dorling Kindersley Handbooks: Rocks and Minerals by Chris Pellant ISBN 0 7513 2741 7
Larousse Field Guide to the Rocks and Minerals of the World ISBN 0 7523 0051 2
A really adequate handbook would have at least two different colour pictures of each rock and mineral. Alternatively, get two different handbooks.

TEXTBOOKS

Geology of Britain: an Introduction by Peter Toghill (Airlife, 2000) ISBN 1 84037 404 7
Thorough, with excellent diagrams and pretty good photos. Just occasionally degenerates into fact-listing. Slight Shropshire bias, but why not.

Principles of Physical Geology by Arthur Holmes (revised edition Thomas Nelson, 1965, or any more recent edition)
A magisterial tome, revised and developed over 50 years. Undergraduate-level geology, but all clearly explained and readable. This will help you understand not only what is known, but also why, and what the evidence is. Very inexpensive second-hand, presumably from ex-students unloading their textbooks.

Volcanoes by Peter Francis (Oxford University Press, 1993,

BELOW: Dawn granite above Glen Kinglass, Argyll

ISBN 0 19 854033 7).
University-level, but written in an enthusiastic and completely understandable way, low in jargon and with lots of diagrams and photos. Quite hard work, but worth it.

Hutton's Arse by Malcolm Rider, pb (Rider-French, 2005) ISBN 0 9541906 1 0
Irresistibly titled account of the Northern and Western Highlands. Not a textbook, but an exploration of some currently hot topics such as the Rum volcano and 'Snowball Earth'. Extremely lively and entertaining.

The Earth: An Intimate History by Richard Fortey, pb (HarperCollins, 2005) ISBN 978 0 0065 5137 9
A well-written, non-technical account of many of the rocks described in this book but with a world-wide perspective.

HISTORY AND BIOGRAPHY

With 17 rocks, I've tried not to crowd this book with too many human characters. So while James Hutton rambles with his little hammer through several chapters, I've excluded four or five others who also spent their lives out in the mountains in the rain, trying to find out about the world. With their clear heads and wet socks, they are the spirit of scientific enquiry; and (with the exception of Roderick Impey Murchison) a very likeable bunch.

The Man who found Time: James Hutton and the discovery of the Earth's antiquity by Jack Repcheck (Pocket, 2004) ISBN 0 7434 5087 6
An easy read, good on Hutton's social surroundings.

The Map that Changed the World by Simon Winchester, pb (Penguin, 2002) ISBN 0 140 28039 1
Biography of another attractive character, 'Strata' Smith, father of English geology. Rather lightweight in style, but good on the Jurassic limestone.

The Highlands Controversy by David R Oldroyd (University of Chicago Press, 1990) ISBN 0 226 62653 0
The untangling of the Moine Thrust: the geological evidence, and the personal disputes that clouded it. A serious and scholarly account of perhaps the most acrimonious chapter in the history of geology.

GLOSSARY
a'a to xenolith

A'A basalt lava-flow of a turbulent sort with a splintery crust that's extremely uncomfortable to walk on

ALLUVIUM a layer of gravel, pebbles etc left by a river or lake

ANTICLINE an upward-bulging rock fold (think 'arch') as opposed to a downward-bulging syncline (think 'sink')

ARENACEOUS sandy

ARGILLACEOUS clayey

ARKOSE a sandstone unusually rich in feldspar. As feldspar decomposes readily to clay, an arkose will have formed close (in time and space) to the original source of eroded sediment. Torridonian Sandstone and Millstone Grit are both examples of arkose.

ASH term loosely applied to fine solid particles ejected by a volcano. Volcanoes don't burn so this isn't ash in the normal sense.

BATHOLITH a very large lump of granite. Originally having cooled several kilometres underground, erosion may have exposed its top as granite mountains. One rather lumpy batholith underlies Dartmoor and Bodmin Moor; another forms the Cairngorms.

BIOTITE a black form of mica, commonly supplying the black specks in granite

CLAST a broken (rather than smoothly rounded) chunk of rock, often embedded in a lava or breccia

CONCRETION a lump, often of silica, formed within an already-existing rock by chemical action. Flint is the commonest concretion.

DIABASE another name for dolerite

DIORITE coarsely crystalline igneous rock that's the underground equivalent of andesite lava (see table in Chapter 18). It's dark grey, sometimes with white specks.

DOLOMITE a form of limestone where the calcium has been replaced by magnesium. Dolomite usually forms in super-salty seas. It makes, and takes its name from, the Dolomite mountains of northern Italy, where it gives splendid and very exposed scrambling and climbing.

DRIFT a layer of boulder clay and rubble left by a glacier; same as till

DRUMLIN small hill of glacier rubble (till) left behind after the glacier melts. Drumlins collectively occur in 'swarms'.

DYKE an igneous rock intruded across older beds. A dyke will normally be roughly vertical, unless shifted by later earth movements. Where the earth's crust is under tension, dykes occur (like drumlins, above) in 'swarms'.

FAULT a surface where two rock bodies have moved past each other. 'Normal fault': the upper rock body has moved downwards (the crust has stretched) – two large normal faults together form a rift valley. 'Reverse fault': the upper rock body has moved upwards (the crust has been compressed). 'Thrust fault': the upper body has moved horizontally over the top of the lower. 'Imbricate fault': several adjacent parallel faults combining into, effectively, one big one.

GRANOPHYRE a form of granite containing scattered large crystals – a granite porphyry

GREISEN an igneous rock composed of quartz and mica only. A granite, but without feldspar; can be formed from granite by further heating or chemical attack

KNOCK AND LOCHAN knock (Gaelic 'cnoc') is a small rugged hillock: lochan is a small lake. The typical landscape of Lewisian Gneiss involves many knocks interspersed with many lochans.

HORNFELS a featureless, brittle rock produced metamorphically from various starting rocks (e.g. slates, mudstones, tuff) by the heat of a nearby intrusion, such as some granite

IGNIMBRITE a volcanic rock formed from an airborne avalanche of red-hot volcanic ash. On coming to rest, the ash welds itself together. Lumps of pumice within the ashpile are flattened, to appear in the resulting rock as narrow discs (*fiamme*)

LAHAR a hot mud-slide down the side of a volcano, typically caused by the escape of a caldera lake during an eruption. An ancient lahar is on Arran

LAVA rock in a melted state at the Earth's surface

LITHIC stony

MAGMA rock in a melted state below the earth's surface.

MANTLE the part of the earth's interior immediately below the crust. It is mechanically separate from the oceanic crust, although made of similar basalt-like material.

MANTLE PLUME a localised upward current in the mantle, persisting over tens of millions of years, and producing a volcanic hot-spot at the earth's surface. Diagram page 16

MICROGRANITE a granite but with smaller crystals, not individually visible without a hand lens: the intrusive, rather than plutonic, form of granite

MORAINE unsightly rubble piling on, or at the end of, a glacier

MUSCOVITE a white form of mica (cf. biotite, the commoner, black form).

OPHIOLITE at a subduction zone (page 16), the heavier oceanic crust goes down underneath. Occasionally a fragment is scraped onto the continental crust and is preserved on the land surface – an ophiolite. The UK example is at Ballantrae, Ayrshire.

ORTHOCLASE a form of feldspar containing potassium rather than calcium/sodium, white or pink in colour. Orthoclase is the commonest form of potassium feldspar (K-feldspar, alkali feldspar.) Pink granites are coloured by orthoclase.

PEGMATITE a granite containing very large crystals (of quartz, feldspar, mica) 1cm upwards, formed in intrusions that have cooled very slowly or in several stages. When a gneiss is metamorphosed to the point of partially melting, the melted potions will typically solidify as pegmatite. Would go underneath granite in the diagram page 182.

PERIDOTITE an 'ultramafic' rock that belongs to the right of gabbro in the table on page 182. It's a coarsely crystalline igneous rock, even rougher than gabbro, and weathering blackish-orange.

PHENOCRYST single large crystals in a generally fine-grained rock. Any rock with phenocrysts is referred to as porphyry.

PLAGIOCLASE a form of feldspar containing calcium/sodium rather than potassium. It is transparent or white in colour, but sometimes pink.

PORPHYRY any igneous rock that is generally fine-grained, but scattered with individual large crystals. Such rocks will have had a complex history of cooling, possibly in distinct phases.

PSAMMITE a mica-schist type rock that's relatively low in mica and high in quartz; before metamorphosis, the original sediment was sandy rather than muddy. Thus, psammite is intermediate between mica schist itself and quartzite, which has no mica at all.

PYROCLAST a solid rock fragment ejected by a volcano: same as volcaniclast

PYROCLASTIC FLOW any flow of volcanic material other than a lava flow, such as a volcano landslide; or more specifically, an airborne avalanche of red-hot volcanic ash such as produces ignimbrite rocks

SILL an igneous rock intruded as a layer between two older beds. A sill will normally be roughly horizontal, unless shifted by earth movements

STRIAE the technical term for the scratches on rocks caused by glaciers

SUBDUCTION ZONE the edge of a tectonic plate, where ocean crust is being drawn down under the edge of either continental crust or another oceanic crust. The result is a deep ocean trench, and a range of wrinkle-mountains on the overriding continent. Diagrams pages 16 and 88.

SYNCLINE a downward-bulging rock fold (think 'sink') as opposed to an upward-bulging anticline (think 'arch').

TILL same as drift; rubble and boulder clay left by a glacier

TILLITE rock formed out of compacted till

TUFA a spongy-looking kind of limestone, formed by calcite that has dissolved in water precipitating back out again

TUFF rock formed of volcanic ash

TUFFITE rock formed of volcanic ash that has been laid down in water; sometimes called 'volcaniclastic sandstone'. Technically, it's a sedimentary rather than an igneous rock

TURBIDITE sedimentary rock formed from a turbidity current (see Chapter 7). Most greywackes are turbidites, and vice versa

VARISCAN OROGENY another name for the Hyrcanian Orogeny

VESICLE in lava, a small hole formed by a gas bubble

VOLCANICLAST a broken rock-chunk flung out by a volcano

VOLCANICLASTIC ROCK tuff made of broken chunks and ash; also known as 'block tuff'.

WHINSTONE a common name for dolerite, as in the Whinstone Sill, but in southern Scotland used for the local greywacke. Geologically quite different, the two stones are both tough and unworkable, and carry thin infertile soils often clothed in gorse (whin)

XENOLITH a foreign rock embedded inside another. In a magma such as granite, a xenolith could be a broken-off part of the magma chamber wall, or a speck of mantle material (peridotite) brought up from the depths

INDEX

References in *italics* are only to a diagram or picture and its caption (where image and caption are on different pages, the image is referenced). Those in **bold** mark the main definition or explanation of a term.

A

a'a *175, 176*
Aber Falls 180
Africa crunch (Hyrcanian Orogeny) **21–22**, 91, 154, 156
Agassiz, Louis 31–32, 35
Ailsa Craig *167*
Aletsch Glacier 28–29
Alpine Orogeny 15, **25–26**
Alpine Schistus *127*
Alps 15, 16, 26, 28–30 *125, 159*
ammonites 23, 25
amphibole 64
Amphitheatre Buttress 101
An Teallach *7, 49*
Andes 16, 176, 182
andesite 11–12, *96,* **114–119**, 142, *146,* 176, 181–182, *196*
anticline 14, and see Harlech Dome
Antrim 139, 166, 178
Aonach Eagach *118*
Aonachs (Nevis Range) 117
Ardnamurchan *166*
Arkle *17*
Arran *127,* 129–130, *132,* 162, 166
Arthur's Seat *108,* 128–129, 138–139, 142–145, 148
ash 62–63, **93**, 96–99, 103–104, 182
see also Tuff
Ashgill Force *161*
Assynt 60, 184
Atlantic Ocean (opening of) 16, **24–26**, 145, 166, 175–176, 194
Avon Slabs, Cairngorms *30*

B

Bach, J.S. 122
bacteria, early history of 51–52
banded ironstone 51–52
barite 188–190
Barn Wall climb, Bidean nam Bian *119*
basalt 54, 64, *127,* 139, 145, 166–167, 170–171, *172,* **174–179**, 181–182
    Lake District 176
    Snowdonia 101–104, 176–177
    viscosity of 143, 176
Beinn Alligin *49,* 60
Beinn Bhan (Applecross) *47*

Beinn Eighe 8–9, 56, *57,* 59–60
    Mountain Trail *46,* 198
Ben Cruachan 20, 69
Ben Nevis *2–3, 32, 107,* 114–120, 131
Ben Starav *115*
Ben Vorlich (Loch Earn) *68*
Bhasteir Tooth back cover, *171*
Bidean nam Bian 115, 117, *119, 120*
biotite mica 54, 66, 125, **130**
Black Combe *62, 88*
Black Ladders 145–146
block tuff *96, 118*
Borrowdale Volcanic Series 8, 11–12, 88, **93–96**, 106–107, 186–187, 195
Boval Glacier *28*
Bowfell *27, 36,* 93
BPF (Bedded Pyroclastic Formation) 102–104
breccia *108, 188,* 190
Brecon Beacons 20, 150–153
Bristly Ridge, Glyder Fach *104*
Brontë, Emily 160
Brown, Joe 163
Buachaille Etive Mor 117, *120*
Buckland, William 32
buried landscape *50,* 51
Buttermere 11–12, *95,* 131, *196*

C

Cadair Idris *74,* 138, 180
Cairngorms 30–31, 35–36, 69, 126, **130–136**, 164, 200
calcite 54, **156**, 188, 190
caldera 99, 101, **114–115**, *118,* 175
Caledonian Orogeny (mountain building) **19–20**, 59–60, 66, 68–69, 82, *86,* 150, 154, 194
Cambrian Period 17, 75, 156
Cambrian Quartzite 8–9, 17, *46, 50, 51,* **56–60**
Campsie Fells 145
Capel Curig Volcanic Formation *104*
Carboniferous Period 21, 156
Carn Deag (Ben Nevis) *2–3*
Carn Mor Dearg 115, *116,* 117
Carn Mor Dearg Arete 115, *116*
Carnedd Dafydd 145–146
Carnedd Llewelyn *98,* 145
Carneddau *75,* 145–146, *196*
Cathedral Cave, Little Langdale *62*
cauldron subsidence 114–117, 166
Chalamain Gap, Cairn Gorm 35
chalk **24**, *55*
Cheddar *156*
Cheviot 20, *129, 142*
Cioch Nose Direct (climb), Applecross *9, 49*
Cir Mhor *129, 166*

D

Clach Glas *165, 172*
Claus, Santa 9
cleavage **62–63**, 65–66, 69
Cleveland Dyke *142,* 166
Clogwyn Du'r Arddu 101, 102
Clogwyn Mawr, Snowdon *14*
Coal Measures **21**, 150, *160,* 175
Cobbler, the (Arrochar) *70*
columnar jointing *120,* **139–141**, 145–146, 178–179
concretion
    flint 55–56
    quartz *100*
conglomerate 50, 124, 150–152, 154, 194
Coniston Limestone 88, **91**, 156
Coniston Old Man *36,* 94
continental drift **15–16**, 143–145
coral, fossil 21, *125,* 152, 156, *158,* 175, 188–190
corries 12, *29,* 32–34, 114
Cotswolds 23
crater 114
Creag Meagaidh *34, 70*
Cretaceous Period **24–25**, 35, 175
Crete, White Mountains 25
Crib Goch 146
Crib y Ddysgl *104*
Cross Fell *125,* 184–188
cross-bedding *49,* **148–149**, *153*
Cuillin, Skye 25–26, *34,* 166–172
Cwm Idwal 100–103
cyclopean masonry 131–134

D

Dartmoor 22, *129, 132,* 134, 200
Darwin, Charles 32, 102–103, 138–139
Death Valley, California 52
Devil's Kitchen, Snowdonia 101–104, *177*
Devonian Period **20**
Diabaig, Wester Ross *42*
diorite 182
Dobbs Linn, Moffatdale 78–80
dolerite **138–146**, 176, 182, 190–192
Domed Ridge (climb), Cairn Gorm *133*
Dorset 23, *24,* 55
Dow Crag *142, 146, 181*
drift 196
drumlins 32–33, 102–103, *112*
Dufton Microgranite 186–188, 192
Dufton Pike 184–188
Dufton Shale 186–187
Dumbarton Rock 145
Dumfriesshire *82–85,* 153–154, 194
Durness Limestone *46,* 156
dykes 42–43, *142,* 166, *172*

E

earthquakes 9–10
Edinample Falls, Loch Earn *64*
Edinburgh *32, 108,* 124, 128, 138–139, 143, 145, 148
Edinburgh Geological Society 32
erratic boulders **31**, *35, 42,* 188–190, 194–195
Esk Hause *106,* 109–110
Esk Pike *18, 110*
Eskdale 92–93, 109 and see granite, Eskdale
Etive Slabs 131–133
Everest 16, 124, *159*
exfoliation (of granite) *123,* **131**
extinctions 19, 23, 24, 174–175, 194

F

faulting 10, 44, 54–55, 93, 101, **106–107**
    Glen Coe ring-fault 115
    Rossett Fault, Lakeland 106–112
    Loch Maree *46, 50*
    Moine Thrust *46,* **59–60**
    Pennine 186–190
    Scottish Lowlands rift valley 143–144
    Southern Uplands 80–82
feldspar 43, 54, 103–104, **130,** 138–139, 162–163, 171, *181,* 188–190
felsic (igneous) rocks 182
Fingal's Cave 139, 178
Fleetwith Edge 11–12
flint 55–56
Flying Buttress (climb), Stanage Edge *21*
Foinaven *17*
Forcan Ridge *65*
frost striping *36*
Fucoid Beds *46, 57*

G

gabbro **168–172,** 182
Galloway Hills *4, 9, 35, 73,* 125, 131
Gargunnock Hills 145
garnets *39, 42,* 54, *65,* **66,** 69
Gauguin, Paul 69
Giant's Causeway 139, 166, 178
Giant's Staircase scramble, Grey Corries 58
glacier-smoothed rocks *2,* 28–30, *32, 58*
glaciers (current) 28–30
glaciers, evidence of former **30–35,** 134–136
Glen Affric 67
Glen Coe *20,* 114–120
    ring-fault 115
Glen Etive 69, 115, *132*
Glen Feshie 68

Glen Tilt *108,* 128–129
global warming *26,* 51, 175, 196–197
Glyder Fach *63*
Glyder Fawr 101, *112*
Glyders *18,* 99–101
gneiss 62, *63,* 66, 69
    Malverns 44–45
    see also Lewisian Gneiss
Goats Water *31, 96,* 195
graded bedding *74*
granite 20, 122–129, **130–133,** *142,* 179, 182, 194–195
    and gritstone 162–164
    Ben Nevis 115, *116,* 120
    Dartmoor 22
    Eskdale/Ennerdale **92–93,** *122,* 125,
    Galloway *2, 9*
    Mountains of Mourne 10, *126*
    Shap 187–190
    Skiddaw 92
    tors *126,* 132–136
granophyre *92–93, 95*
graptolites *18,* 23, **78–82**
Great Gable *36, 94,* 107–108, *109*
Great Glen 65, 69, 107
Great Langdale *8, 33,* 109, *112*
Great Rundale 185–190
Great Scar Limestone cover, *157,* 159
Great Whin Sill 139–142, 176, *186–187,* 190–192
Grey Corries *9,* 58–59
greywacke **72–76,** 78–84, 89, *125,* 143, *157, 196*
gritstone 159–164 see also Millstone Grit

H

Hadrian's Wall *142*
Half Dome 122–123
Hargreaves' Original Route *149*
Harlech Dome *73,* 74
Hart Fell *81, 83*
Heaton Cooper, William 107
High Cup Nick 140–142, 191–192
Highland Boundary Fault *143*
Himalaya 15, 16
history of Britain, very brief 16
Holmes, Arthur 168, 198
hornfels 113, *196*
hot-spot (mantle plume) 16, 144–145, 175–176, 197
Howgill Fells 82, *86,* 159
Hutton, James 122–130, 148, 197, 199
    Hutton's Riverbank (Glen Tilt) 128–129
    Hutton's Section (Salisbury Crags) 138–139
    Hutton's Unconformity (Arran) 127–130

Hutton's Unconformity (Siccar Point) **10–11,** 130
Hyrcanian or Variscan Orogeny (Africa crunch) **21–23,** 150, 154–156

I

Iappetus Ocean *18,* 88
Ice Age *18, 26,* **28–36,** 103, 175
ice effects **30–35,** 134–136
ice-smoothed rocks *2, 4, 30, 31*–32
ice-scratched rocks 31–32, 169
Idwal Slabs *55, 100,* 101
Idwal Syncline 101–102
igneous rocks **181–182** and see andesite, basalt, dolerite, gabbro, granite, ignimbrite, rhyolite, tuff
ignimbrite *96, 98,* **99–101,** 104, 139
Ingleborough cover, 157–158, 160
Isle of Man *82, 86*

J

Jameson, Robert 138
Jurassic Period **23,** 194

K

Kinder Scout *164*
knock and lochan 39, *40, 43,* 93

L

Lake District **88–96,** 106–112, 184
    southern 90–91
landslip landscape 178–179
lapilli *96*
Lapworth, Charles 78–80, 82, 197
lava *95, 103,* 181–182 and see andesite, basalt, rhyolite
Law of Superposition 186–187
Lewisian Gneiss *9,* **38–43,** *46,* 50–51
Liathach *9, 42, 46, 48,* 49–50, 56, 60
limestone *63,* **156–161,** 175, 185–192 see also mountain limestone
limestone pavement cover, 156, *157–158, 186*
Lindisfarne Castle *142*
Lingmoor Fell *19,* 109, *112*
Llyn Ogwen 101
Llyn y Cwn, Glyders *102,* 104, *181*
Loch Avon *30*
Loch Lomond re-advance 103
Loch Maree *46, 50*
Loch Monar 67
Loch Mullardoch 67

Loch Ness monster 197
Loch Skeen 81
Lochnagar *124, 129*
Lomonds of Fife 145
Lowther Hills (Dumfriesshire) 82, *84*
LRTF (Lower Rhyolitic Tuff Formation) 100–102
Lundy Island 166
Lynas, Bryan 198

M

mafic (igneous) rocks 54, 182
magma 16, 22, 182 and see andesite, basalt, rhyolite
magnetite 52, 169
Malverns 44–45, 139, *174*
Mamores 69, 117
mantle 16, 143, 171
mantle plume 16, 144–145, 175–176, 197
marble *63, 108*
Mars 125
Mealaisbhal *38*
Mears, Ray 112
Mediterranean 25–26
Mell Fells 150
meltwater channels 33–35, 192, *207*
metamorphic rocks 56–58, **62–63** and see gneiss, phyllite, quartzite, schist, slate
mica 43, 54, **63–66**, 70, 89–90, 187–188 see also biotite, muscovite
mica schist see schist
Mickleden 33, *106*, 109, *112*
microgranite 115, *180*, 182
mid-ocean ridge **16**, 21, 24, 25–26, 143–144
Miller, Hugh 150
Millstone Grit 8, 21, *149, 157*, **162–164**
Moel Siabod 146
Moelwyns *74*
Moine Thrust *46, 50*, **59–60**, *65*, 199
Mont Blanc 125
moraine 28–30 see also drumlins
Morteratsch Glacier *28–29*
mountain building 15–16 see also Alpine Orogeny, Caledonian Orogeny, Hyrcanian Orogeny
Mountain Limestone 21, *150*, 152, **156–159**, 190–192
Mourne Mountains 10, *126, 129*, 166
mudstone 49, 62–64, 69, 75, **82**, *86*
Mull 166–167, *174, 179*
 volcano *142*, 166, 176
Murchison, Roderick Impey 22, 31–32, 199
Muscovite 66, **188**
Mynydd Mawr, Snowdonia 20

N

Naismith's Route, Bhasteir Tooth *171*
Narrow Buttress (climb), Stanage Edge *164*
Neptunism 138, 179
Neptunism vs Plutonism 124–130
Nevis Gorge 69, *70*
New Red Sandstone 22–23, 72, **153–154**, 194
Noah's Flood 25, 31–32, 125–126, 138
North Yorks Moors 23, *163, 166*
Nuclear Winter 175
nuée ardente 98–99, 182

O

obsidian 55
Ochils 143
Old Etonians, infestations of 163
Old Red Sandstone 20, 22, 72, 143, **150–153**, 180
Old Red Sandstone (period) see Devonian Period
Old Red Sandstone continent 20, 22, 144
olivine 171
Ordovician Period **18–19**, 80, 90
oxygen (arrives in atmosphere) 51–52

P

Palü Glacier *30*
Pangaea 22, 24, *174*
Peak District 21, 156–158, 160, 162–164
pegmatite *45*
Pen y Fan 153
Pen-y-ghent 160
Pen yr Ole Wen 99–100
Pennine Faults 186–190
Pennines 16, 139–142, 156, 186–192
Penrith Sandstone 88
Pentlands *144*
periglacial effects 36
Permian Period **22–23**, 174, 194
Perthshire 10, 69
phyllite **63**, *64*, 69
Picos de Europa *159*
Pikes Crag *95*
pillow lava 102–103, 138
pipe rock *57*, **59**
Pitts Head Tuff 99–101
Piz Badile *13*, 125
Plutonism vs Neptunism 124–130
porphyry 187–188
Precambrian Period *17*, 42, 44, 49, 52
psammite 69, *70*
Pumlumon Fawr (Plynlimon) 82, *86*
Pygmy Ridge *131, 133*

Pyrenees 9, 22, 23, *159*
pyroxene 64, 171

Q

quartz 45, **54–56**, 63, 100, 130, 153, 162–163, 182
quartzite *8–9, 17*, **56–60**, *63*, 65, 69, 115, 117, 136, 196 see also Cambrian Quartzite
Quaternary Period 26
Queensberry, Dumfriesshire *19, 196*
Quiraing *172*, 178–179

R

Raise (Helvellyn) *175*
Rhinogs *17*, 72–76
rhyolite *96*, 104, **115–120**, 146, 176, 179, 181–182, *188*
ribbon lakes 12, *30*, 32–33
Rift Valley 15, 143–144
roches moutonées 1, 32
rock scratching (striae) 31–32, 169
Roineabhal (Roineval), Harris 39–42
Ruskin, John 157–158

S

St Abbs Head *175, 181*
St Bees Sandstone 88, *95*, 186–187
St Kilda *166*, 176
Salisbury Crags 138–139, 148
sandstone 54, *63*, 72, 124–125, **148**, *152–153* see also Torridonian Sandstone, Old Red Sandstone, New Red Sandstone
Santorini 114
Scafells 88, *94–95, 106*, 109, *110*
schist *17, 19, 62, 63*, **64–70**
 Dalradian 65, 68, 69, *143*
 Moine 65, 67–69
Scourie Dykes *42, 43, 46*, 52
screes 9, 35–36, 89–90, *171*
seashells, fossil *17*, 124–125, 156, *158*
Sedgwick, Adam 25, 31, 102–103, 197
sedimentary rocks 82 see gritstone, greywacke, limestone, quartzite, sandstone, shale
Sgorr Ruadh 46, 58–60
Sgurr nan Eag, Skye 169–170
Sgurr nan Gillean *168, 170*
shale 62–63, **82**, 89, 159–161
 Moffatdale **78–80**
Shap Granite 187–190
Sharp Edge, Blencathra *90*

shells see seashells
Siccar Point, Berwickshire 10–11, 130
silica 54–56, 64, 100, 182
sills *120*, 138–142, 145–146 see also Great
    Whin Sill
Silurian Period **19**, 22, 80, 90
Skew Gill, Scafell Pike 106–109
Skiddaw *86*, 88–90
Skiddaw granite *92*
Skiddaw Slates 11–12, *62, 74,* 82, *88,* **89–90**,
    106, 186
Skye 166–167
    Cuillin 25–26, *34,* 166–172
    Red Cuillin *167*
    Trotternish 171–172, 178–179
slate **62–64**, *75, 86, 89–90, 96, 180*
Slickensides *108*
Slieve Binnian *126*
Slieve Donard 10
Smith, William 'Strata' 197, 199
Snowball Earth *52*
Snowdon 14, *18, 26,* 33, 98–100, 102, 104,
    124, 145
Snowdonia 17–20, *74,* 93, **98–104**, 145–146,
    180 see also Carneddau, Cwm Idwal,
    Glyders, Rhinogs
Southern Upland Fault *143*
Southern Uplands 19, *72,* 75, **78–85**, 125
Staffa 178
Stanage Edge 8, *21, 149,* 162–164
Stiperstones 45, *60,* 136
Stirling Castle 144–145
striae (ice-scratches) 31–32, 169
stromatolites 51–52

Strone Ulladale *42*
Strontian *115*
Stuc a' Chroin *68, 70*
subduction **16**, 18, 75, *88,* 143–144, 176, 182
syncline 14, 93, 101–102

T
Tatras 9
Tenerife *114, 181*
Tertiary Period **25–26**, 134
Tertiary Volcanic Province 166–167
Thearlaich-Dubh Gap 170
Thin Man's Ridge 9
Torridonian Sandstone 9, *12, 46,* **48–52**, *56,*
    59, 153–154, *195*
tors *126,* 132–136, 162–163
trap landscape 176–178
trap rock 170, *172*
Triassic Period **23**, 174
Trichrug, South Wales 152
Trumpet rock *53, 57*
Tryfan *74, 104, 138*
tufa *188*
tuff 63, **93–96** see also Block tuff, Ignimbrite
tuffite *175*
turbidity currents *72, 74,* **75**

U
Unconformity *50,* 127, *157,* 194
    Hutton's (Arran) 130
    Hutton's (Siccar Point) **10–11**, 130

Universal Ocean 127
Ussher, Bishop 25

V
Vale of Eden 186–187
Variscan or Hyrcanian Orogeny (Africa
    crunch) *21–23,* 150, 154–156
Venus 175
vesicle 138–139, *181,* 187–188
viscosity 143, 176, 182
volcanoes 16, *88,* 114–115, 143, 166,
    175, 182

W
Wegener, Alfred 15
Werner, Abraham 124
Wester Ross 9, 12, 46
Wet Side Edge Member 93–95
Wheel Stones *163*
Wordsworth, Dorothy 82

X, Y, Z
Xenolith 127–129
Y Garn (Glyders) 100
Y Gribin (Glyders) *99–100*
Y Lliwedd *98,* 101
Yoredale Series *157,* **159–160**, 191–192
Yorkshire Dales cover, 156–160, 184
Yosemite 9, 122–123
younger Dryas 103

INDEX OF PLACES

ENGLAND: SOUTH & EAST

Cheddar *156*
Cotswolds 23
Dartmoor *22*, *129*, 132, 134, 200
Dorset 23, *24*, *55*
Lundy Island 166
Malverns 44–45, 139, *174*
North Yorks Moors 23, *163*, 166
Stiperstones 45, *60*, 136

ENGLAND: PENNINES

Pennines: general 16, 139–142, 156, 186–192
Ashgill Force *161*
Cheviot 20, *129*, *142*
Cross Fell *125*, 184–188
Dufton Pike 184–188
Great Rundale 185–190
Hadrian's Wall *142*,
High Cup Nick 140–142, 191–192
Howgill Fells 82, *86*, *159*,
Ingleborough cover, 157–158, 160
Kinder Scout *164*,
Lindisfarne Castle *142*,
Peak District 21, 156–158, 160, 162–164
Pen-y-ghent 160
Stanage Edge 8, *21*, *149*, 162–164
Vale of Eden 186–187
Yorkshire Dales cover, 156–160, 184

ENGLAND: LAKE DISTRICT

Lake District: general **88–96**, 106–112, 184
Black Combe *62*, 88
Bowfell *27*, *36*, 93
Buttermere 11–12, *95*, 131, *196*,
Coniston Old Man *34*, *94*,
Dow Crag *142*, *146*, *181*
Esk Hause *106*, 109–110
Esk Pike *18*, *110*
Eskdale 92–93, 109
Fleetwith Edge 11–12
Goats Water *31*, *96*, 195
Great Gable *36*, *94*, 107–108,
Great Langdale 8, *33*, 109, *112*
Lingmoor Fell *19*, 109, *112*
Mell Fells 150
Mickleden 33, *106*, 109, *112*
Pikes Crag *95*
Raise (Helvellyn) *175*
Scafells 88, *94*–95, *106*, 109, *110*
Sharp Edge, Blencathra *90*
Skew Gill 106–109
Skiddaw *86*, 88–90
Southern Lake District 90–91

WALES: SOUTHERN & CENTRAL

Brecon Beacons 20, 150–153

Pen y Fan 153
Pumlumon Fawr (Plynlimon) 82, *86*
Trichrug, South Wales 152

WALES: SNOWDONIA

Snowdonia: general 17–20, *74*, 93, **98–104**,
   145–146, 180
Aber Falls 180
Cadair Idris *74*, 138, 180
Carnedd Dafydd 145–146
Carnedd Llewelyn *98*, *145*
Carneddau *75*, 145–146, *196*
Clogwyn Du'r Arddu 101, 102
Clogwyn Mawr, Snowdon *14*
Crib Goch 146
Crib y Ddysgl 104
Cwm Idwal 100–103
Devil's Kitchen 101–104, *177*
Glyder Fach *63*
Glyder Fawr 101, *112*
Glyders *18*, 99–101
Harlech Dome *73*, *74*
Llyn Ogwen 101
Llyn y Cwn (Glyders) *102*, 104, *181*
Moel Siabod 146
Moelwyns *74*
Mynydd Mawr (Snowdonia) 20
Pen yr Ole Wen 99–100
Rhinogs 17, *72*–76
Snowdon 14, *18*, *26*, 33, 98–100, 102, 104,
   124, 145
Tryfan *74*, *104*, 138
Y Garn (Glyders) 100
Y Gribin (Glyders) *99–100*
Y Lliwedd *98*, 101

SCOTLAND: SOUTHERN

Arthur's Seat *108*, 128–129, 138–139,
   142–145, 148
Campsie Fells 145
Dobbs Linn, Moffatdale 78–80
Dumbarton Rock 145
Dumfriesshire 82–85, 153–154, 194
Edinburgh 32, *108*, 124, 128, 138–139, 143,
   145, 148
Galloway Hills *4*, *9*, *35*, *73*, 125, 131
Gargunnock Hills 145
Hart Fell 81, *83*
Loch Skeen 81
Lomonds of Fife 145
Lowther Hills 82, *84*
Ochils 143
Pentlands *144*
Queensberry *19*, *196*
St Abbs Head *175*, *181*
Salisbury Crags 138–139, 148

Siccar Point 10–11, 130
Southern Uplands 19, *72*, 75, **78–85**, 125
Stirling Castle 144–145

SCOTLAND: HIGHLANDS

An Teallach *7*, *49*
Aonach Eagach *118*
Aonachs (Nevis Range) 117
Ardnamurchan *166*
Arkle 16
Assynt 60, 184
Avon Slabs *30*
Beinn Alligin *49*, 60
Beinn Bhan, Applecross *47*
Beinn Eighe 8–9, 56, *57*, 59–60
Ben Cruachan 20, 69
Ben Nevis *2*, *32*, *107*, 114–120, 131
Ben Starav 115
Ben Vorlich, Loch Earn 68
Bidean nam Bian 115, 117, *119*, *120*
Buachaille Etive Mor 117, *120*
Cairngorms 30–31, 35–36, 69, 126, **130–136**,
   164, 200
Carn Deag, Ben Nevis *2*
Carn Mor Dearg 115, *116*, 117
Chalamain Gap, Cairn Gorm 35
Cobbler, Arrochar *70*
Creag Meagaidh *34*, *70*
Edinample Falls, Loch Earn *64*
Etive Slabs 131–133
Foinaven *17*
Forcan Ridge 65
Glen Affric 67
Glen Coe 20, 114–120
Glen Etive 69, 115, *132*
Glen Feshie 68
Glen Tilt *108*, 128–129
Great Glen 65, 69, 107
Grey Corries *9*, 58–59
Liathach *9*, *42*, *46*, *48*, 49–50, 56, 60
Loch Avon *30*,
Loch Maree *46*, *50*,
Loch Monar 67
Loch Mullardoch 67
Lochnagar *124*, *129*
Mamores 69, 117
Nevis Gorge 69, *70*,
Perthshire 10, 69
Sgorr Ruadh *46*, 58–60
Strontian *115*
Stuc a' Chroin *68*, *70*
Wester Ross *9*, 12, 46

SCOTLAND: ISLANDS

Ailsa Craig *167*,
Arran *127*, 129–130, *132*, 162, 166

Bhasteir Tooth back cover, *171*
Cir Mhor 129, *166*
Clach Glas *165, 172*
Cuillin, Skye 25–26, *34*, 166–172
Fingal's Cave 139, 178
Mealaisbhal, Harris *38*
Mull 166–167, *174, 179*
Quiraing *172*, 178–179
Roineabhal (Roineval), Harris 39–42
St Kilda *166*, 176
Sgurr nan Eag 169–170
Sgurr nan Gillean *168, 170*
Skye 166–167
Staffa 178
Strone Ulladale *42*
Trotternish 171–172, 178–179

REST OF UK
Antrim 139, 166, 178
Isle of Man 82, *86*
Mourne Mountains 10, *126, 129*, 166
Slieve Binnian *126*
Slieve Donard 10

REST OF WORLD
Aletsch Glacier 28–29
Alps 15, 16, 26, 28–30 , *159*
Andes 16, 176, 182
Boval Glacier *28,*
Crete, White Mountains *25*
Death Valley, California *52*
Everest 16, 124, *159*
Himalaya 15, 16

Mediterranean 25–26
Mont Blanc 125
Morteratsch Glacier *28–29*
Palü Glacier *30*
Picos de Europa *159*
Piz Badile *13, 125*
Pyrenees 9, 22, 23, *159*
Santorini 114
Tatras 9
Tenerife *114, 181*
Yosemite 9, 122–123

OTHER PLANETS
Mars 125
Venus 175

ABOVE: The UK's most spectacular meltwater channel,
Water of Ailnack in the eastern Cairngorms

ACKNOWLEDGEMENTS

More than most scientists, geologists quite often explain themselves in ways that the rest of us, if we work at it, can follow. Thanks in particular to the lucid authors of the text-books listed at the end. Even more thanks to the academics and others who have placed interesting and well-illustrated material on the Internet for no personal gain whatever. I've been enlightened by material from Edinburgh, Oxford, and James Madison (Virginia) Universities, the British and US Geological Surveys, Fettes Academy, and St Abbs Community.

To them must be added the many anonymous contributors to Wikipedia, the open-source encyclopedia on the World Wide Web. As with litter on UK hills, there seem to be many more people picking up mistakes on Wikipedia than depositing them.

Thanks too to various unnamed rock-lovers met on hills; to Barbara Turnbull of Cornell University, currently studying the fluid dynamics of turbidity currents; and Harry Cripps, Stanage climber. Special thanks to Orion Dooley, geophysicist, who checked my geology aboard SS *Geofisik II*

in quiet moments during an investigation of the underwater structure of the Caspian Sea; and to my editor, Roly Smith (in particular for suggesting Cross Fell and Dufton Pike). Warm thanks to book designer Maria Charalambous for her artistry, but even more for her patience in the face of my tiresome demands over text, images and captions. Remaining errors are my fault, not theirs.

Finally, thanks to my hill companions of the last two years for standing so patiently while I took photos of stones.

Parts of Chapters 4 and 7 have appeared in *Trail Walker* magazine: Chapters 11 and 19 are adapted from articles in *Lakeland Walker*. Geological and topographic mapping are based on out-of-copyright OS and BGS material, are illustrative only, and are not intended for navigation on the hill. The Landranger extract on page 110 is reproduced by permission of Ordnance Survey on behalf of HMSO © Crown Copyright 2008. All rights reserved. Ordnance Survey Licence number 100043293. The geological map extract on the same page is reproduced with permission from the British Geological Survey (IPR/99-08CA).